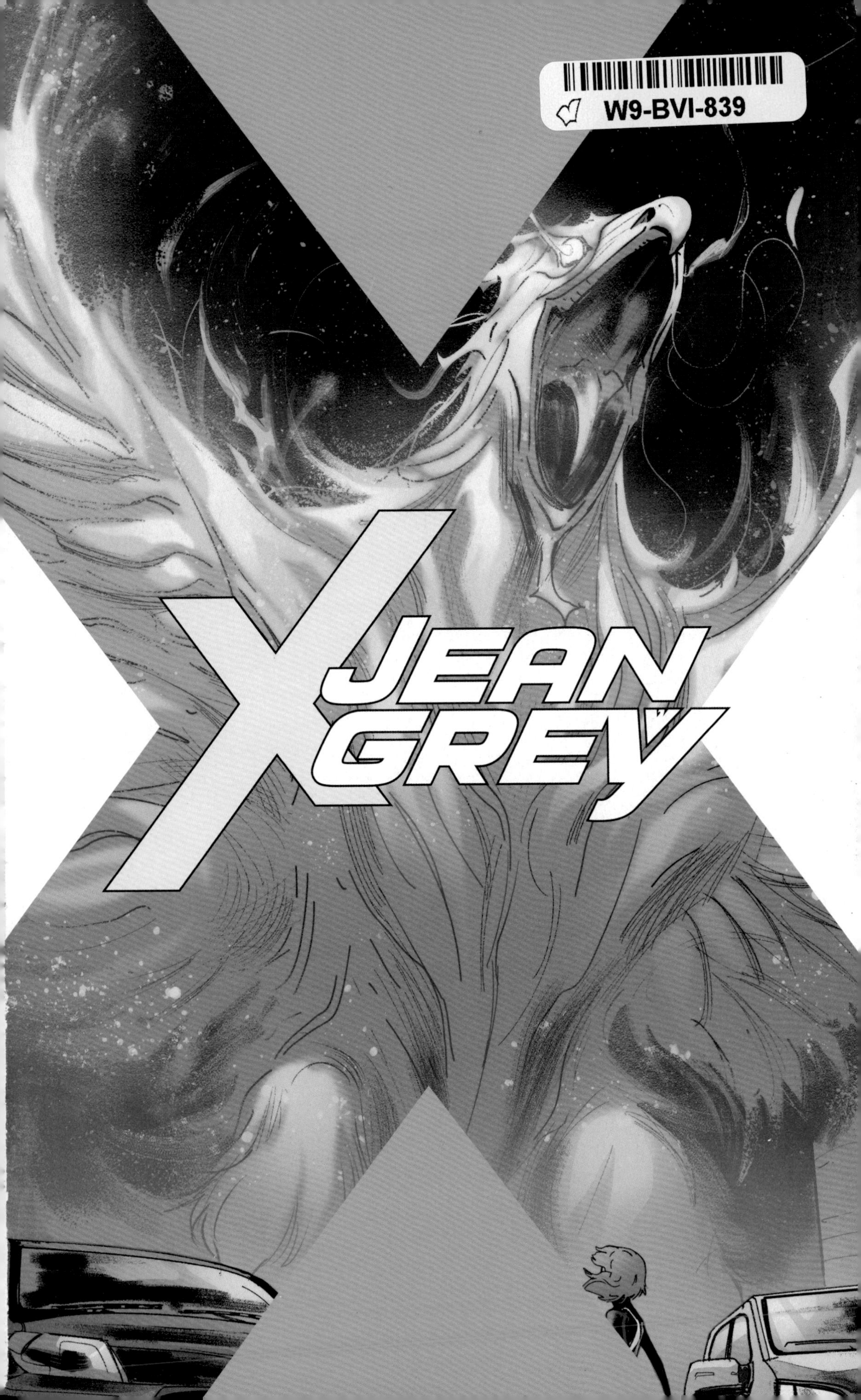
JEAN
GREY

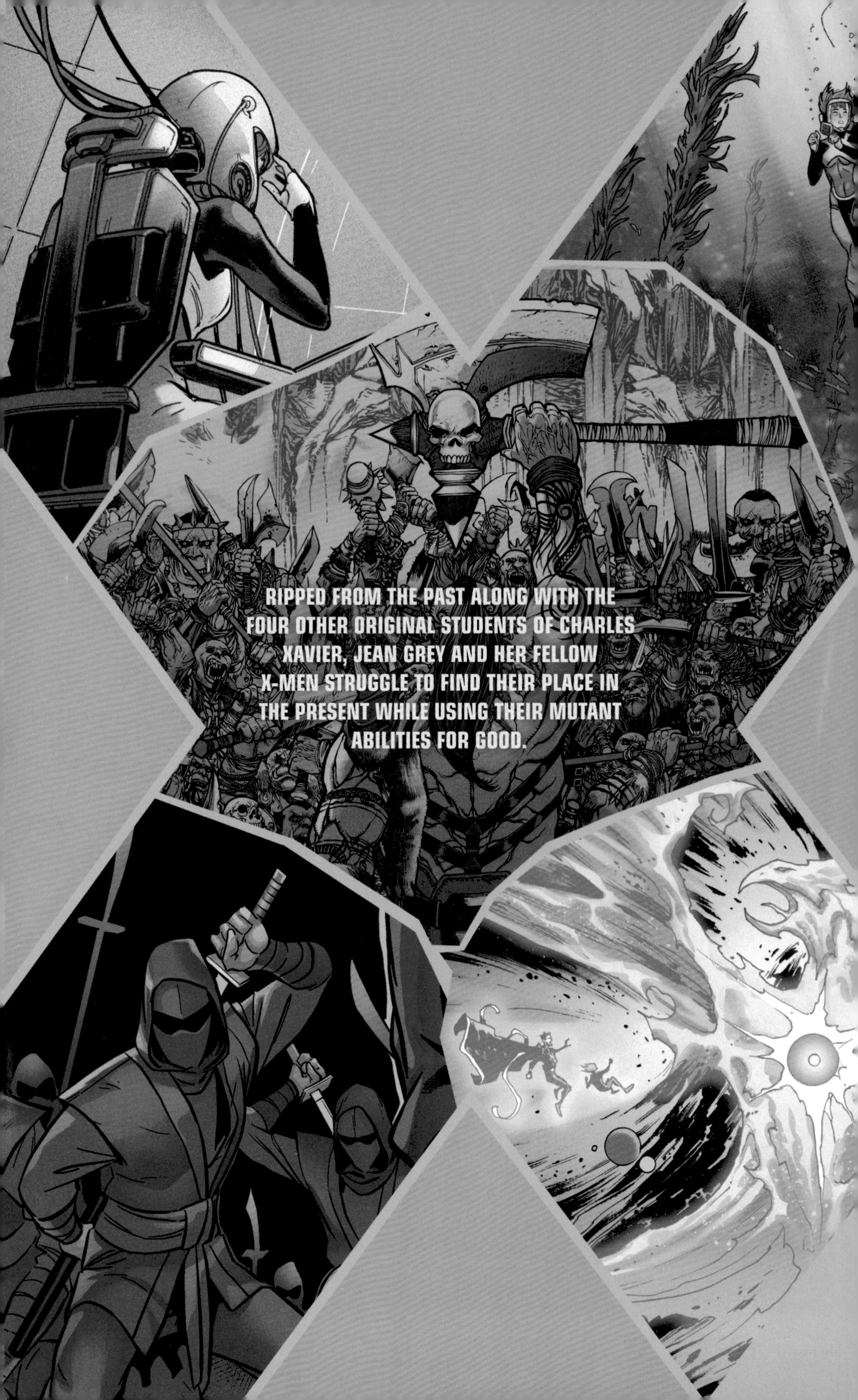
RIPPED FROM THE PAST ALONG WITH THE FOUR OTHER ORIGINAL STUDENTS OF CHARLES XAVIER, JEAN GREY AND HER FELLOW X-MEN STRUGGLE TO FIND THEIR PLACE IN THE PRESENT WHILE USING THEIR MUTANT ABILITIES FOR GOOD.

JEAN GREY

NIGHTMARE FUEL

Writer/**DENNIS HOPELESS**

Artists/**VICTOR IBÁÑEZ** (#1-3), **HARVEY TOLIBAO** (#4), **ANTHONY PIPER** (#5) & **PAUL DAVIDSON** (#6)

Layout Artist, #3/**AL BARRIONUEVO**

Colorists/**JAY DAVID RAMOS** with **CHRIS SOTOMAYOR** (#2) & **DONO SÁNCHEZ-ALMARA** (#3-4)

Letterers/**VC'S TRAVIS LANHAM** (#1, #3-6) & **JOE CARAMAGNA** (#2)

Cover Art/**DAVID YARDIN**

Assistant Editor/**CHRIS ROBINSON**
Editors/**DANIEL KETCHUM** & **DARREN SHAN**
X-Men Group Editor/**MARK PANICCIA**

JEAN GREY CREATED BY **STAN LEE** & **JACK KIRBY**

Collection Editor/**JENNIFER GRÜNWALD** • Assistant Editor/**CAITLIN O'CONNELL**
Associate Managing Editor/**KATERI WOODY** • Editor, Special Projects/**MARK D. BEAZLEY**
VP Production & Special Projects/**JEFF YOUNGQUIST** • SVP Print, Sales & Marketing/**DAVID GABRIEL**
Book Designer/**JAY BOWEN**

Editor in Chief/**AXEL ALONSO** • Chief Creative Officer/**JOE QUESADA**
President/**DAN BUCKLEY** • Executive Producer/**ALAN FINE**

JEAN GREY VOL. 1: NIGHTMARE FUEL. Contains material originally published in magazine form as JEAN GREY #1-6. First printing 2017. ISBN# 978-1-302-90877-5. Published by MARVEL WORLDWIDE, INC., a subsidiary of MARVEL ENTERTAINMENT, LLC. OFFICE OF PUBLICATION: 135 West 50th Street, New York, NY 10020. **Printed in Canada.** DAN BUCKLEY, President, Marvel Entertainment; JOE QUESADA, Chief Creative Officer; TOM BREVOORT, SVP of Publishing; DAVID BOGART, SVP of Business Affairs & Operations, Publishing & Partnership; C.B. CEBULSKI, VP of Brand Management & Development, Asia; DAVID GABRIEL, SVP of Sales & Marketing, Publishing; JEFF YOUNGQUIST, VP of Production & Special Projects; DAN CARR, Executive Director of Publishing Technology; ALEX MORALES, Director of Publishing Operations; SUSAN CRESPI, Production Manager; STAN LEE, Chairman Emeritus. For information regarding advertising in Marvel Comics or on Marvel.com, please contact Vit DeBellis, Integrated Sales Manager, at vdebellis@marvel.com. For Marvel subscription inquiries, please call 888-511-5480. **Manufactured between 8/25/2017 and 9/26/2017 by SOLISCO PRINTERS, SCOTT, QC, CANADA.**

10 9 8 7 6 5 4 3 2 1

1

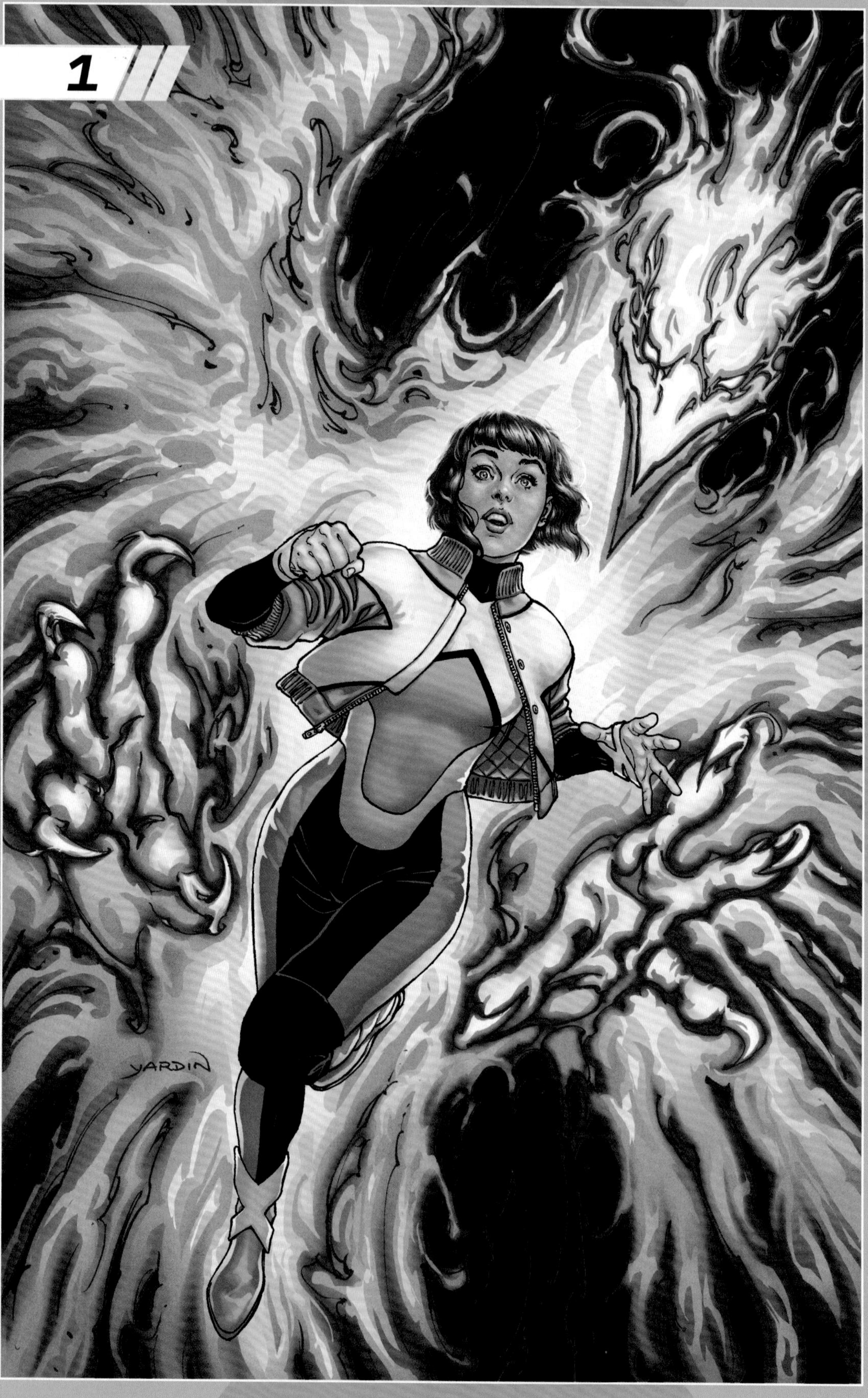
YARDIN

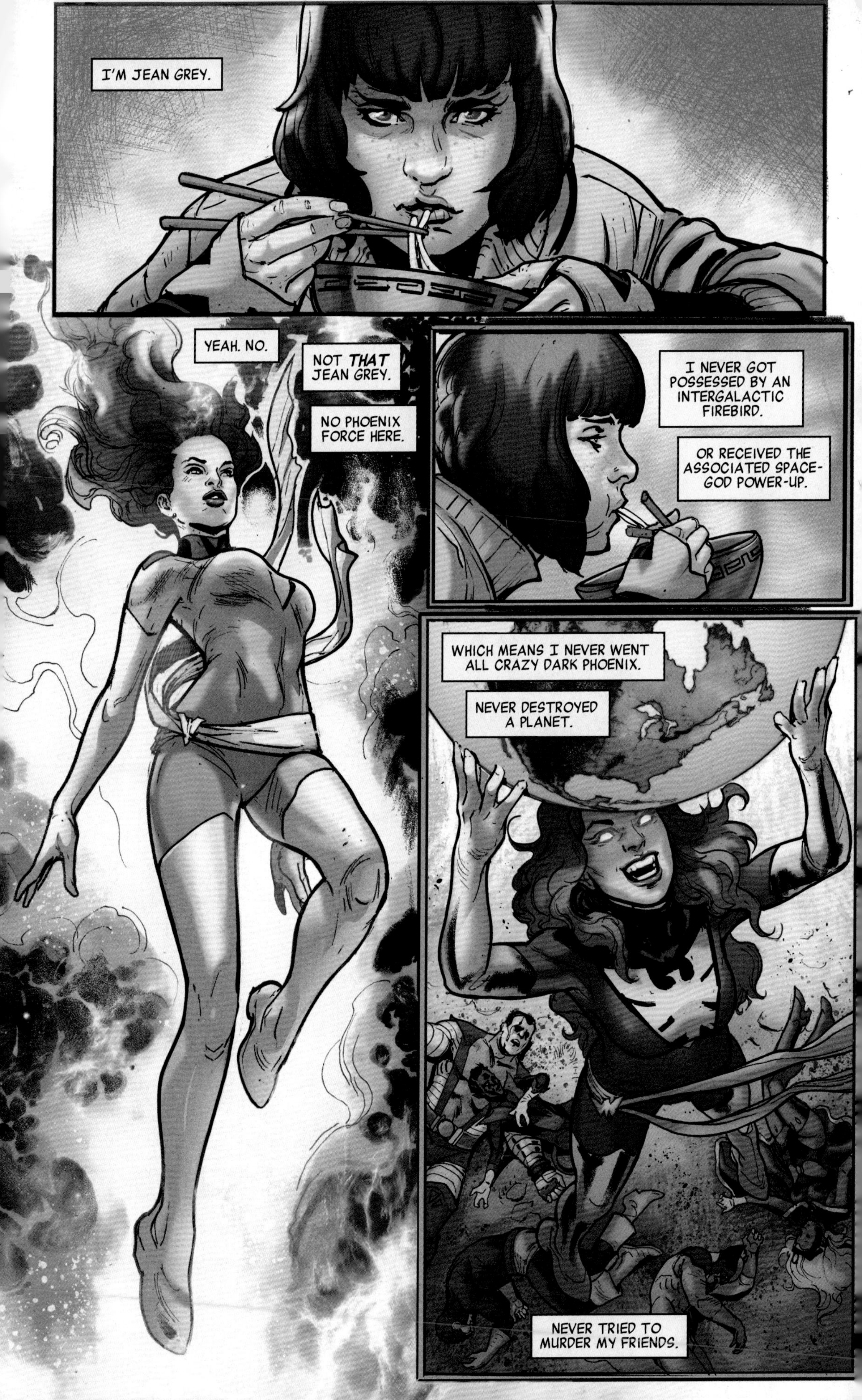
I'M JEAN GREY.
YEAH. NO.
NOT THAT JEAN GREY.
NO PHOENIX FORCE HERE.
I NEVER GOT POSSESSED BY AN INTERGALACTIC FIREBIRD.
OR RECEIVED THE ASSOCIATED SPACE-GOD POWER-UP.
WHICH MEANS I NEVER WENT ALL CRAZY DARK PHOENIX.
NEVER DESTROYED A PLANET.
NEVER TRIED TO MURDER MY FRIENDS.

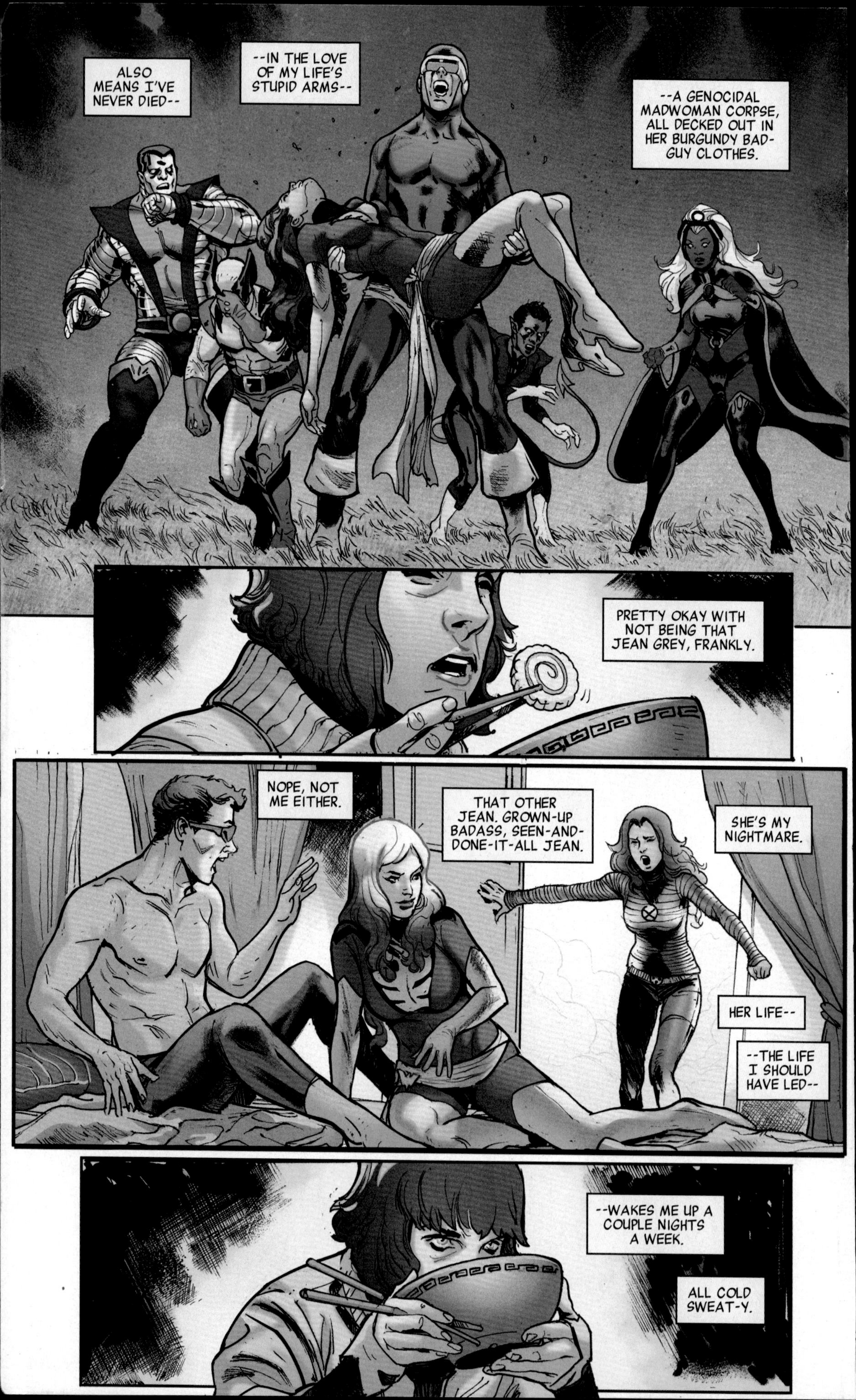
ALSO MEANS I'VE NEVER DIED--
--IN THE LOVE OF MY LIFE'S STUPID ARMS--
--A GENOCIDAL MADWOMAN CORPSE, ALL DECKED OUT IN HER BURGUNDY BAD-GUY CLOTHES.
PRETTY OKAY WITH NOT BEING THAT JEAN GREY, FRANKLY.
NOPE, NOT ME EITHER.
THAT OTHER JEAN. GROWN-UP BADASS, SEEN-AND-DONE-IT-ALL JEAN.
SHE'S MY NIGHTMARE.
HER LIFE--
--THE LIFE I SHOULD HAVE LED--
--WAKES ME UP A COUPLE NIGHTS A WEEK.
ALL COLD SWEAT-Y.

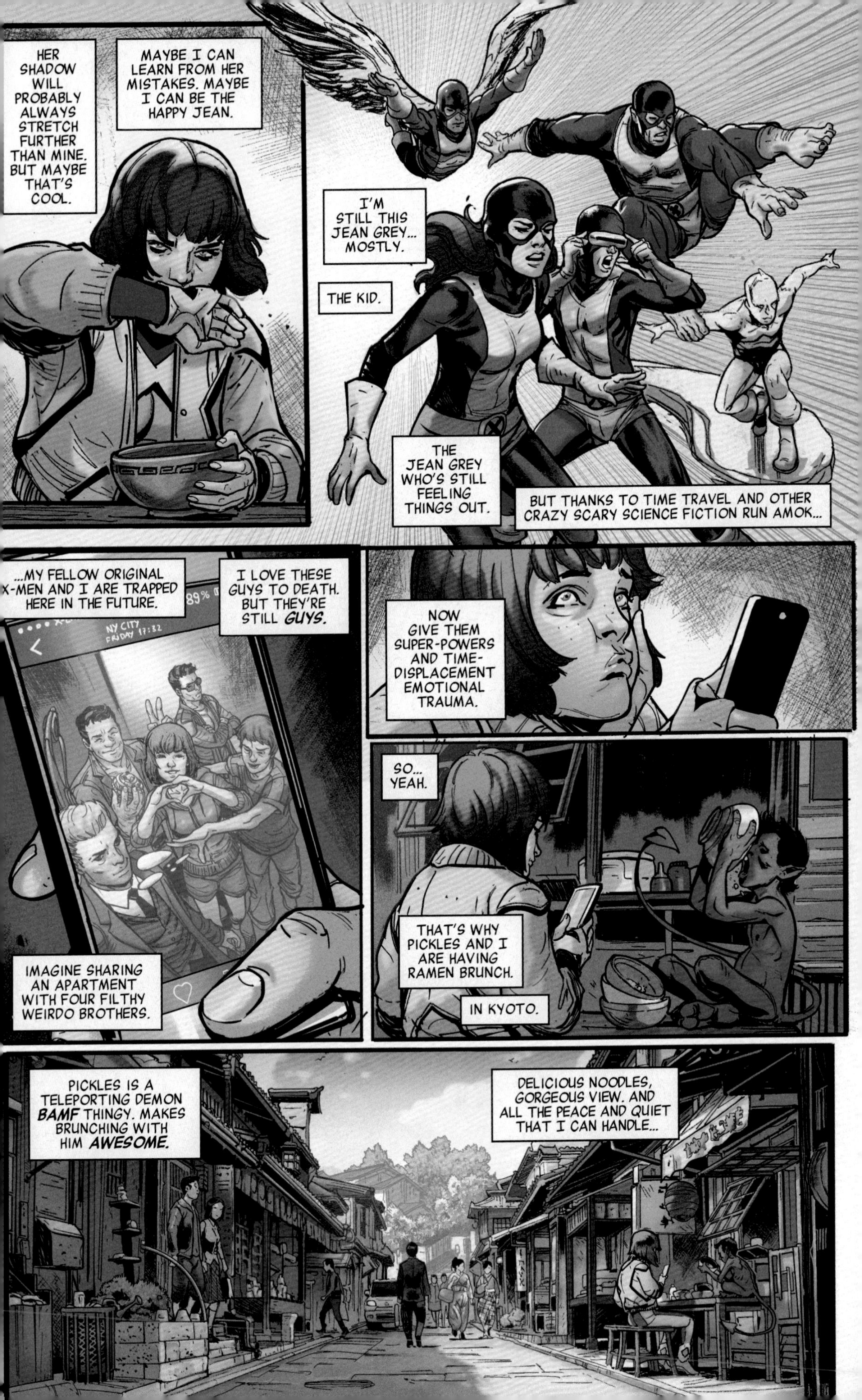

HER SHADOW WILL PROBABLY ALWAYS STRETCH FURTHER THAN MINE. BUT MAYBE THAT'S COOL.
MAYBE I CAN LEARN FROM HER MISTAKES. MAYBE I CAN BE THE HAPPY JEAN.
I'M STILL THIS JEAN GREY... MOSTLY.
THE KID.
THE JEAN GREY WHO'S STILL FEELING THINGS OUT.
BUT THANKS TO TIME TRAVEL AND OTHER CRAZY SCARY SCIENCE FICTION RUN AMOK...
...MY FELLOW ORIGINAL X-MEN AND I ARE TRAPPED HERE IN THE FUTURE.
I LOVE THESE GUYS TO DEATH. BUT THEY'RE STILL *GUYS.*
89%
NY CITY FRIDAY 17:32
IMAGINE SHARING AN APARTMENT WITH FOUR FILTHY WEIRDO BROTHERS.
NOW GIVE THEM SUPER-POWERS AND TIME-DISPLACEMENT EMOTIONAL TRAUMA.
SO... YEAH.
THAT'S WHY PICKLES AND I ARE HAVING RAMEN BRUNCH.
IN KYOTO.
PICKLES IS A TELEPORTING DEMON ***BAMF*** THINGY. MAKES BRUNCHING WITH HIM ***AWESOME.***
DELICIOUS NOODLES, GORGEOUS VIEW. AND ALL THE PEACE AND QUIET THAT I CAN HANDLE...

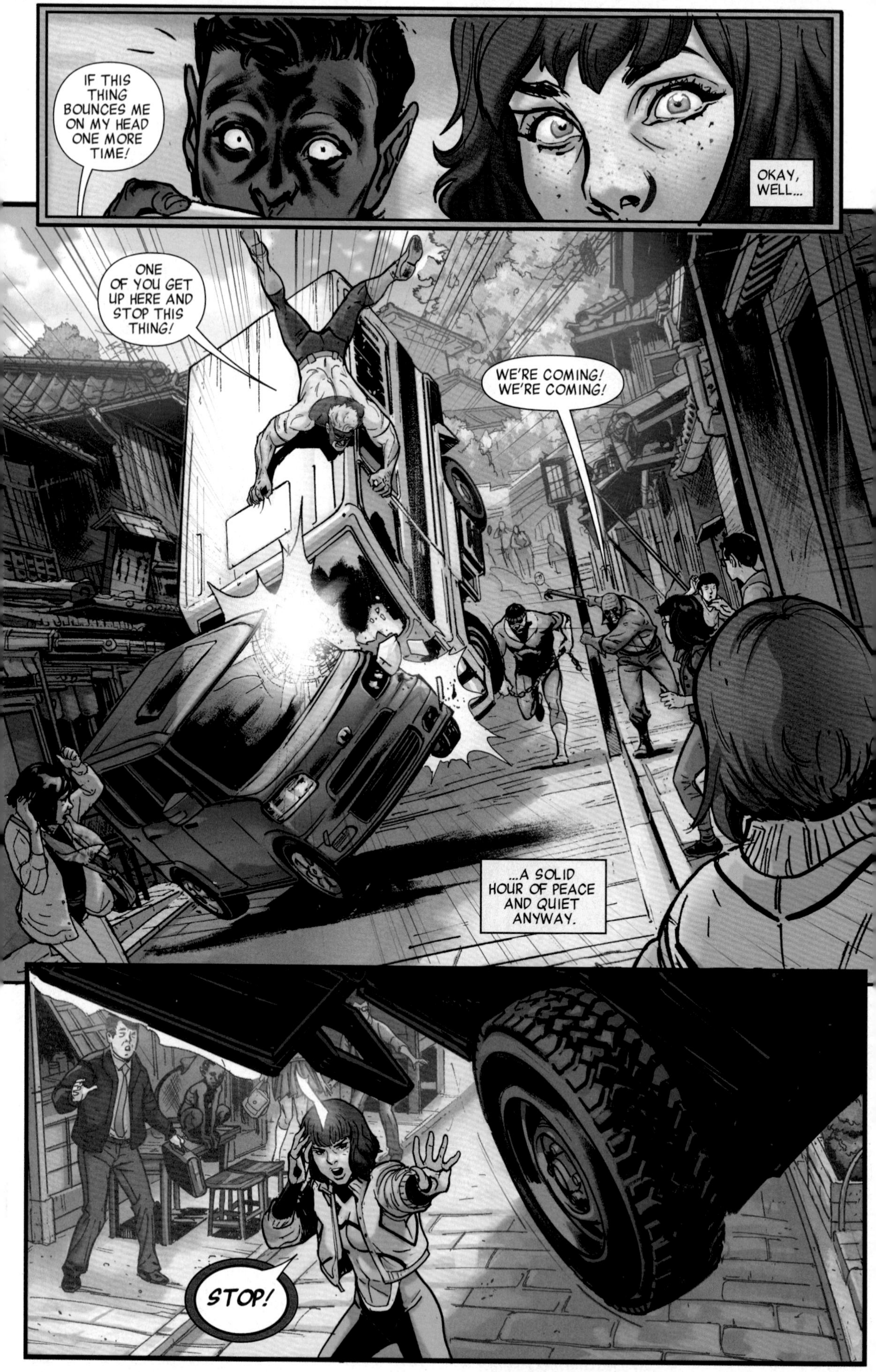
IF THIS THING BOUNCES ME ON MY HEAD ONE MORE TIME!
OKAY, WELL...
ONE OF YOU GET UP HERE AND STOP THIS THING!
WE'RE COMING! WE'RE COMING!
...A SOLID HOUR OF PEACE AND QUIET ANYWAY.
STOP!

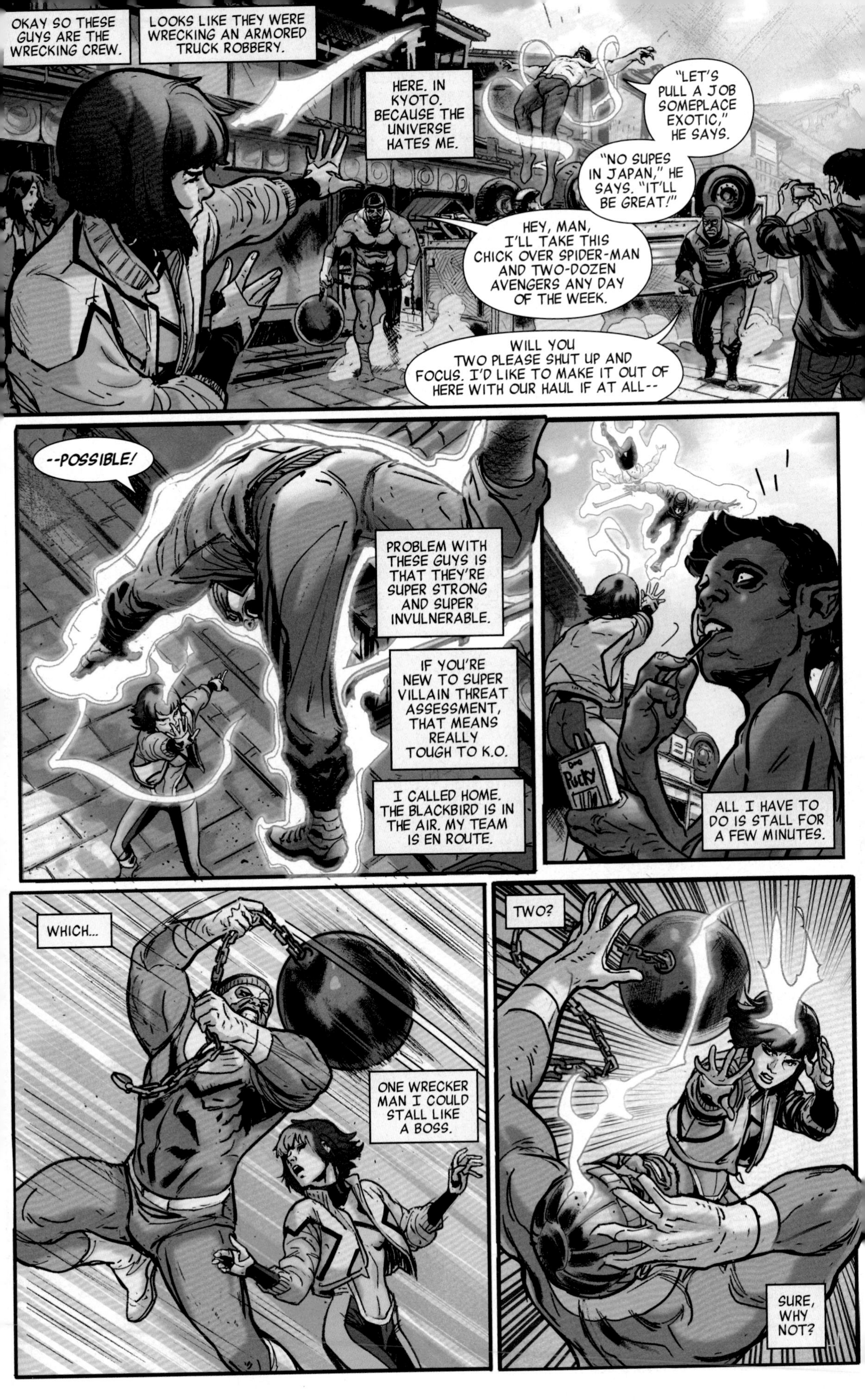
OKAY SO THESE GUYS ARE THE WRECKING CREW.
LOOKS LIKE THEY WERE WRECKING AN ARMORED TRUCK ROBBERY.
HERE. IN KYOTO. BECAUSE THE UNIVERSE HATES ME.
"LET'S PULL A JOB SOMEPLACE EXOTIC," HE SAYS.
"NO SUPES IN JAPAN," HE SAYS. "IT'LL BE GREAT!"
HEY, MAN, I'LL TAKE THIS CHICK OVER SPIDER-MAN AND TWO-DOZEN AVENGERS ANY DAY OF THE WEEK.
WILL YOU TWO PLEASE SHUT UP AND FOCUS. I'D LIKE TO MAKE IT OUT OF HERE WITH OUR HAUL IF AT ALL--
--POSSIBLE!
PROBLEM WITH THESE GUYS IS THAT THEY'RE SUPER STRONG AND SUPER INVULNERABLE.
IF YOU'RE NEW TO SUPER VILLAIN THREAT ASSESSMENT, THAT MEANS REALLY TOUGH TO K.O.
I CALLED HOME. THE BLACKBIRD IS IN THE AIR. MY TEAM IS EN ROUTE.
Pucky
ALL I HAVE TO DO IS STALL FOR A FEW MINUTES.
WHICH...
ONE WRECKER MAN I COULD STALL LIKE A BOSS.
TWO?
SURE, WHY NOT?

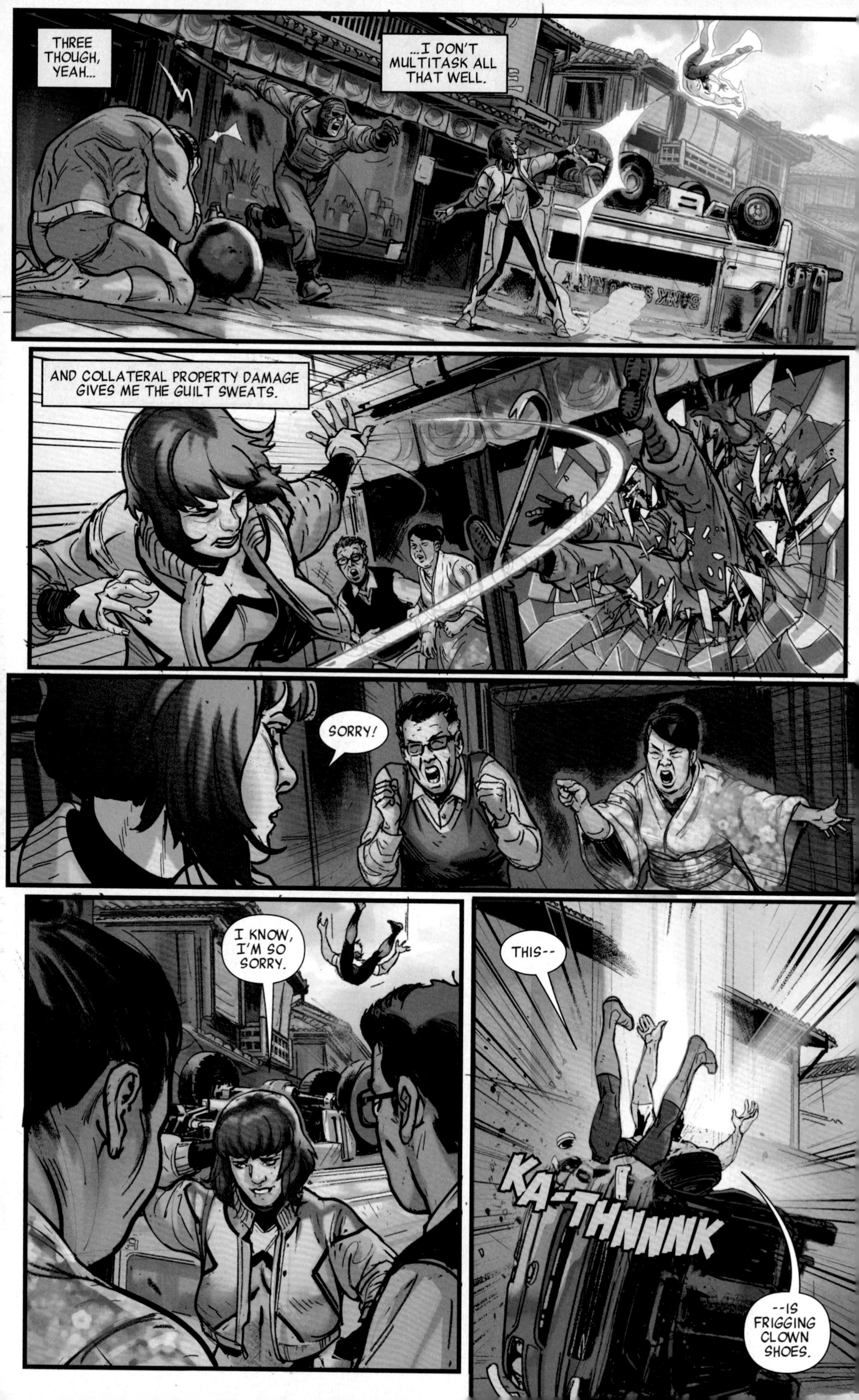
THREE THOUGH, YEAH...
...I DON'T MULTITASK ALL THAT WELL.
AND COLLATERAL PROPERTY DAMAGE GIVES ME THE GUILT SWEATS.
SORRY!
I KNOW, I'M SO SORRY.
THIS--
KA-THNNNNK
--IS FRIGGING CLOWN SHOES.

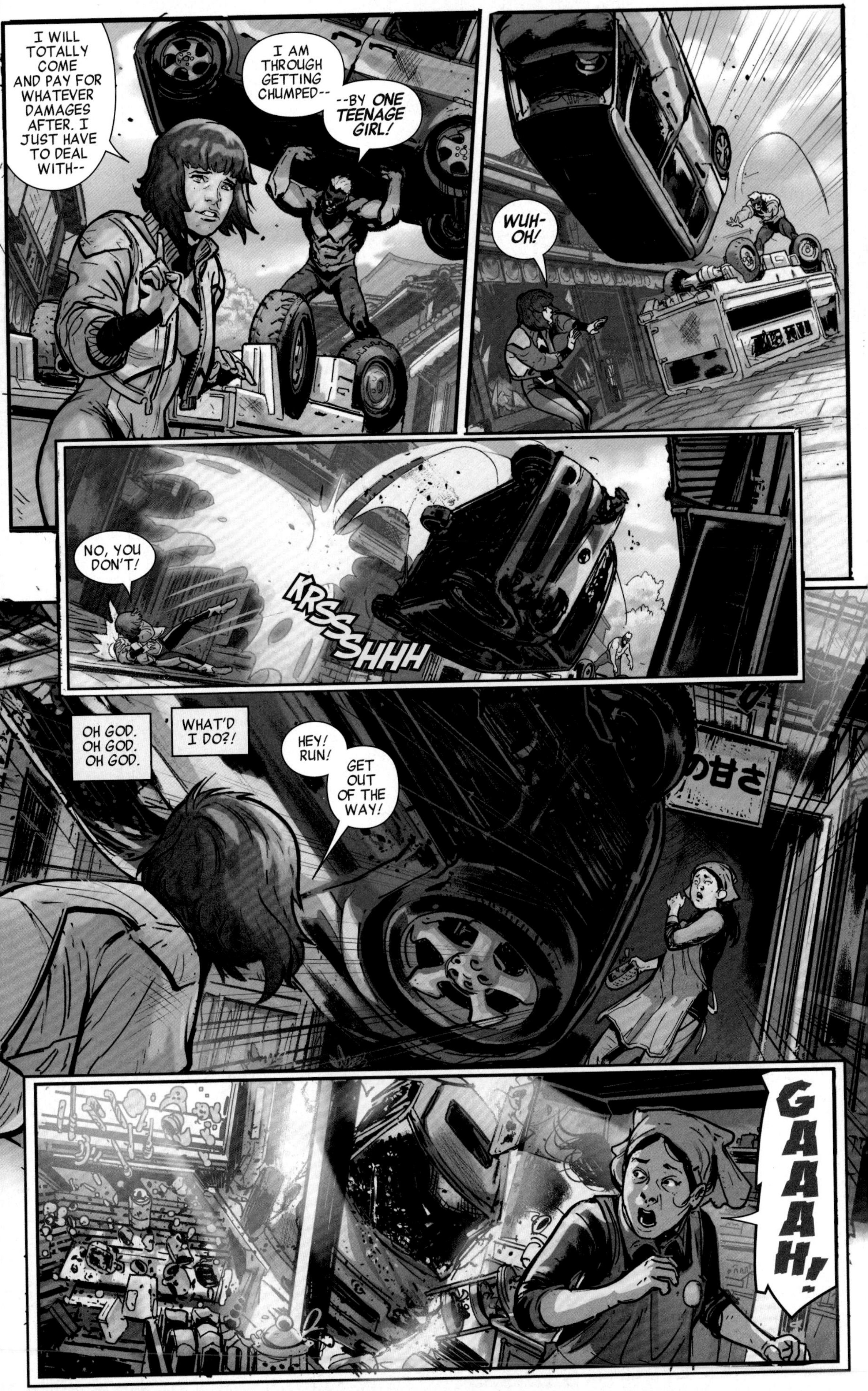
I WILL TOTALLY COME AND PAY FOR WHATEVER DAMAGES AFTER. I JUST HAVE TO DEAL WITH--
I AM THROUGH GETTING CHUMPED--
--BY ONE TEENAGE GIRL!
WUH-OH!
NO, YOU DON'T!
KRSSSHHH
OH GOD. OH GOD. OH GOD.
WHAT'D I DO?!
HEY! RUN!
GET OUT OF THE WAY!
の甘さ
GAAAH!

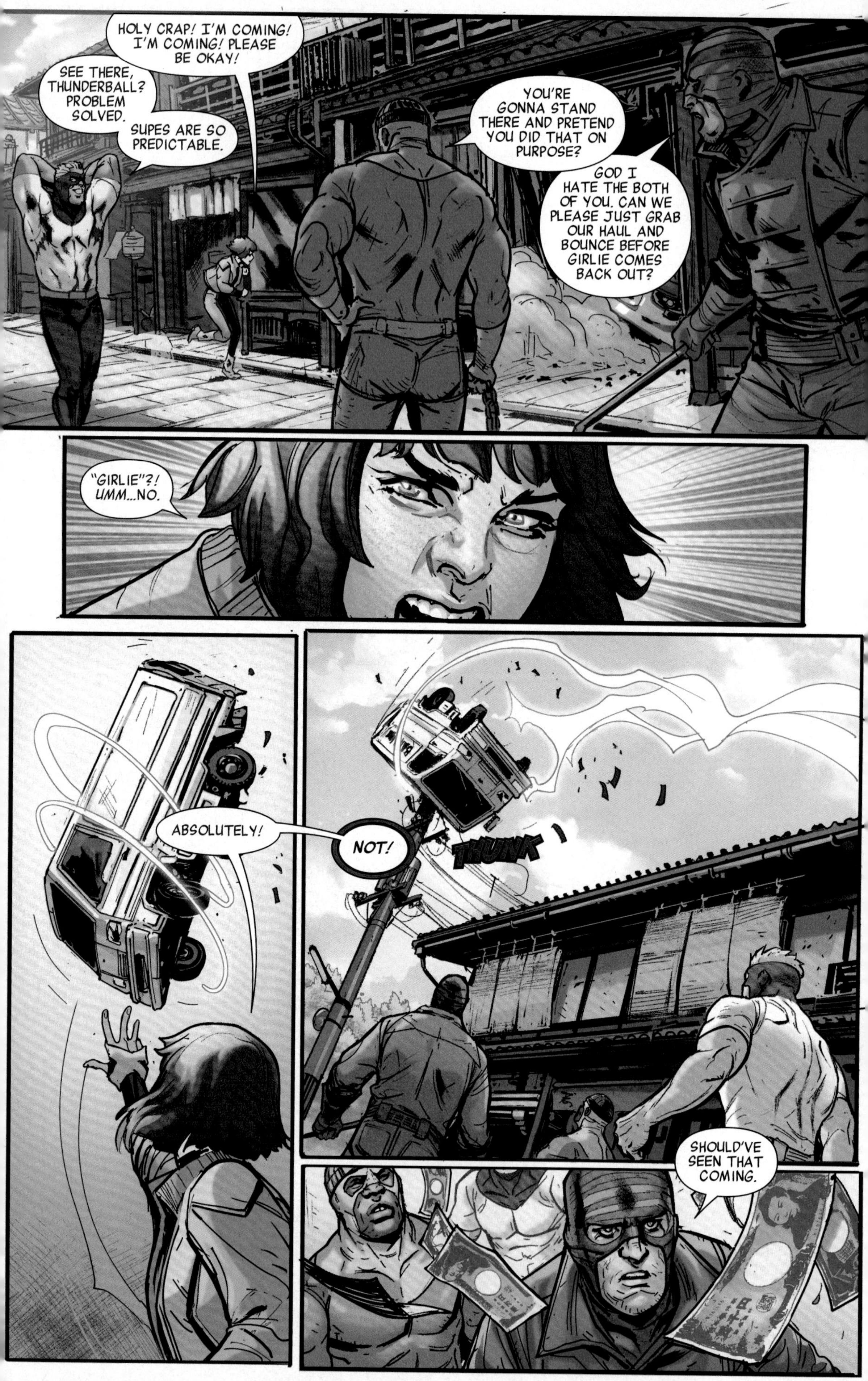
SEE THERE, THUNDERBALL? PROBLEM SOLVED.
SUPES ARE SO PREDICTABLE.
HOLY CRAP! I'M COMING! I'M COMING! PLEASE BE OKAY!
YOU'RE GONNA STAND THERE AND PRETEND YOU DID THAT ON PURPOSE?
GOD I HATE THE BOTH OF YOU. CAN WE PLEASE JUST GRAB OUR HAUL AND BOUNCE BEFORE GIRLIE COMES BACK OUT?
"GIRLIE"?! UMM...NO.
ABSOLUTELY!
NOT!
THUNK
SHOULD'VE SEEN THAT COMING.

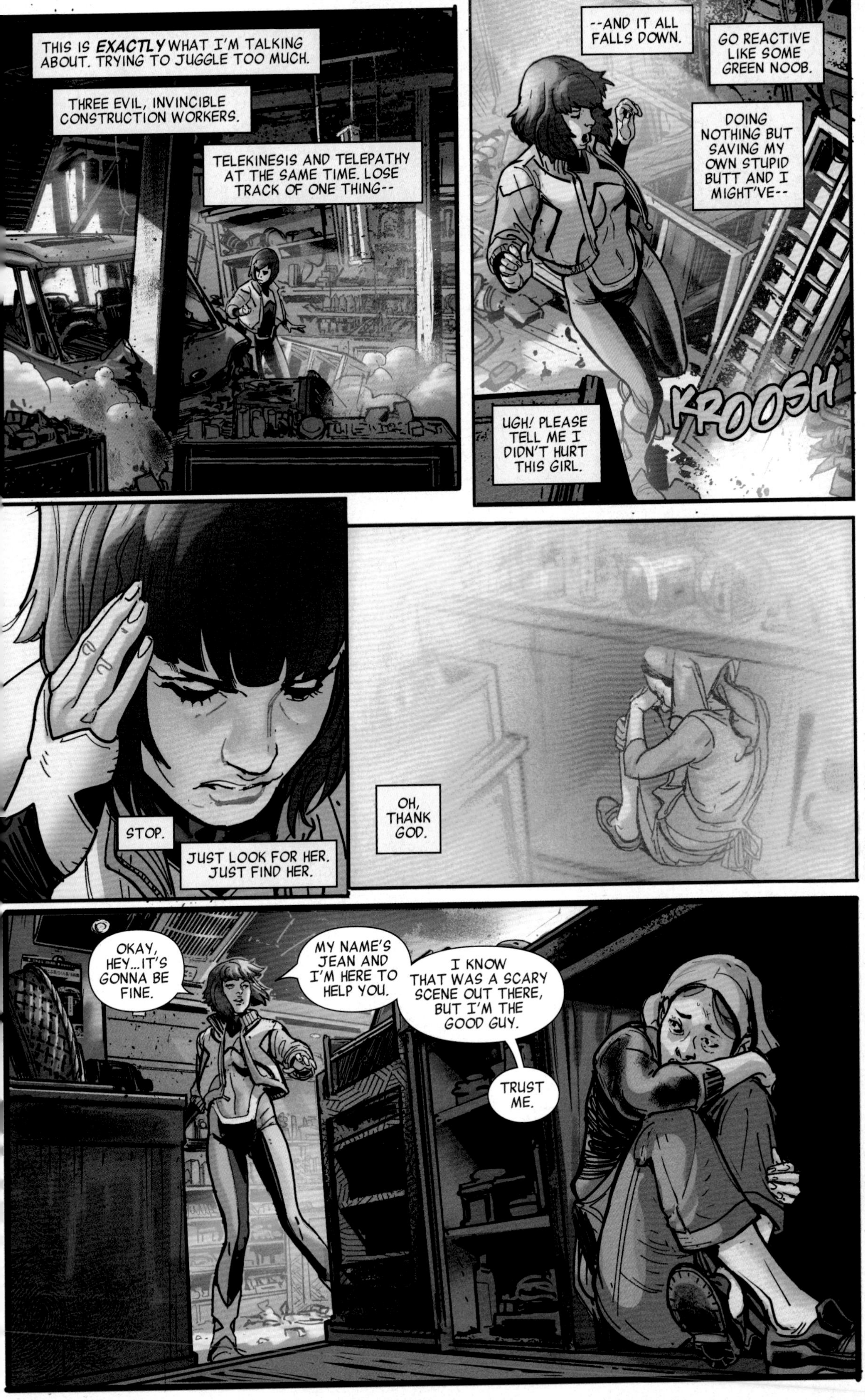
THIS IS EXACTLY WHAT I'M TALKING ABOUT. TRYING TO JUGGLE TOO MUCH.
THREE EVIL, INVINCIBLE CONSTRUCTION WORKERS.
TELEKINESIS AND TELEPATHY AT THE SAME TIME. LOSE TRACK OF ONE THING--
--AND IT ALL FALLS DOWN.
GO REACTIVE LIKE SOME GREEN NOOB.
DOING NOTHING BUT SAVING MY OWN STUPID BUTT AND I MIGHT'VE--
KROOSH
UGH! PLEASE TELL ME I DIDN'T HURT THIS GIRL.
STOP.
JUST LOOK FOR HER. JUST FIND HER.
OH, THANK GOD.
OKAY, HEY...IT'S GONNA BE FINE.
MY NAME'S JEAN AND I'M HERE TO HELP YOU.
I KNOW THAT WAS A SCARY SCENE OUT THERE, BUT I'M THE GOOD GUY.
TRUST ME.

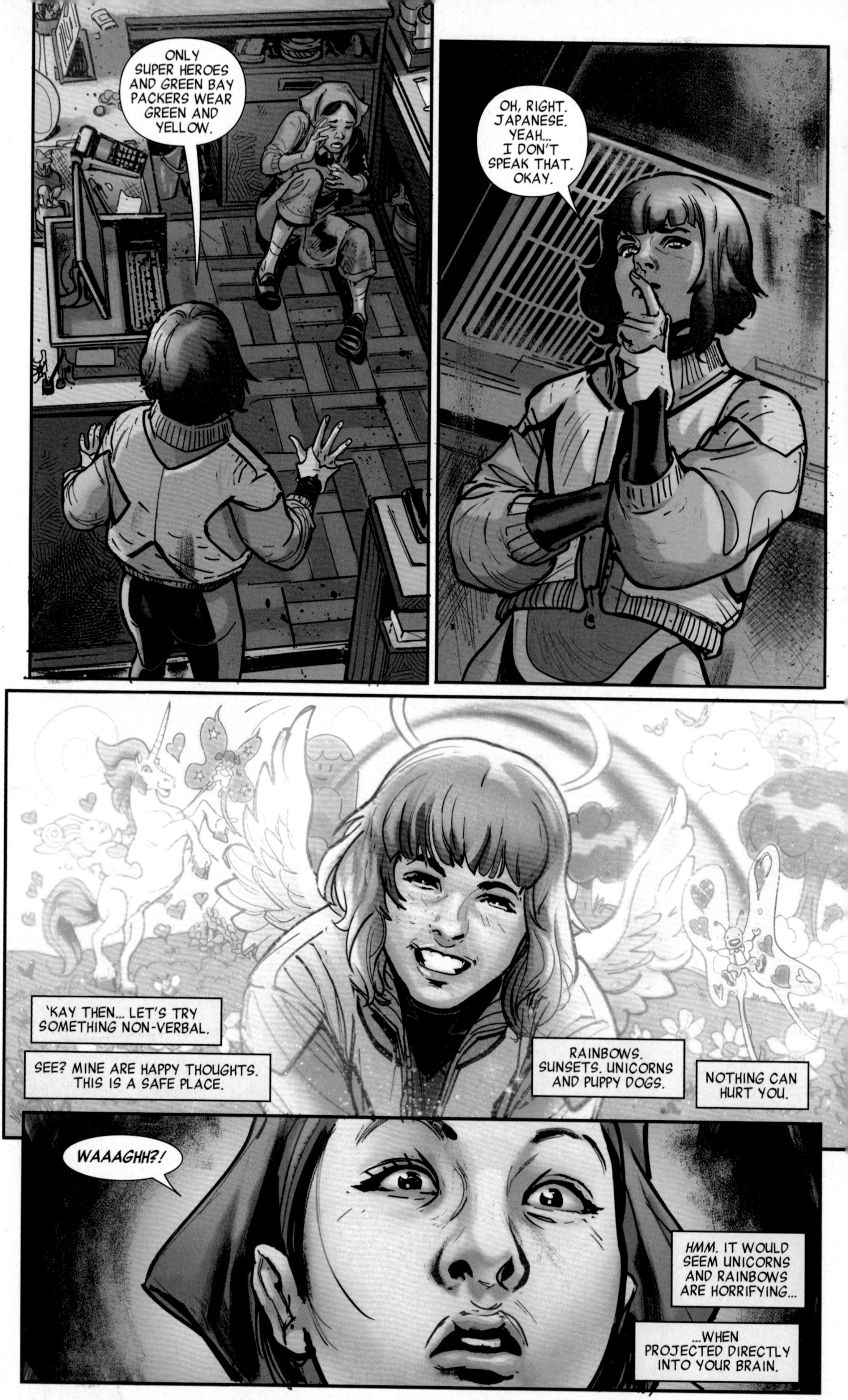

ONLY SUPER HEROES AND GREEN BAY PACKERS WEAR GREEN AND YELLOW.
OH, RIGHT. JAPANESE. YEAH... I DON'T SPEAK THAT. OKAY.
'KAY THEN... LET'S TRY SOMETHING NON-VERBAL.
SEE? MINE ARE HAPPY THOUGHTS. THIS IS A SAFE PLACE.
RAINBOWS. SUNSETS. UNICORNS AND PUPPY DOGS.
NOTHING CAN HURT YOU.
WAAAGHH?!
HMM. IT WOULD SEEM UNICORNS AND RAINBOWS ARE HORRIFYING...
...WHEN PROJECTED DIRECTLY INTO YOUR BRAIN.

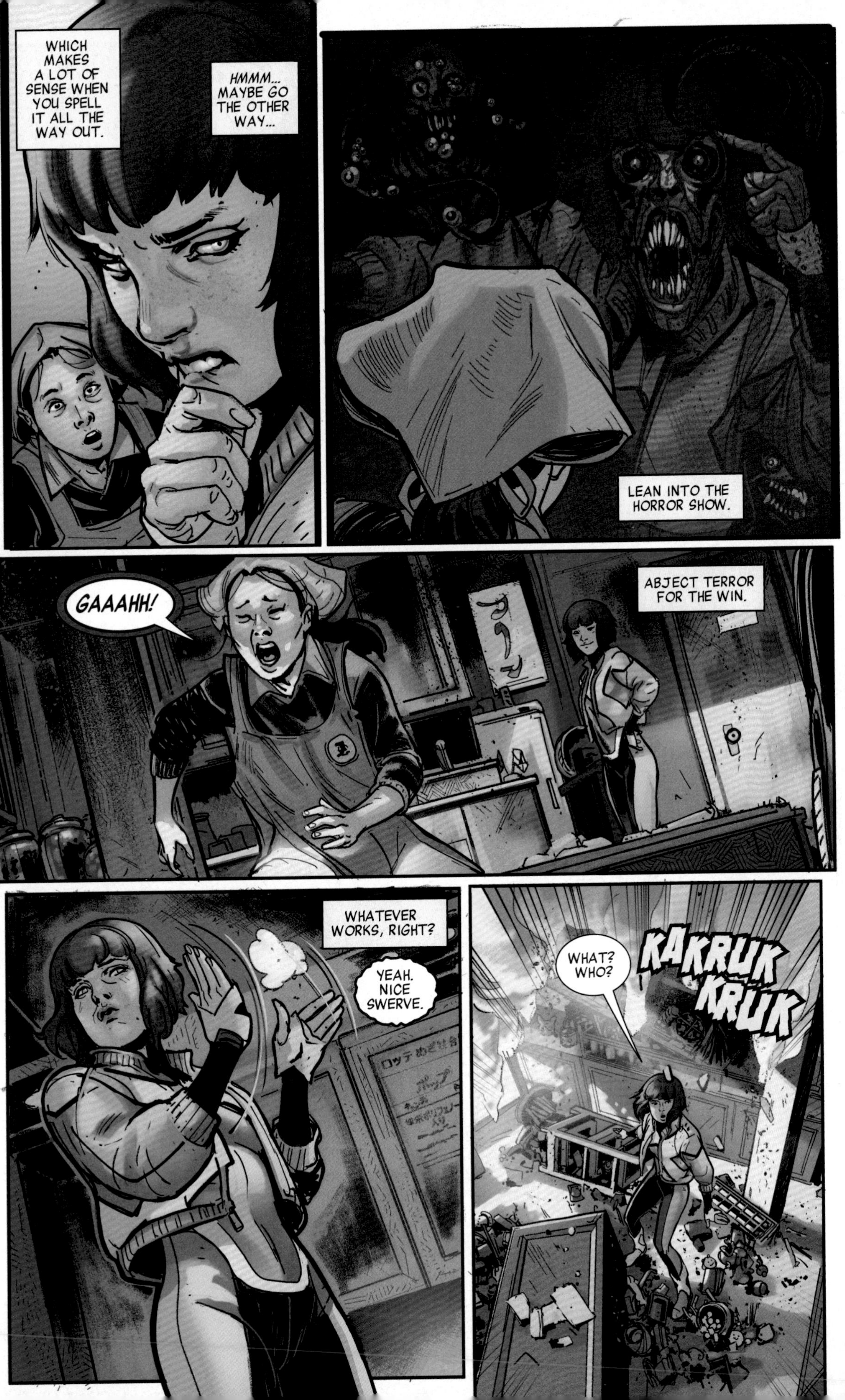
WHICH MAKES A LOT OF SENSE WHEN YOU SPELL IT ALL THE WAY OUT.
HMMM... MAYBE GO THE OTHER WAY...
LEAN INTO THE HORROR SHOW.
GAAAHH!
ABJECT TERROR FOR THE WIN.
WHATEVER WORKS, RIGHT?
YEAH. NICE SWERVE.
WHAT? WHO?
KAKRUK KRUK

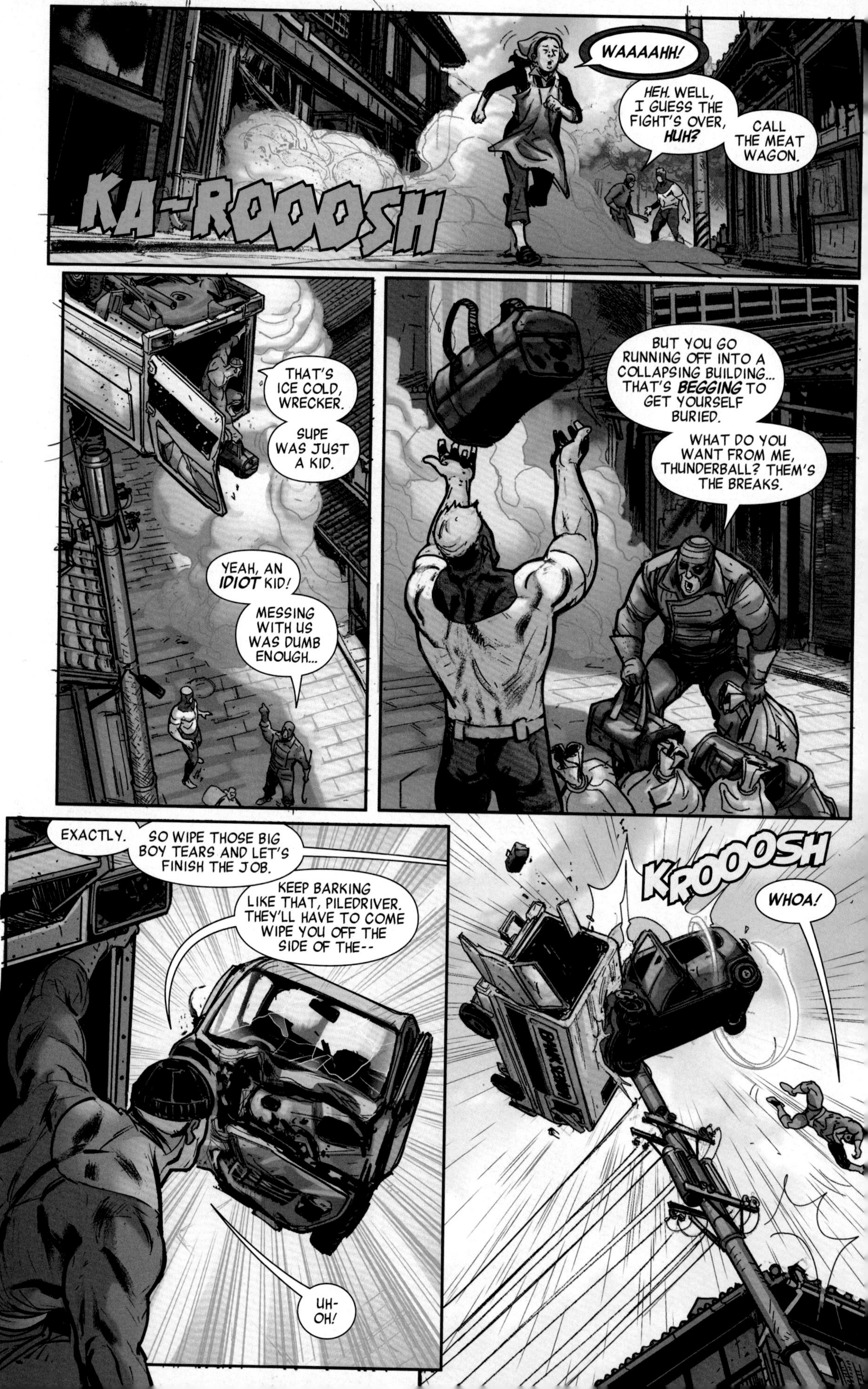
KA-ROOOSH
WAAAAHH!
HEH. WELL, I GUESS THE FIGHT'S OVER, HUH?
CALL THE MEAT WAGON.
THAT'S ICE COLD, WRECKER.
SUPE WAS JUST A KID.
YEAH, AN IDIOT KID!
MESSING WITH US WAS DUMB ENOUGH...
BUT YOU GO RUNNING OFF INTO A COLLAPSING BUILDING... THAT'S BEGGING TO GET YOURSELF BURIED.
WHAT DO YOU WANT FROM ME, THUNDERBALL? THEM'S THE BREAKS.
EXACTLY.
SO WIPE THOSE BIG BOY TEARS AND LET'S FINISH THE JOB.
KEEP BARKING LIKE THAT, PILEDRIVER. THEY'LL HAVE TO COME WIPE YOU OFF THE SIDE OF THE--
UH-OH!
KROOOSH
WHOA!

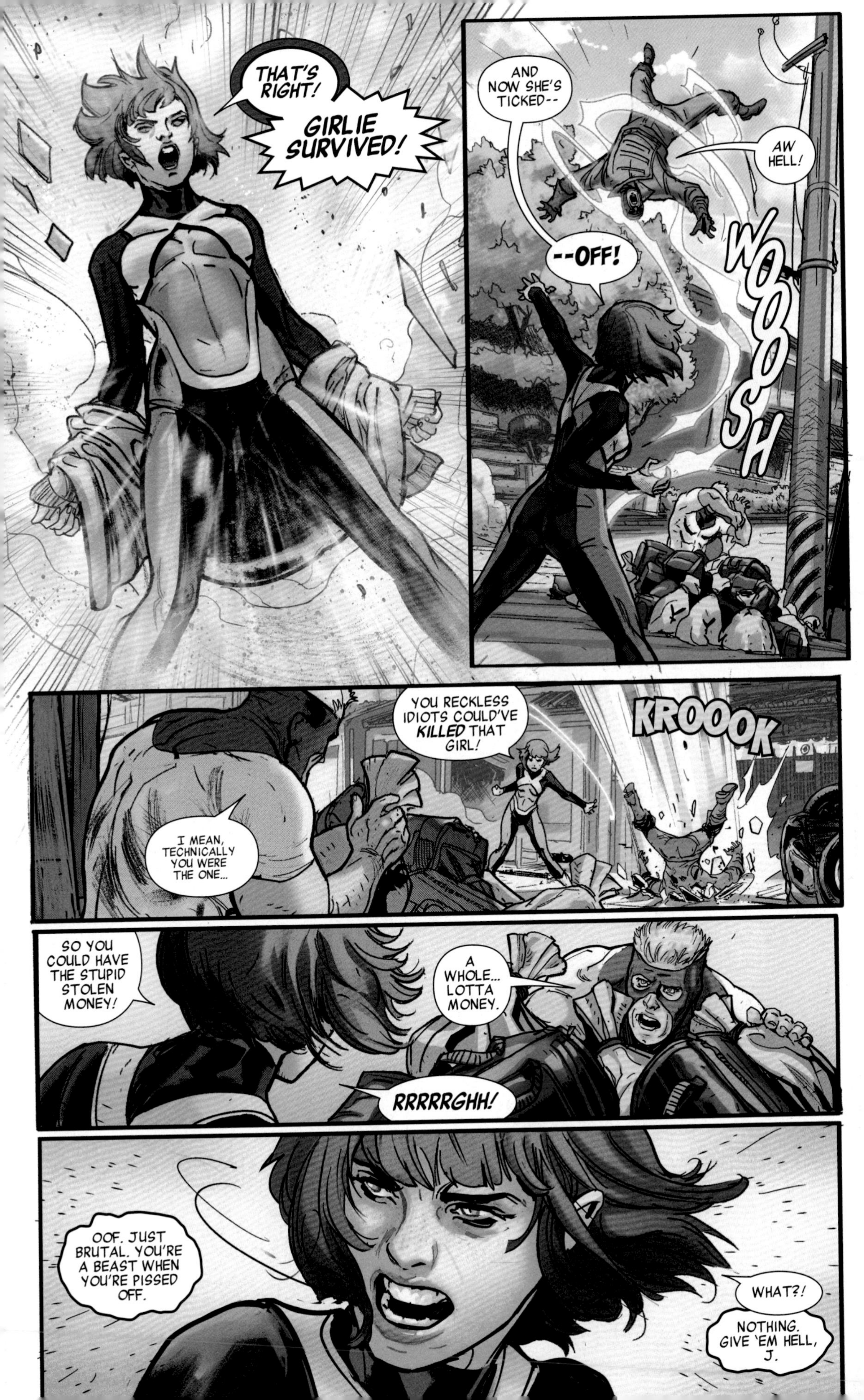
THAT'S RIGHT!
GIRLIE SURVIVED!
AND NOW SHE'S TICKED--
--OFF!
AW HELL!
WOOOOSH
YOU RECKLESS IDIOTS COULD'VE KILLED THAT GIRL!
KROOOK
I MEAN, TECHNICALLY YOU WERE THE ONE...
SO YOU COULD HAVE THE STUPID STOLEN MONEY!
A WHOLE... LOTTA MONEY.
RRRRRGHH!
OOF. JUST BRUTAL. YOU'RE A BEAST WHEN YOU'RE PISSED OFF.
WHAT?!
NOTHING. GIVE 'EM HELL, J.

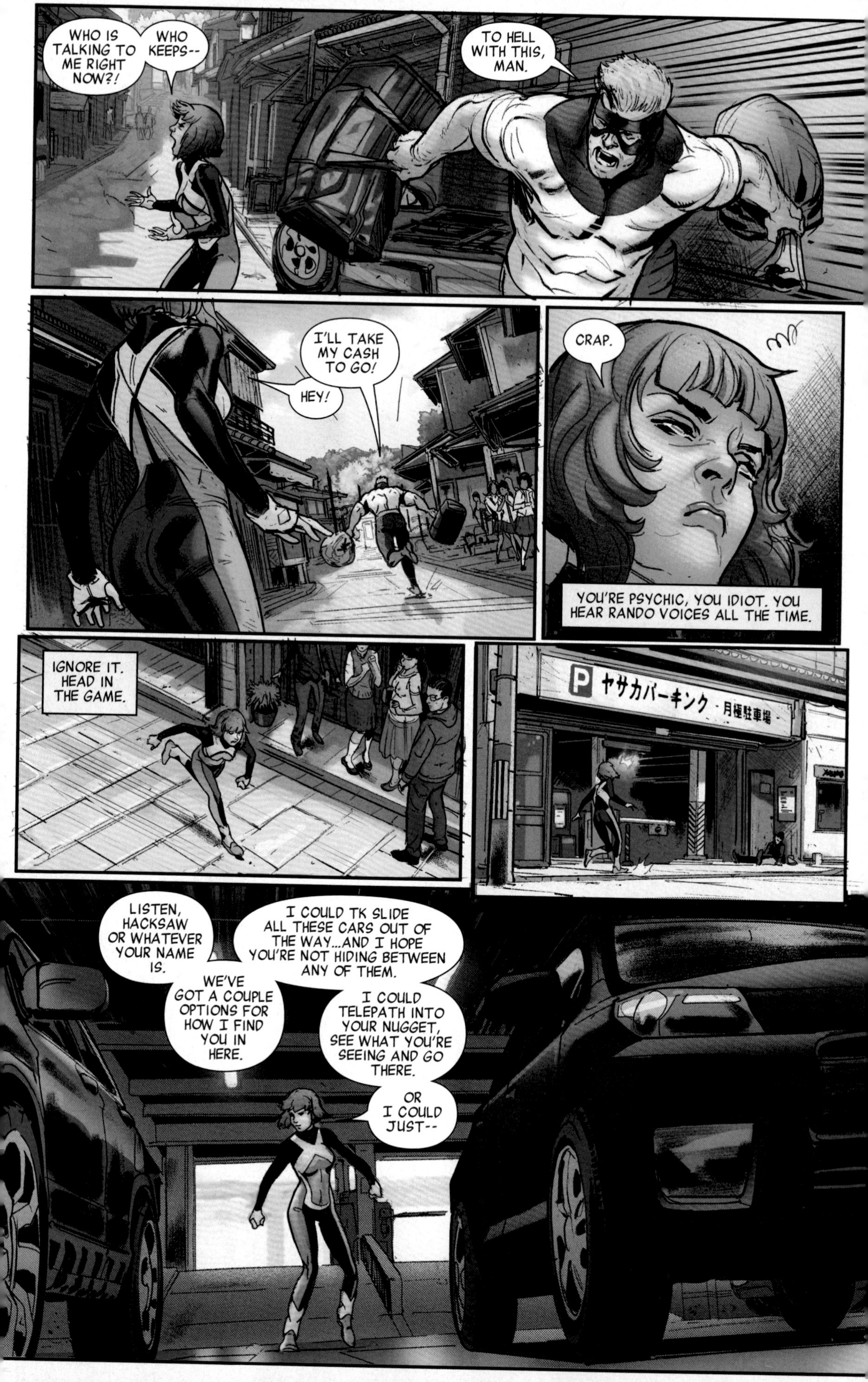
WHO IS TALKING TO ME RIGHT NOW?!
WHO KEEPS--
TO HELL WITH THIS, MAN.
I'LL TAKE MY CASH TO GO!
HEY!
CRAP.
YOU'RE PSYCHIC, YOU IDIOT. YOU HEAR RANDO VOICES ALL THE TIME.
IGNORE IT. HEAD IN THE GAME.
P ヤサカパーキング -月極駐車場
LISTEN, HACKSAW OR WHATEVER YOUR NAME IS.
WE'VE GOT A COUPLE OPTIONS FOR HOW I FIND YOU IN HERE.
I COULD TK SLIDE ALL THESE CARS OUT OF THE WAY...AND I HOPE YOU'RE NOT HIDING BETWEEN ANY OF THEM.
I COULD TELEPATH INTO YOUR NUGGET, SEE WHAT YOU'RE SEEING AND GO THERE.
OR I COULD JUST--

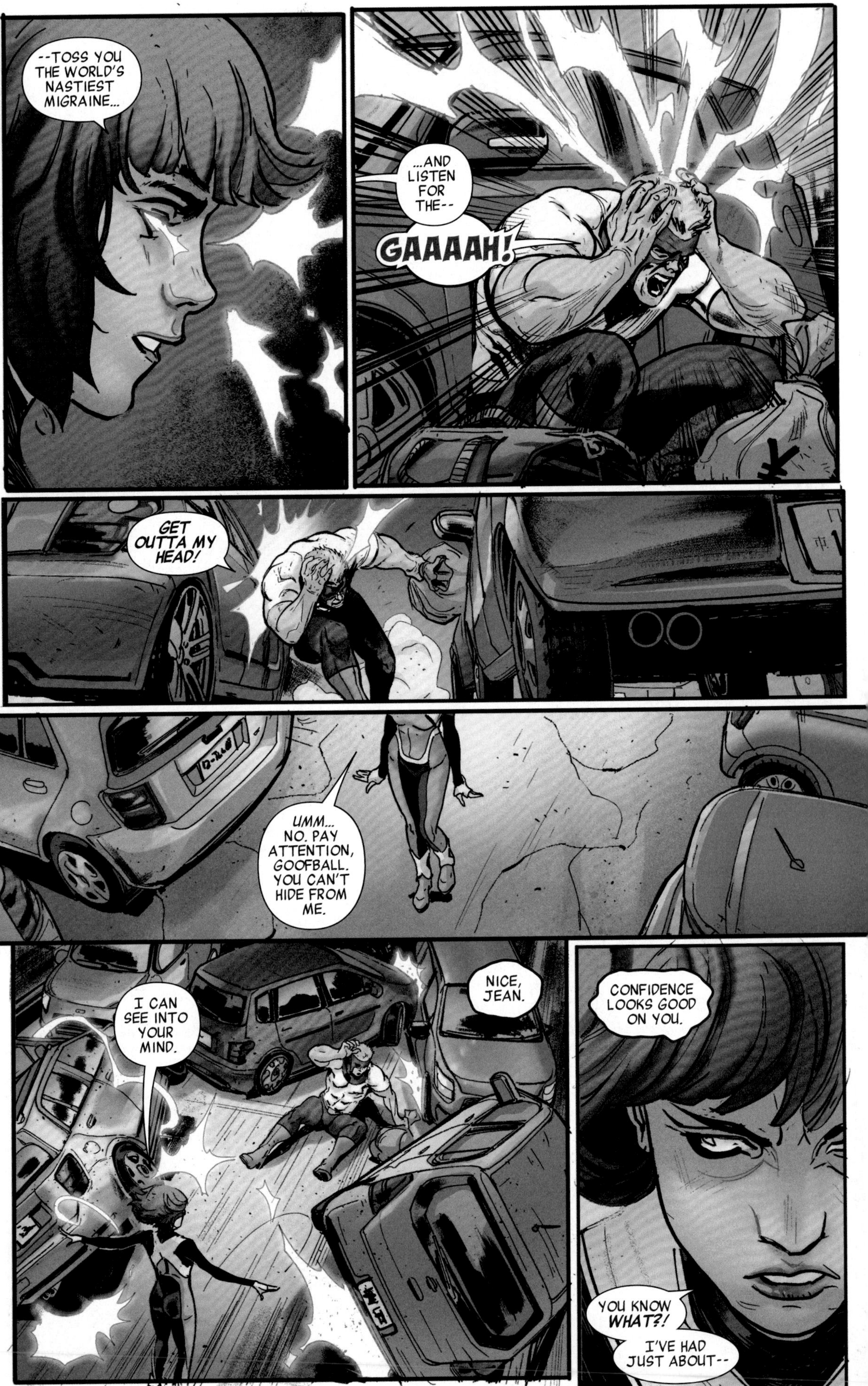
--TOSS YOU THE WORLD'S NASTIEST MIGRAINE...
...AND LISTEN FOR THE--
GAAAAH!
GET OUTTA MY HEAD!
UMM... NO. PAY ATTENTION, GOOFBALL. YOU CAN'T HIDE FROM ME.
I CAN SEE INTO YOUR MIND.
NICE, JEAN.
CONFIDENCE LOOKS GOOD ON YOU.
YOU KNOW WHAT?!
I'VE HAD JUST ABOUT--

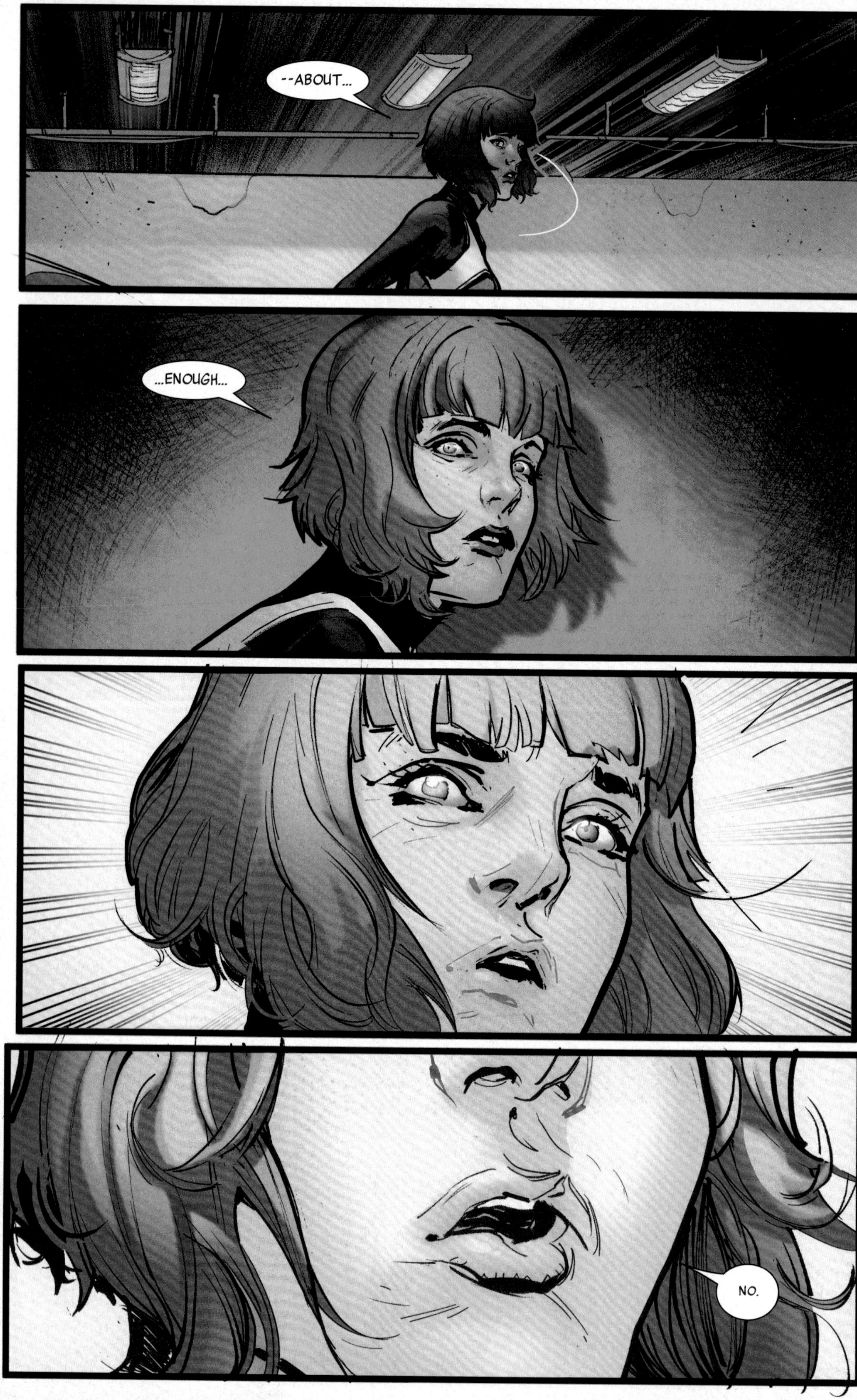
--ABOUT...
...ENOUGH...
NO.

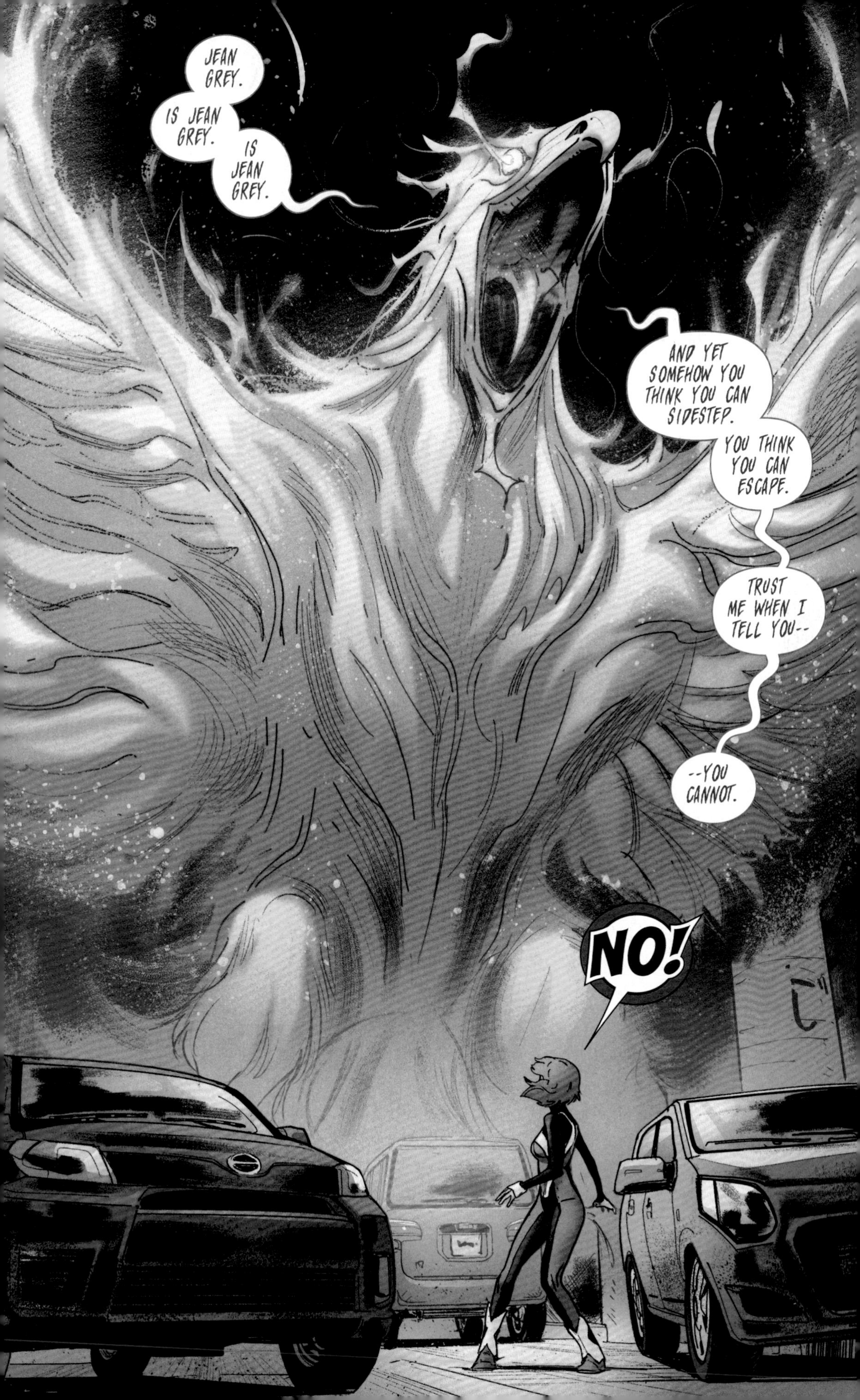
JEAN GREY.
IS JEAN GREY.
IS JEAN GREY.
AND YET SOMEHOW YOU THINK YOU CAN SIDESTEP.
YOU THINK YOU CAN ESCAPE.
TRUST ME WHEN I TELL YOU--
--YOU CANNOT.
NO!

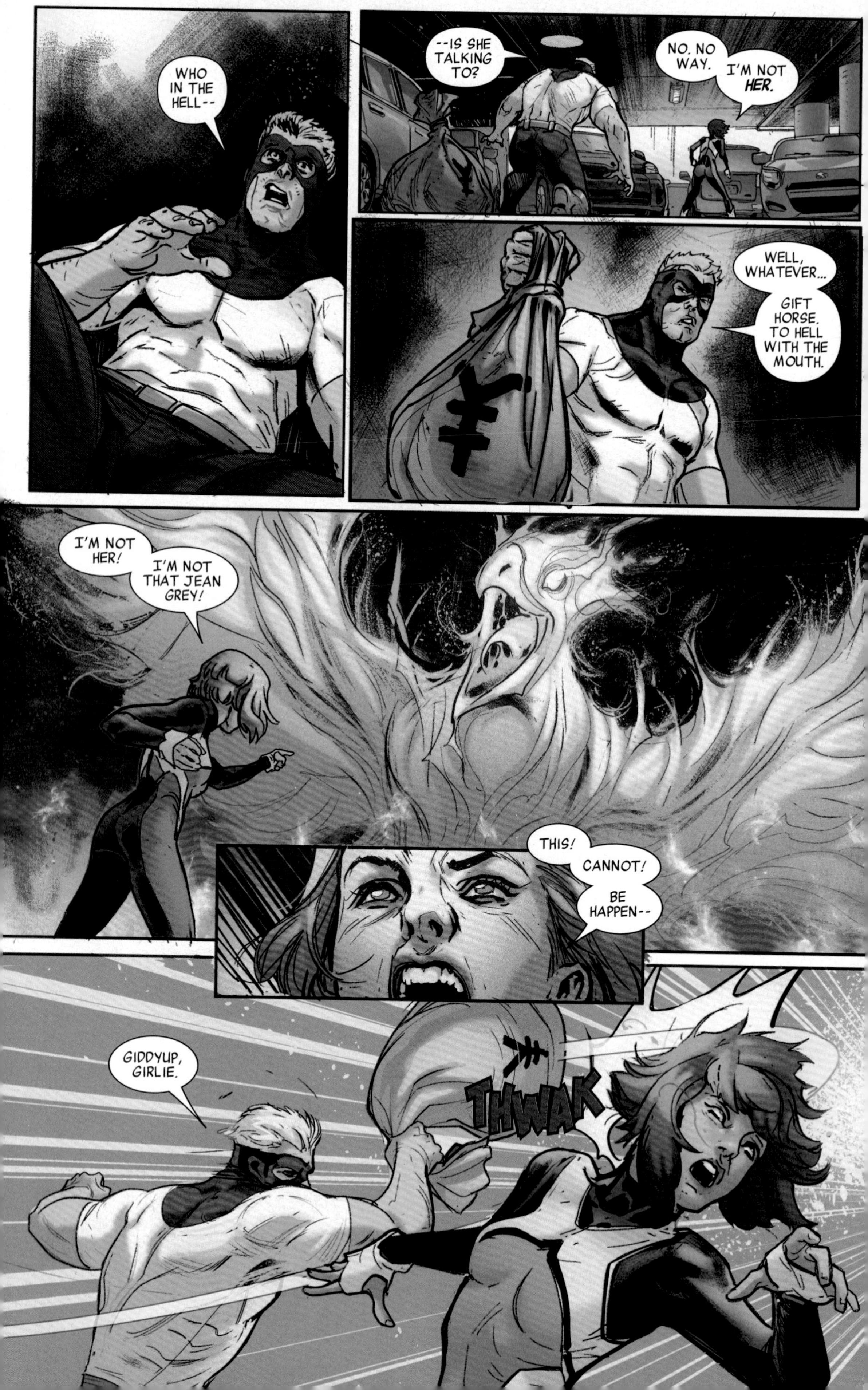
WHO IN THE HELL--
--IS SHE TALKING TO?
NO. NO WAY.
I'M NOT HER.
WELL, WHATEVER...
GIFT HORSE. TO HELL WITH THE MOUTH.
I'M NOT HER!
I'M NOT THAT JEAN GREY!
THIS!
CANNOT!
BE HAPPEN--
GIDDYUP, GIRLIE.
THWAK

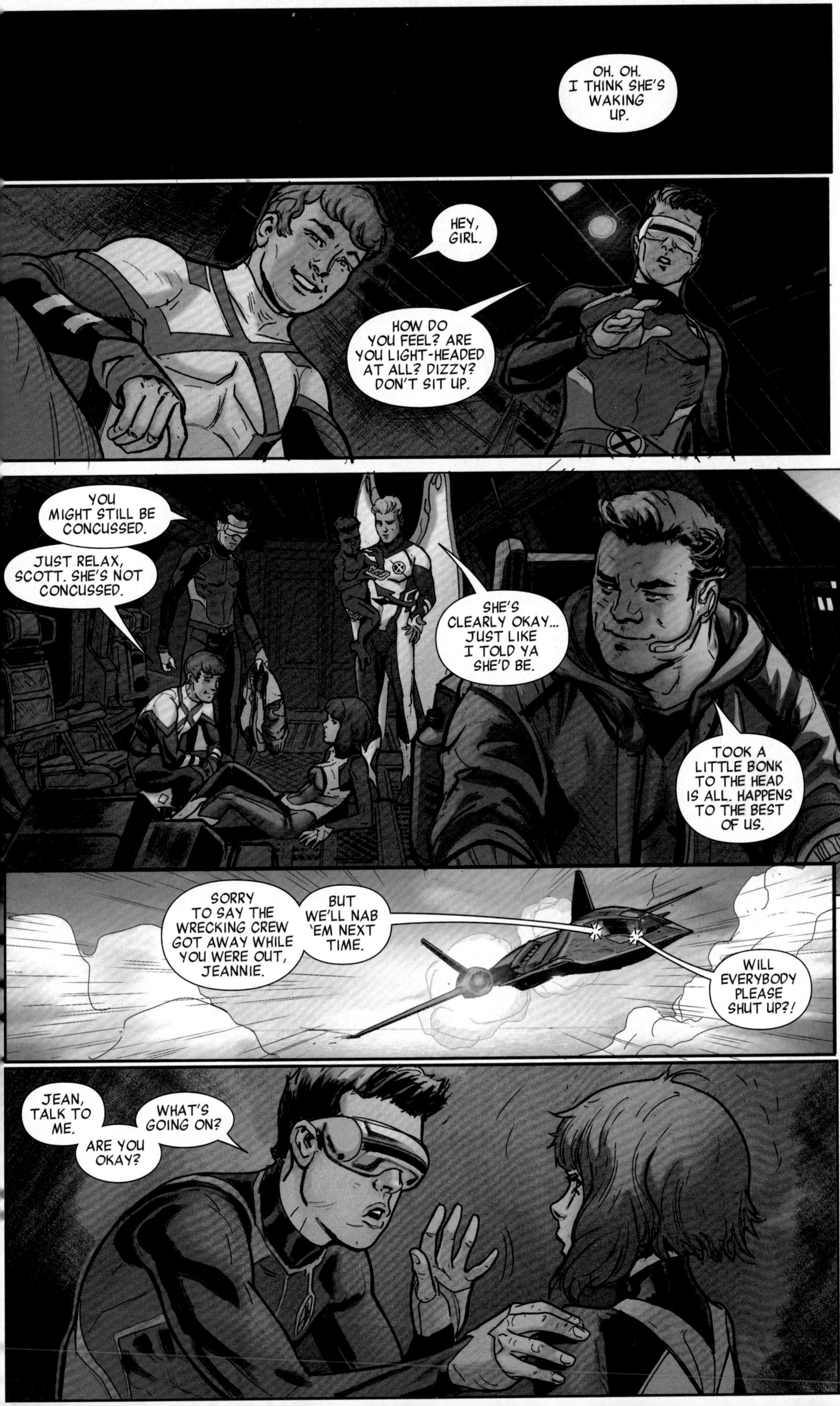
OH. OH. I THINK SHE'S WAKING UP.
HEY, GIRL.
HOW DO YOU FEEL? ARE YOU LIGHT-HEADED AT ALL? DIZZY? DON'T SIT UP.
YOU MIGHT STILL BE CONCUSSED.
JUST RELAX, SCOTT. SHE'S NOT CONCUSSED.
SHE'S CLEARLY OKAY... JUST LIKE I TOLD YA SHE'D BE.
TOOK A LITTLE BONK TO THE HEAD IS ALL. HAPPENS TO THE BEST OF US.
SORRY TO SAY THE WRECKING CREW GOT AWAY WHILE YOU WERE OUT, JEANNIE.
BUT WE'LL NAB 'EM NEXT TIME.
WILL EVERYBODY PLEASE SHUT UP?!
JEAN, TALK TO ME.
ARE YOU OKAY?
WHAT'S GOING ON?

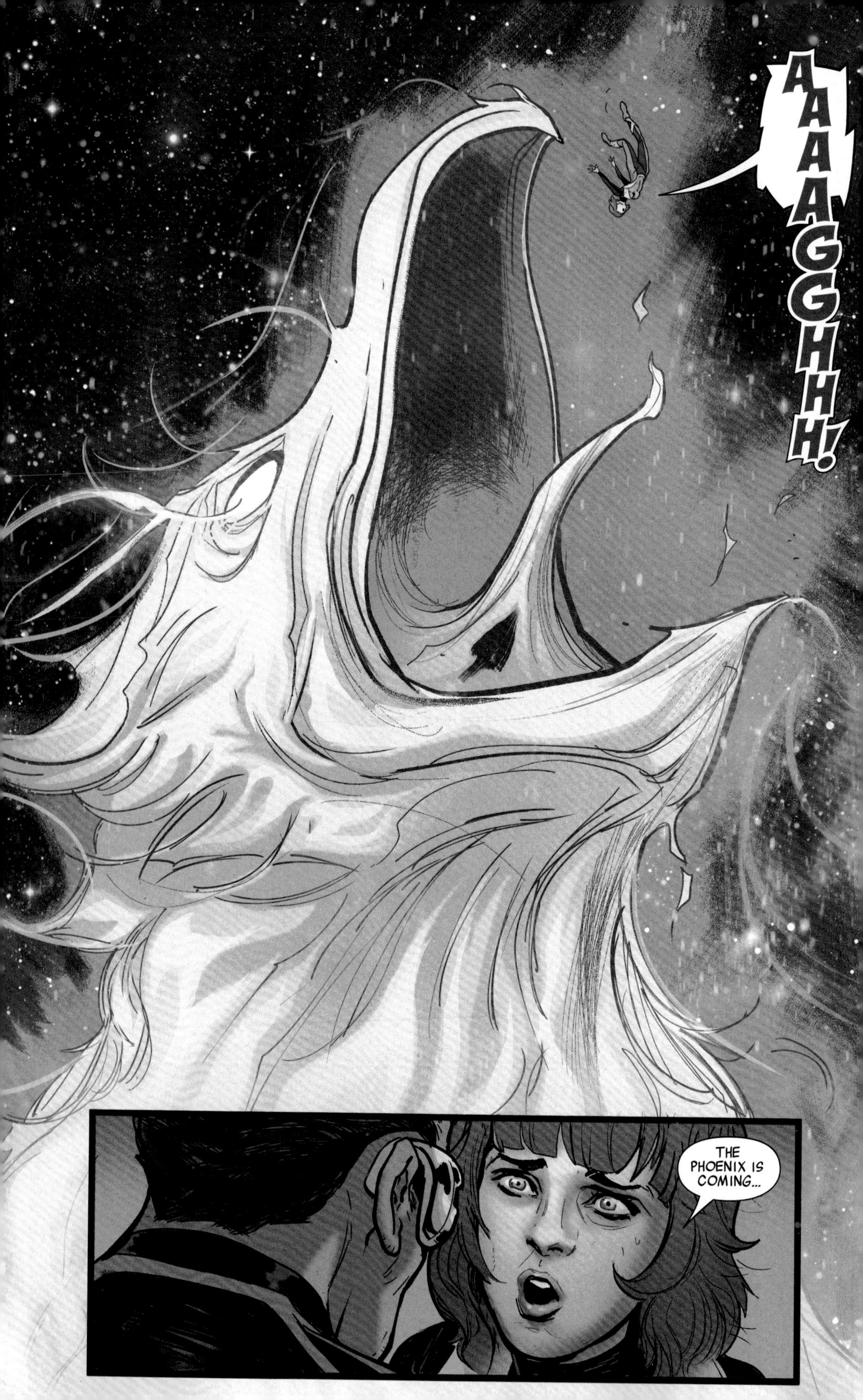
AAAAAGGHHHH!
THE PHOENIX IS COMING...

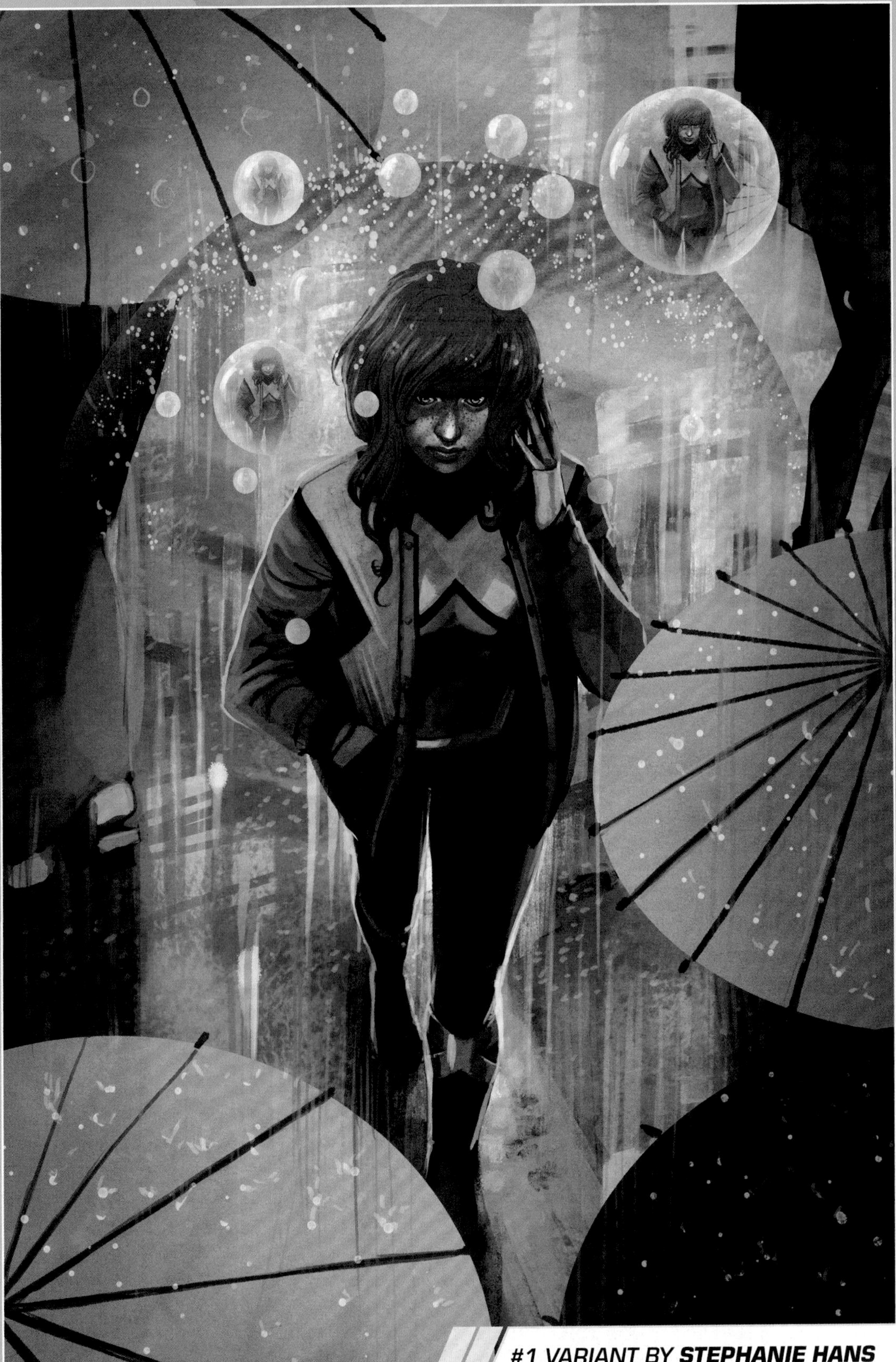

#1 VARIANT BY **STEPHANIE HANS**

2

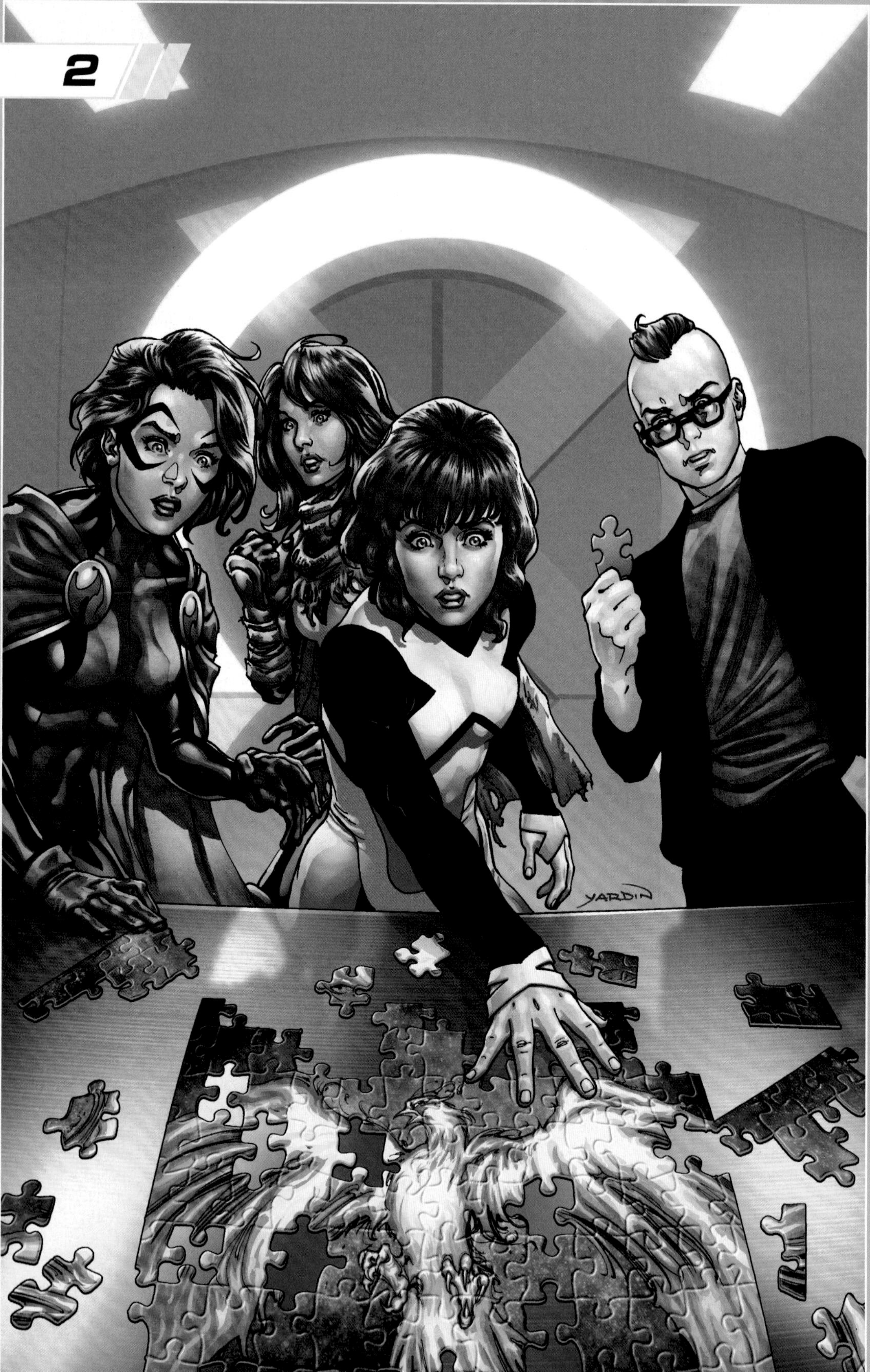
YARDIN

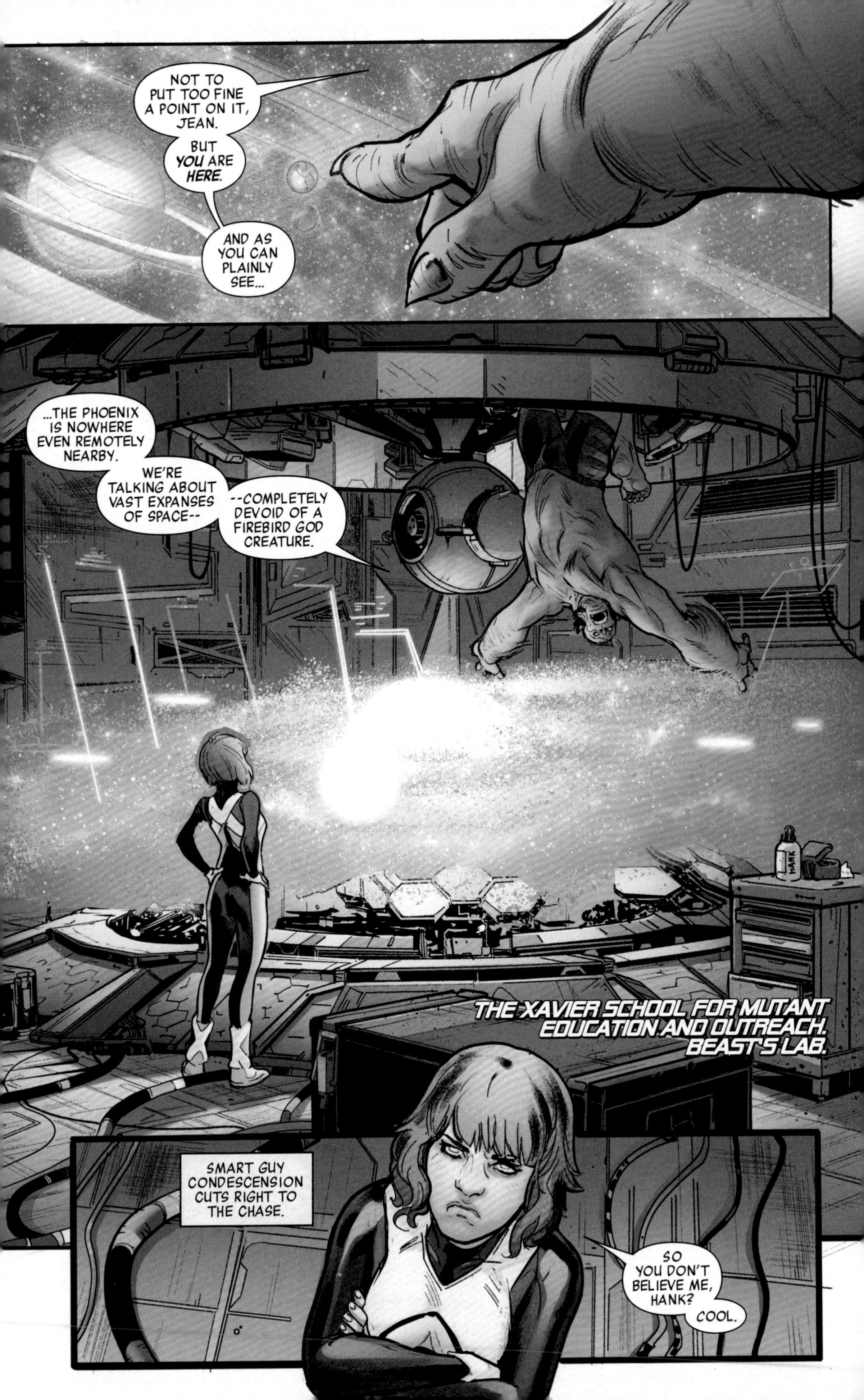
NOT TO PUT TOO FINE A POINT ON IT, JEAN.
BUT *YOU* ARE *HERE*.
AND AS YOU CAN PLAINLY SEE...
...THE PHOENIX IS NOWHERE EVEN REMOTELY NEARBY.
WE'RE TALKING ABOUT VAST EXPANSES OF SPACE--
--COMPLETELY DEVOID OF A FIREBIRD GOD CREATURE.
THE XAVIER SCHOOL FOR MUTANT EDUCATION AND OUTREACH. BEAST'S LAB.
HANK
SMART GUY CONDESCENSION CUTS RIGHT TO THE CHASE.
SO YOU DON'T BELIEVE ME, HANK?
COOL.

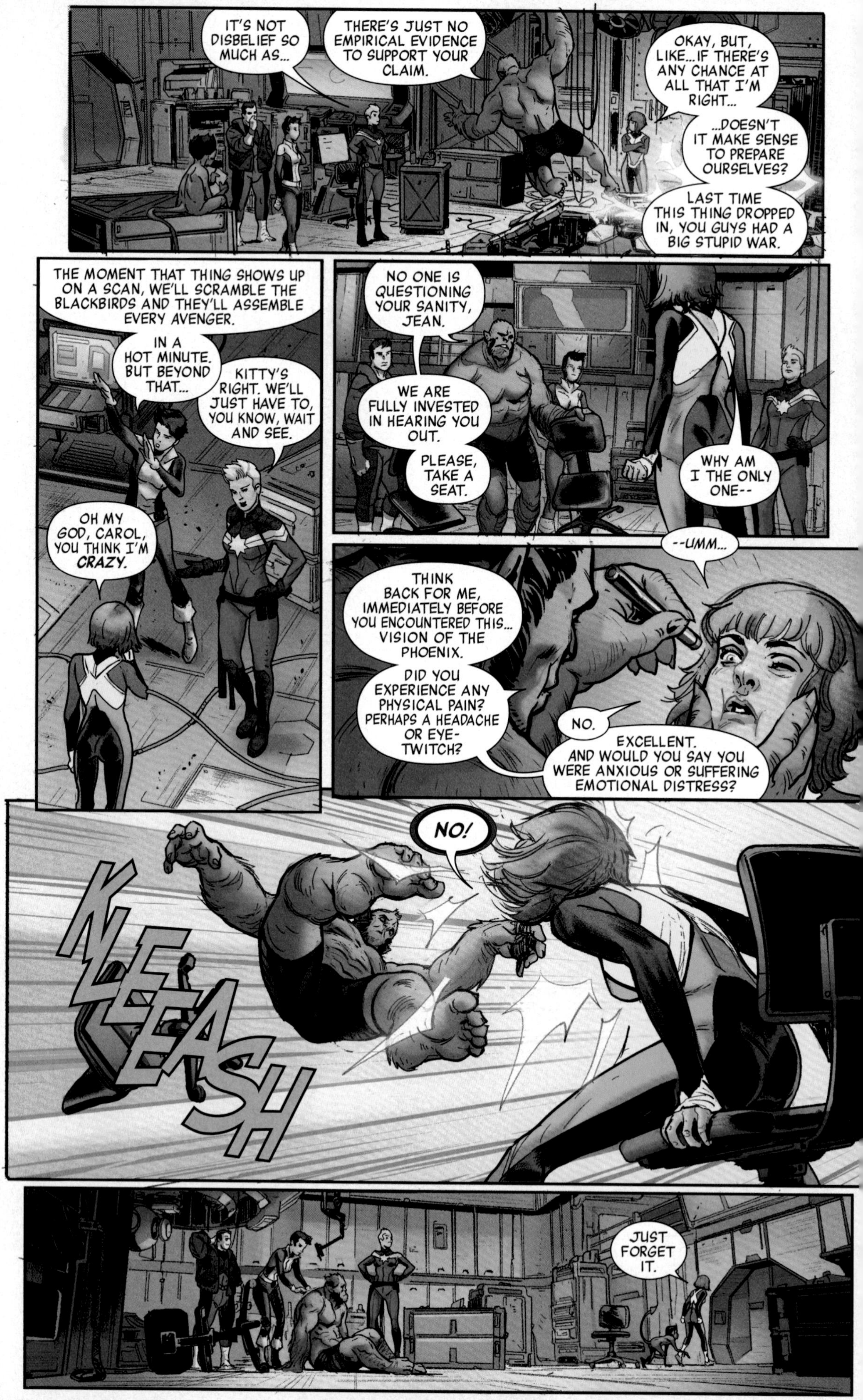
IT'S NOT DISBELIEF SO MUCH AS...
THERE'S JUST NO EMPIRICAL EVIDENCE TO SUPPORT YOUR CLAIM.
OKAY, BUT, LIKE...IF THERE'S ANY CHANCE AT ALL THAT I'M RIGHT...
...DOESN'T IT MAKE SENSE TO PREPARE OURSELVES?
LAST TIME THIS THING DROPPED IN, YOU GUYS HAD A BIG STUPID WAR.
THE MOMENT THAT THING SHOWS UP ON A SCAN, WE'LL SCRAMBLE THE BLACKBIRDS AND THEY'LL ASSEMBLE EVERY AVENGER.
IN A HOT MINUTE. BUT BEYOND THAT...
KITTY'S RIGHT. WE'LL JUST HAVE TO, YOU KNOW, WAIT AND SEE.
OH MY GOD, CAROL, YOU THINK I'M *CRAZY*.
NO ONE IS QUESTIONING YOUR SANITY, JEAN.
WE ARE FULLY INVESTED IN HEARING YOU OUT.
PLEASE, TAKE A SEAT.
WHY AM I THE ONLY ONE--
--UMM...
THINK BACK FOR ME, IMMEDIATELY BEFORE YOU ENCOUNTERED THIS... VISION OF THE PHOENIX.
DID YOU EXPERIENCE ANY PHYSICAL PAIN? PERHAPS A HEADACHE OR EYE-TWITCH?
NO.
EXCELLENT. AND WOULD YOU SAY YOU WERE ANXIOUS OR SUFFERING EMOTIONAL DISTRESS?
NO!
KLEEASH
JUST FORGET IT.

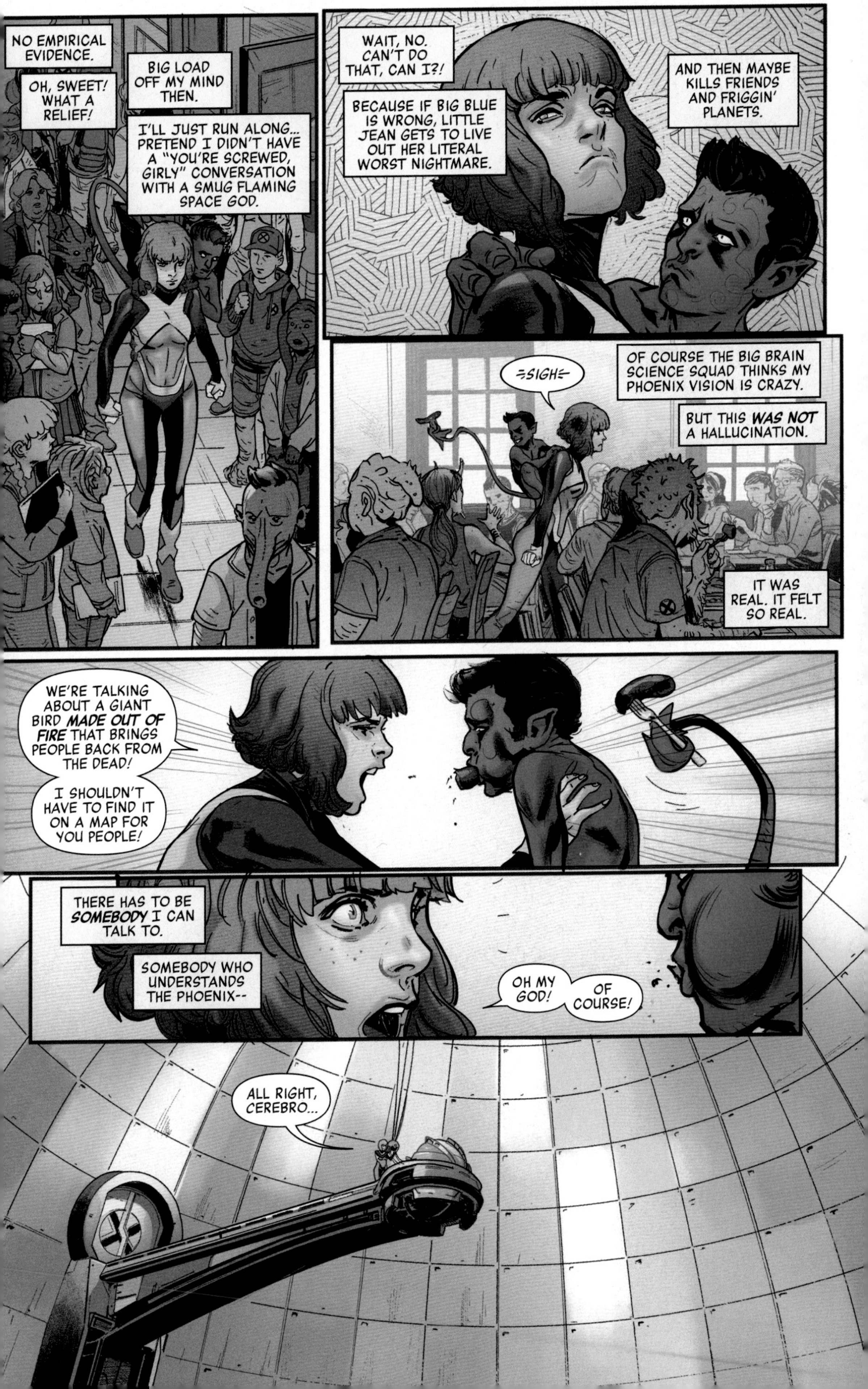

NO EMPIRICAL EVIDENCE.
OH, SWEET! WHAT A RELIEF!
BIG LOAD OFF MY MIND THEN.
I'LL JUST RUN ALONG... PRETEND I DIDN'T HAVE A "YOU'RE SCREWED, GIRLY" CONVERSATION WITH A SMUG FLAMING SPACE GOD.
WAIT, NO. CAN'T DO THAT, CAN I?!
BECAUSE IF BIG BLUE IS WRONG, LITTLE JEAN GETS TO LIVE OUT HER LITERAL WORST NIGHTMARE.
AND THEN MAYBE KILLS FRIENDS AND FRIGGIN' PLANETS.
=SIGH=
OF COURSE THE BIG BRAIN SCIENCE SQUAD THINKS MY PHOENIX VISION IS CRAZY.
BUT THIS WAS NOT A HALLUCINATION.
IT WAS REAL. IT FELT SO REAL.
WE'RE TALKING ABOUT A GIANT BIRD MADE OUT OF FIRE THAT BRINGS PEOPLE BACK FROM THE DEAD!
I SHOULDN'T HAVE TO FIND IT ON A MAP FOR YOU PEOPLE!
THERE HAS TO BE SOMEBODY I CAN TALK TO.
SOMEBODY WHO UNDERSTANDS THE PHOENIX--
OH MY GOD!
OF COURSE!
ALL RIGHT, CEREBRO...

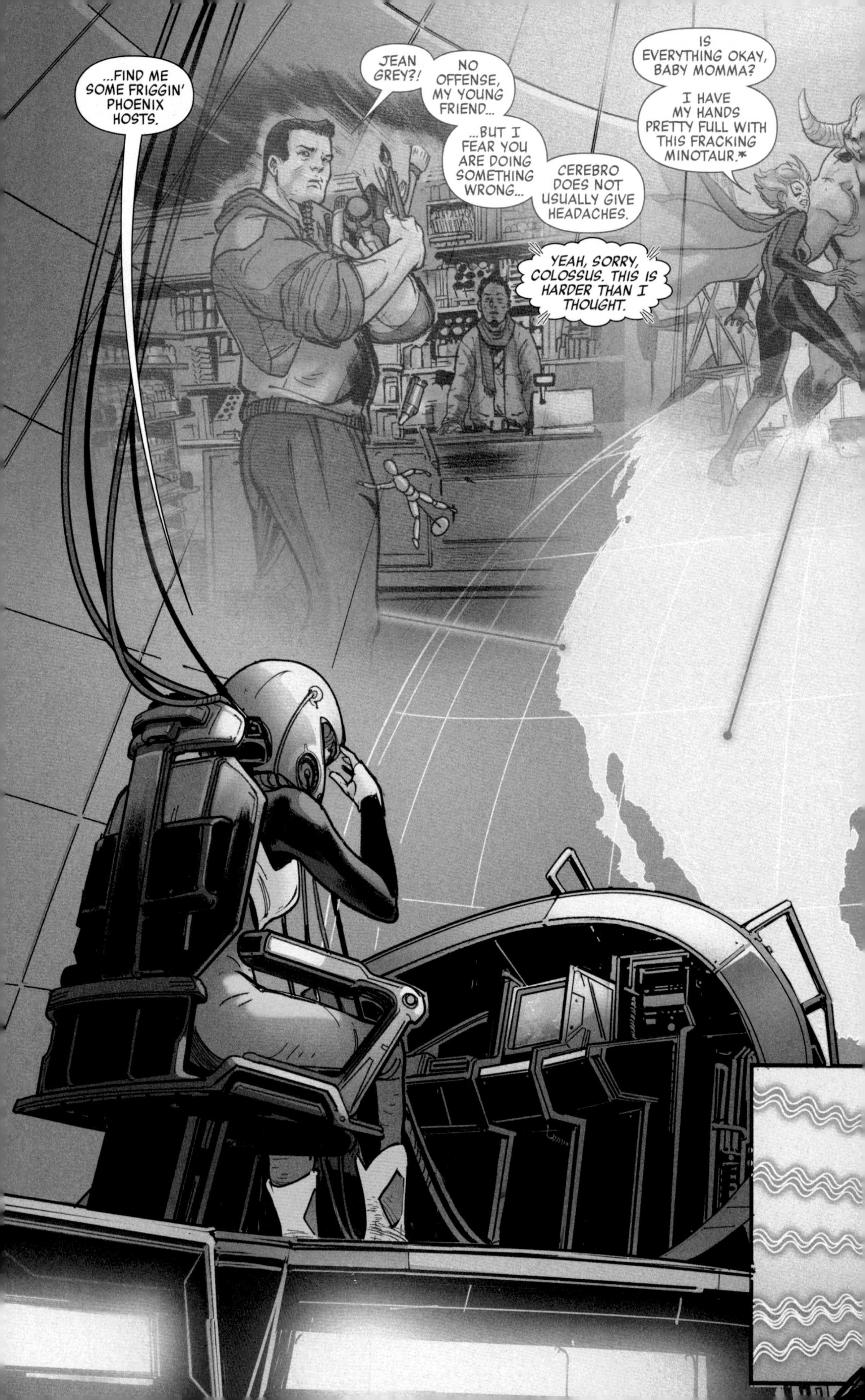
...FIND ME SOME FRIGGIN' PHOENIX HOSTS.
JEAN GREY?!
NO OFFENSE, MY YOUNG FRIEND...
...BUT I FEAR YOU ARE DOING SOMETHING WRONG...
CEREBRO DOES NOT USUALLY GIVE HEADACHES.
IS EVERYTHING OKAY, BABY MOMMA?
I HAVE MY HANDS PRETTY FULL WITH THIS FRACKING MINOTAUR.*
YEAH, SORRY, COLOSSUS. THIS IS HARDER THAN I THOUGHT.

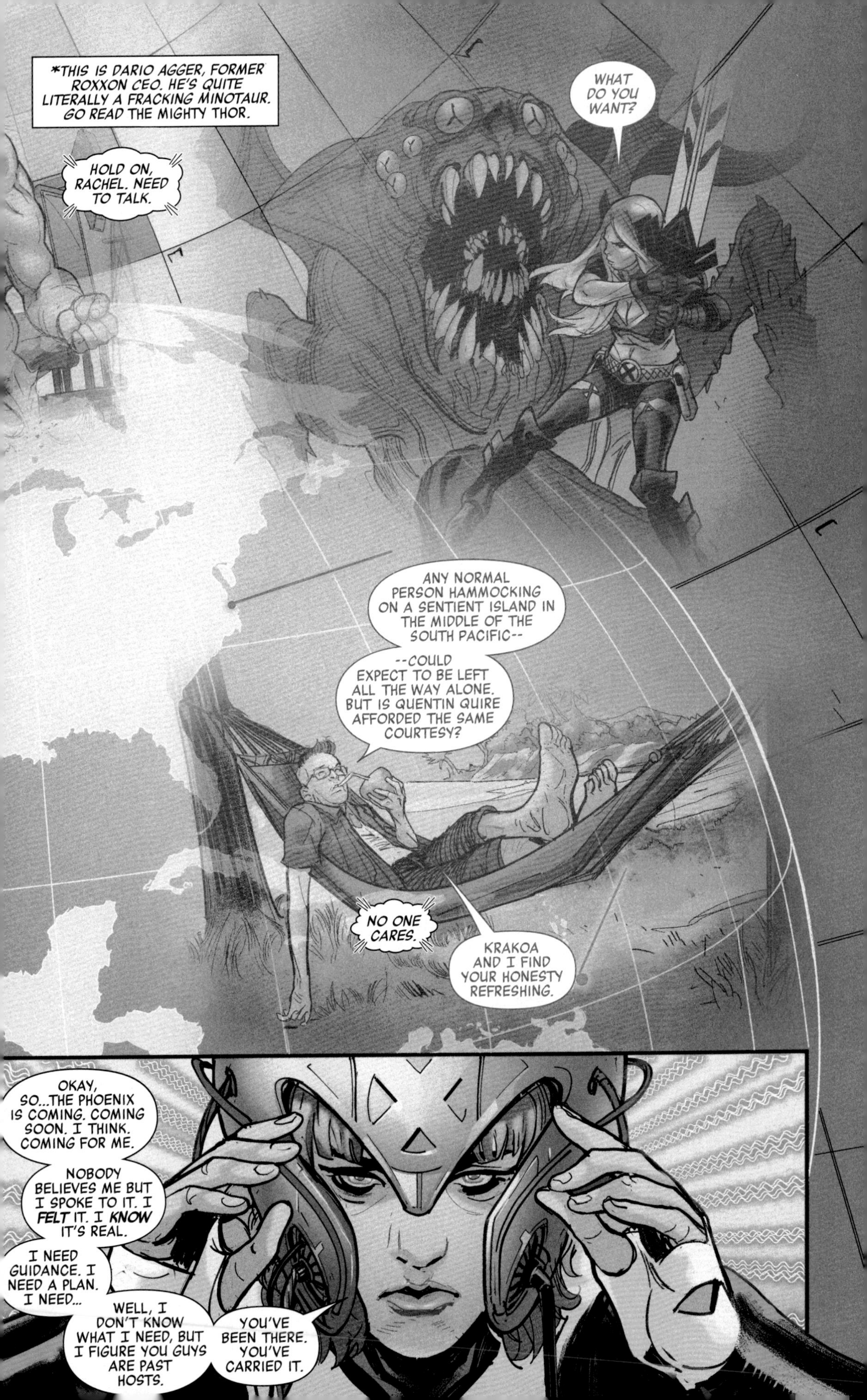
*THIS IS DARIO AGGER, FORMER ROXXON CEO. HE'S QUITE LITERALLY A FRACKING MINOTAUR. GO READ THE MIGHTY THOR.
HOLD ON, RACHEL. NEED TO TALK.
WHAT DO YOU WANT?
ANY NORMAL PERSON HAMMOCKING ON A SENTIENT ISLAND IN THE MIDDLE OF THE SOUTH PACIFIC--
--COULD EXPECT TO BE LEFT ALL THE WAY ALONE. BUT IS QUENTIN QUIRE AFFORDED THE SAME COURTESY?
NO ONE CARES.
KRAKOA AND I FIND YOUR HONESTY REFRESHING.
OKAY, SO...THE PHOENIX IS COMING. COMING SOON. I THINK. COMING FOR ME.
NOBODY BELIEVES ME BUT I SPOKE TO IT. I FELT IT. I KNOW IT'S REAL.
I NEED GUIDANCE. I NEED A PLAN. I NEED...
WELL, I DON'T KNOW WHAT I NEED, BUT I FIGURE YOU GUYS ARE PAST HOSTS.
YOU'VE BEEN THERE. YOU'VE CARRIED IT.

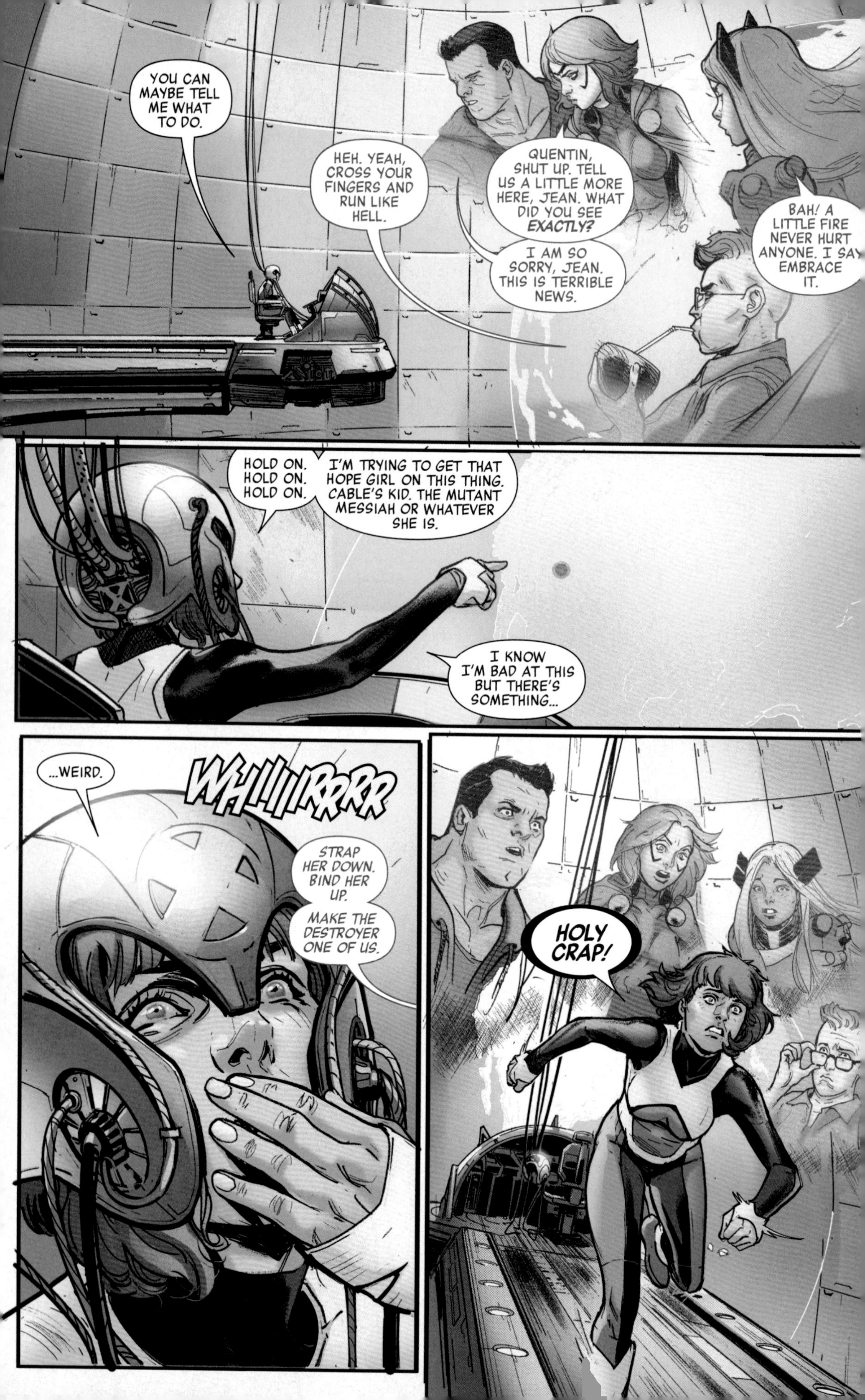
YOU CAN MAYBE TELL ME WHAT TO DO.
HEH. YEAH, CROSS YOUR FINGERS AND RUN LIKE HELL.
QUENTIN, SHUT UP. TELL US A LITTLE MORE HERE, JEAN. WHAT DID YOU SEE *EXACTLY?*
BAH! A LITTLE FIRE NEVER HURT ANYONE. I SAY EMBRACE IT.
I AM SO SORRY, JEAN. THIS IS TERRIBLE NEWS.
HOLD ON. HOLD ON. HOLD ON.
I'M TRYING TO GET THAT HOPE GIRL ON THIS THING. CABLE'S KID. THE MUTANT MESSIAH OR WHATEVER SHE IS.
I KNOW I'M BAD AT THIS BUT THERE'S SOMETHING...
...WEIRD.
WHIIIIRRRR
STRAP HER DOWN. BIND HER UP.
MAKE THE DESTROYER ONE OF US.
HOLY CRAP!

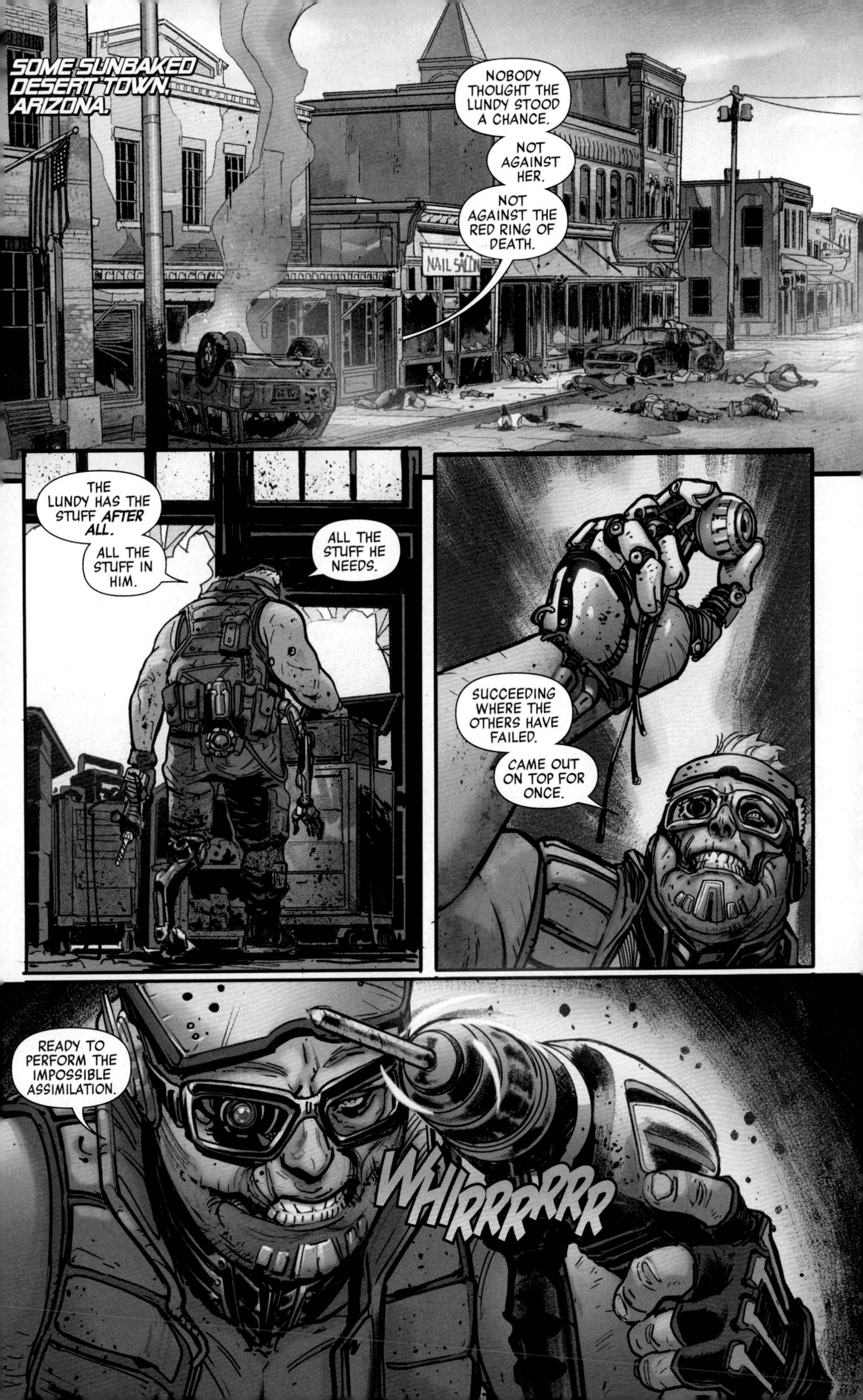
SOME SUNBAKED DESERT TOWN, ARIZONA.
NOBODY THOUGHT THE LUNDY STOOD A CHANCE.
NOT AGAINST HER.
NOT AGAINST THE RED RING OF DEATH.
NAIL SALON
THE LUNDY HAS THE STUFF *AFTER ALL*.
ALL THE STUFF IN HIM.
ALL THE STUFF HE NEEDS.
SUCCEEDING WHERE THE OTHERS HAVE FAILED.
CAME OUT ON TOP FOR ONCE.
READY TO PERFORM THE IMPOSSIBLE ASSIMILATION.
WHIRRRRRR

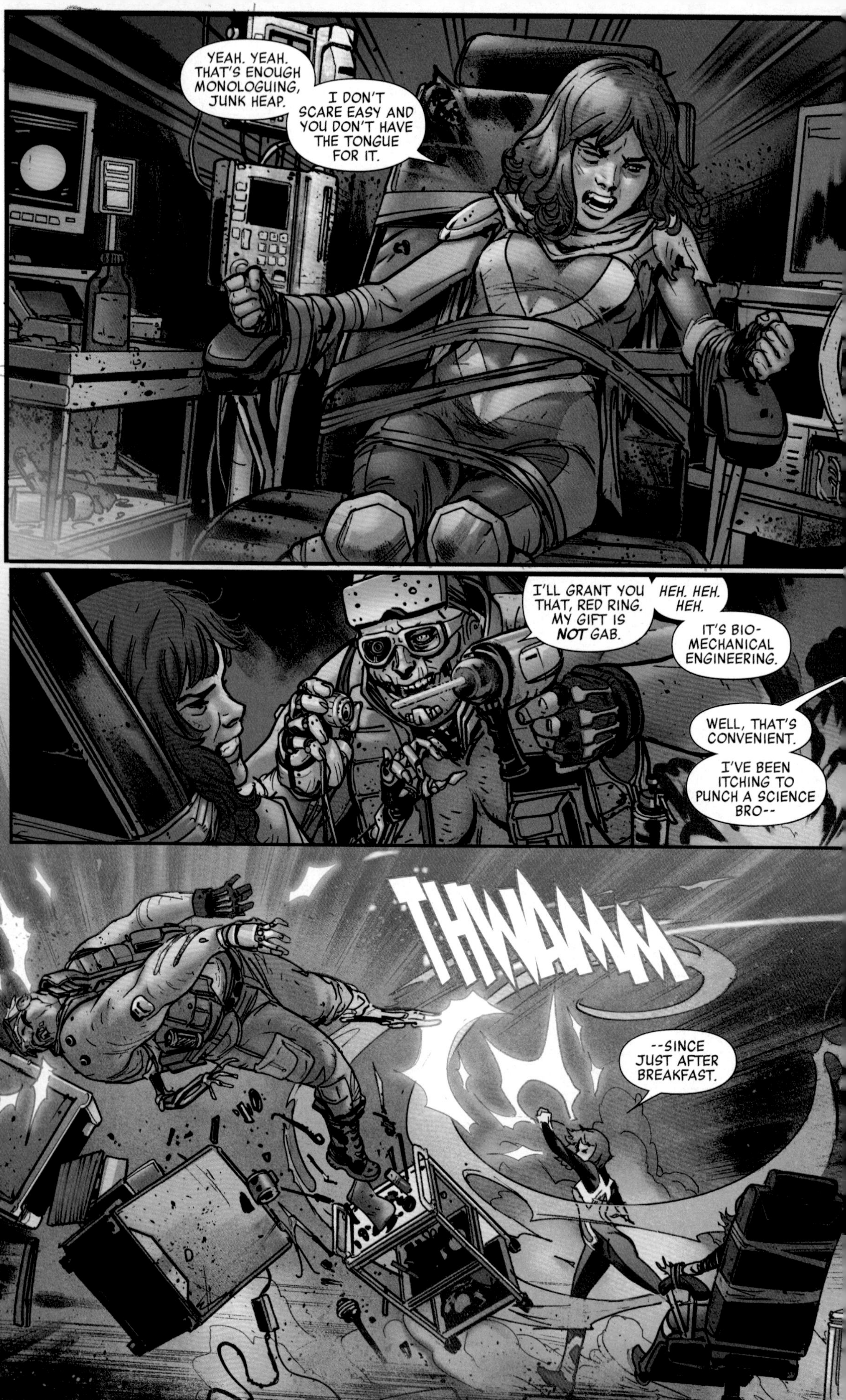
YEAH. YEAH. THAT'S ENOUGH MONOLOGUING, JUNK HEAP.
I DON'T SCARE EASY AND YOU DON'T HAVE THE TONGUE FOR IT.
I'LL GRANT YOU THAT, RED RING. MY GIFT IS NOT GAB.
HEH. HEH. HEH.
IT'S BIO-MECHANICAL ENGINEERING.
WELL, THAT'S CONVENIENT.
I'VE BEEN ITCHING TO PUNCH A SCIENCE BRO--
THWAMM
--SINCE JUST AFTER BREAKFAST.

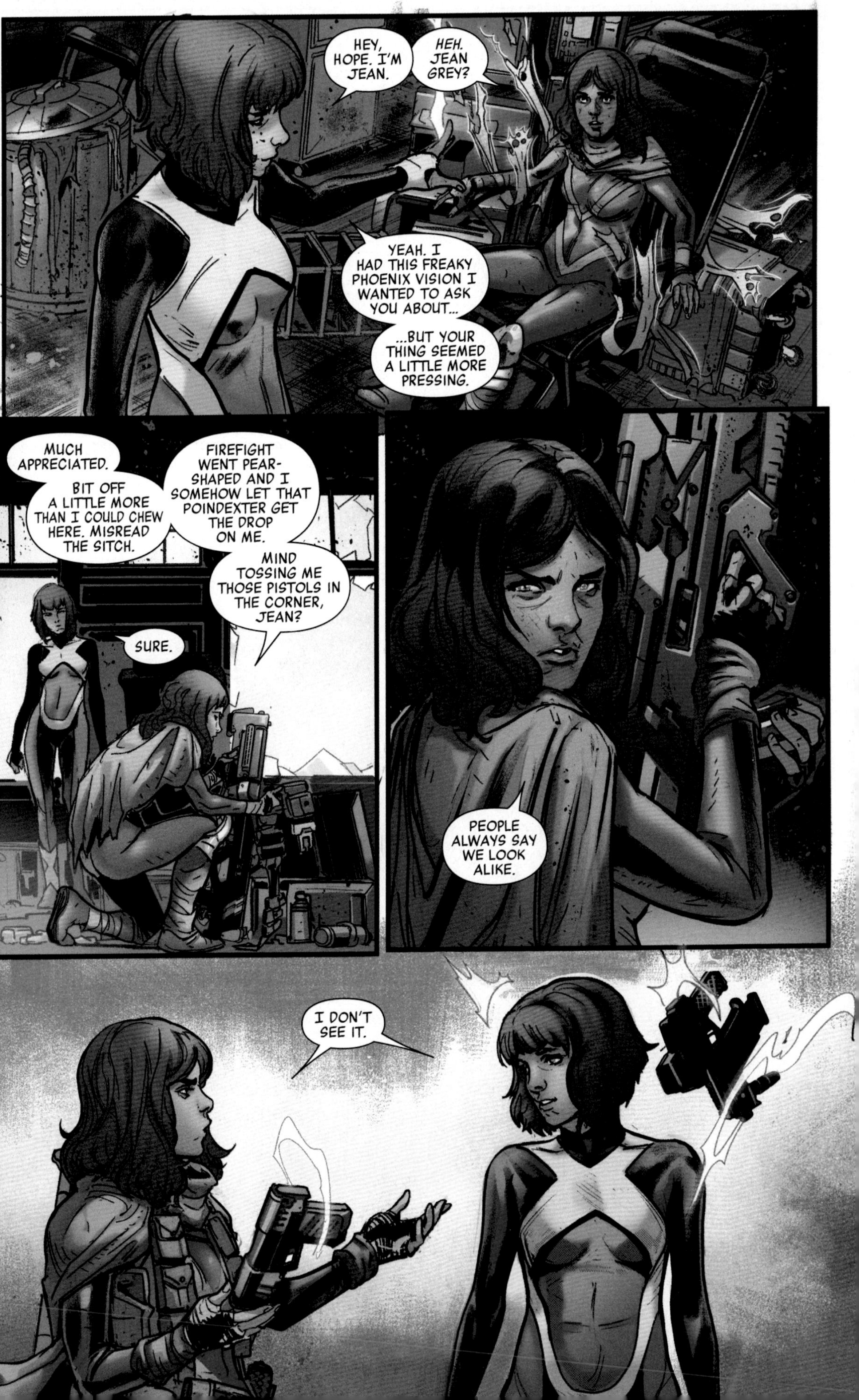
HEY, HOPE. I'M JEAN.
HEH. JEAN GREY?
YEAH. I HAD THIS FREAKY PHOENIX VISION I WANTED TO ASK YOU ABOUT...
...BUT YOUR THING SEEMED A LITTLE MORE PRESSING.
MUCH APPRECIATED.
BIT OFF A LITTLE MORE THAN I COULD CHEW HERE. MISREAD THE SITCH.
FIREFIGHT WENT PEAR-SHAPED AND I SOMEHOW LET THAT POINDEXTER GET THE DROP ON ME.
MIND TOSSING ME THOSE PISTOLS IN THE CORNER, JEAN?
SURE.
PEOPLE ALWAYS SAY WE LOOK ALIKE.
I DON'T SEE IT.

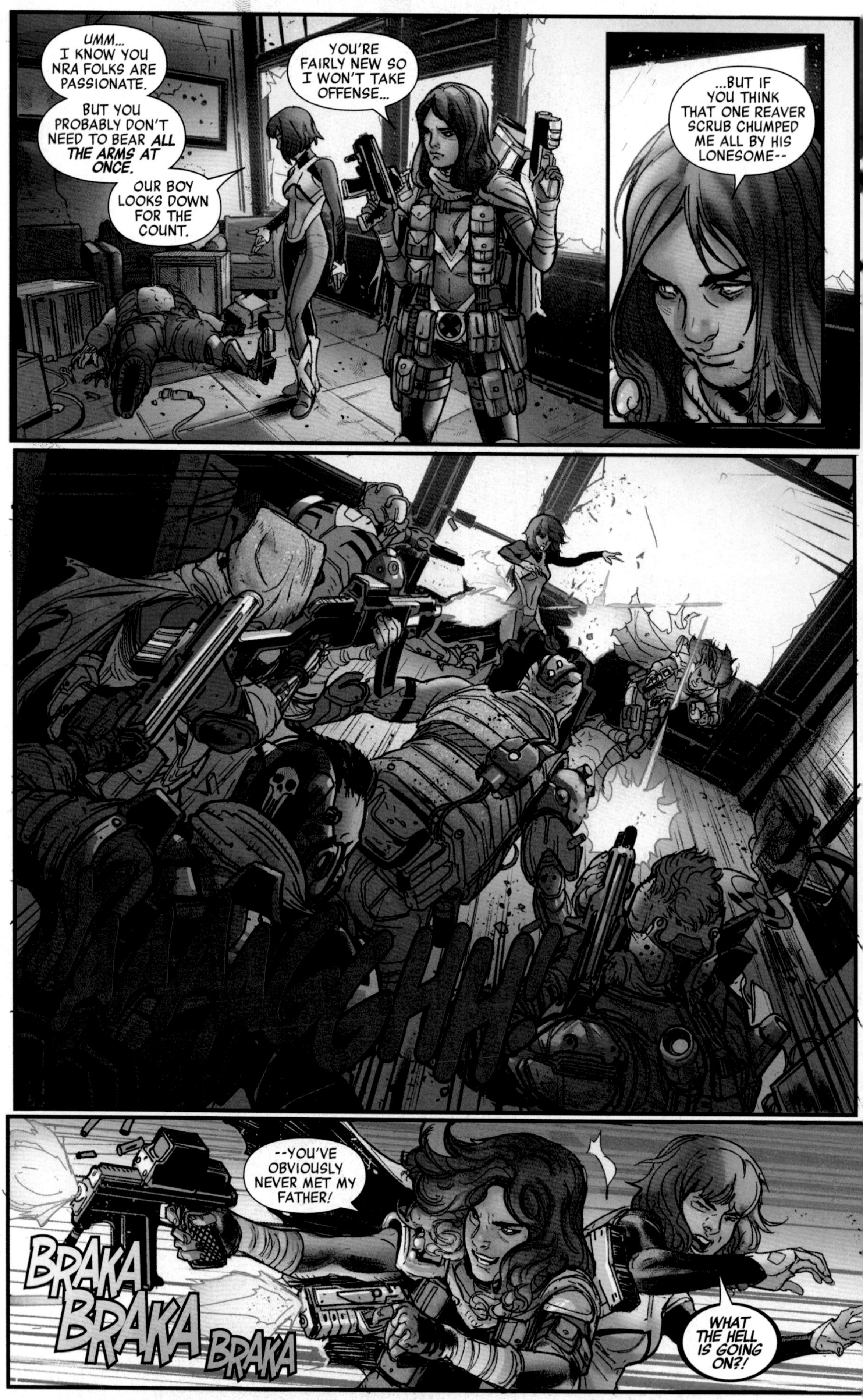
UMM... I KNOW YOU NRA FOLKS ARE PASSIONATE.
BUT YOU PROBABLY DON'T NEED TO BEAR ALL THE ARMS AT ONCE.
OUR BOY LOOKS DOWN FOR THE COUNT.
YOU'RE FAIRLY NEW SO I WON'T TAKE OFFENSE...
...BUT IF YOU THINK THAT ONE REAVER SCRUB CHUMPED ME ALL BY HIS LONESOME--
--YOU'VE OBVIOUSLY NEVER MET MY FATHER!
BRAKA BRAKA BRAKA
WHAT THE HELL IS GOING ON?!

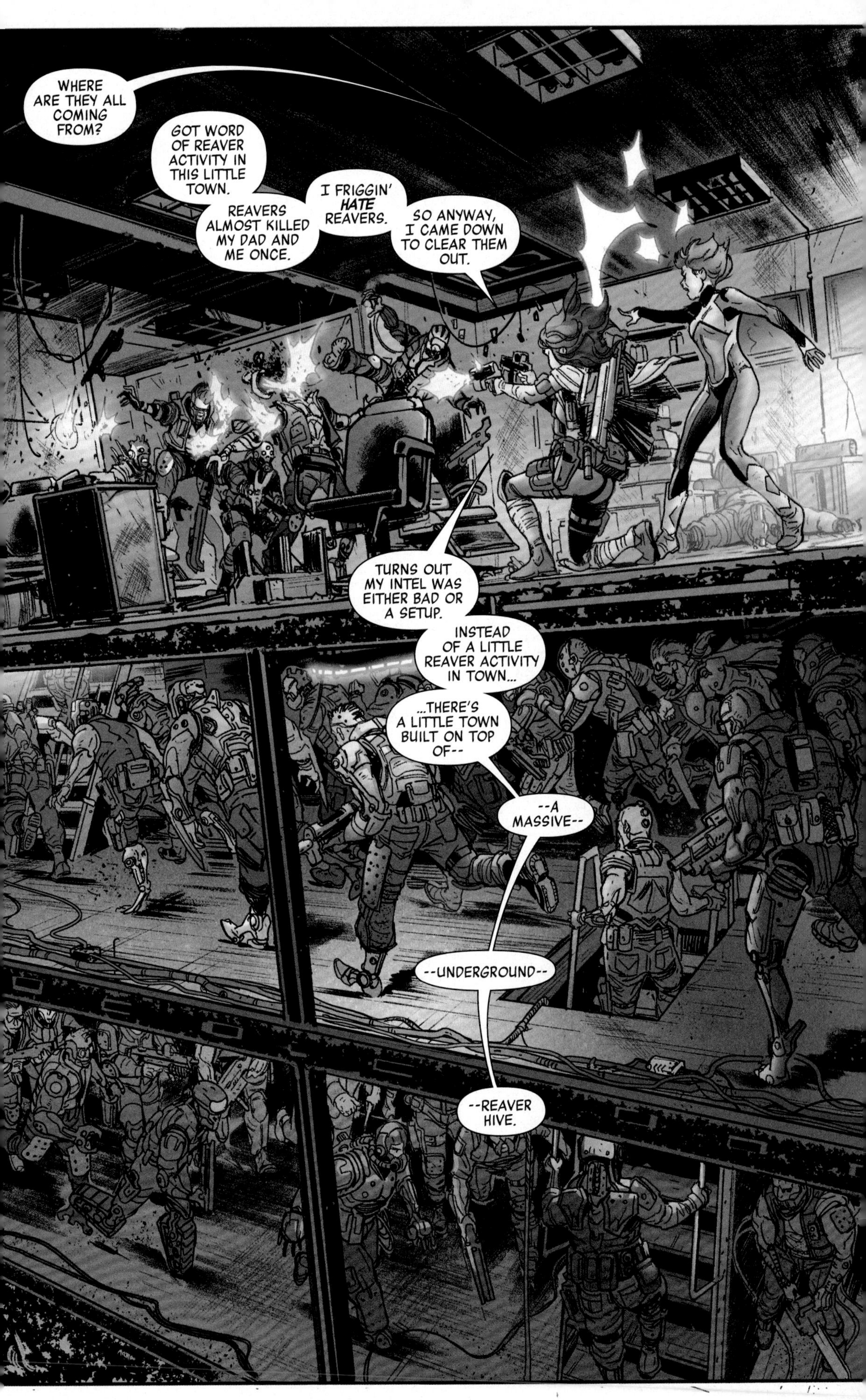
WHERE ARE THEY ALL COMING FROM?
GOT WORD OF REAVER ACTIVITY IN THIS LITTLE TOWN.
REAVERS ALMOST KILLED MY DAD AND ME ONCE.
I FRIGGIN' HATE REAVERS.
SO ANYWAY, I CAME DOWN TO CLEAR THEM OUT.
TURNS OUT MY INTEL WAS EITHER BAD OR A SETUP.
INSTEAD OF A LITTLE REAVER ACTIVITY IN TOWN...
...THERE'S A LITTLE TOWN BUILT ON TOP OF--
--A MASSIVE--
--UNDERGROUND--
--REAVER HIVE.

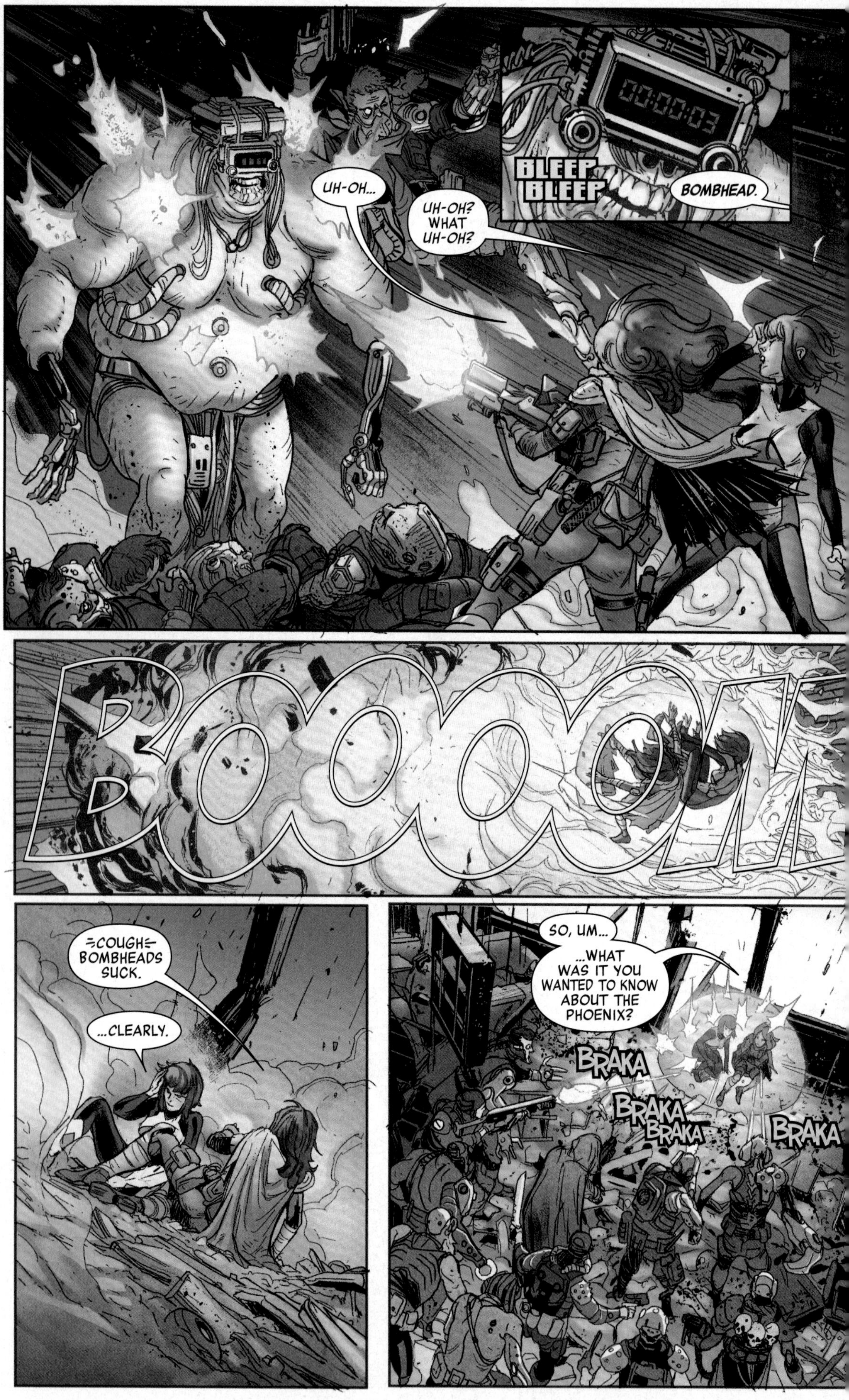
UH-OH...
UH-OH? WHAT UH-OH?
BLEEP BLEEP
BOMBHEAD.
BOOOOM
=COUGH= BOMBHEADS SUCK.
...CLEARLY.
SO, UM...
...WHAT WAS IT YOU WANTED TO KNOW ABOUT THE PHOENIX?
BRAKA
BRAKA BRAKA
BRAKA

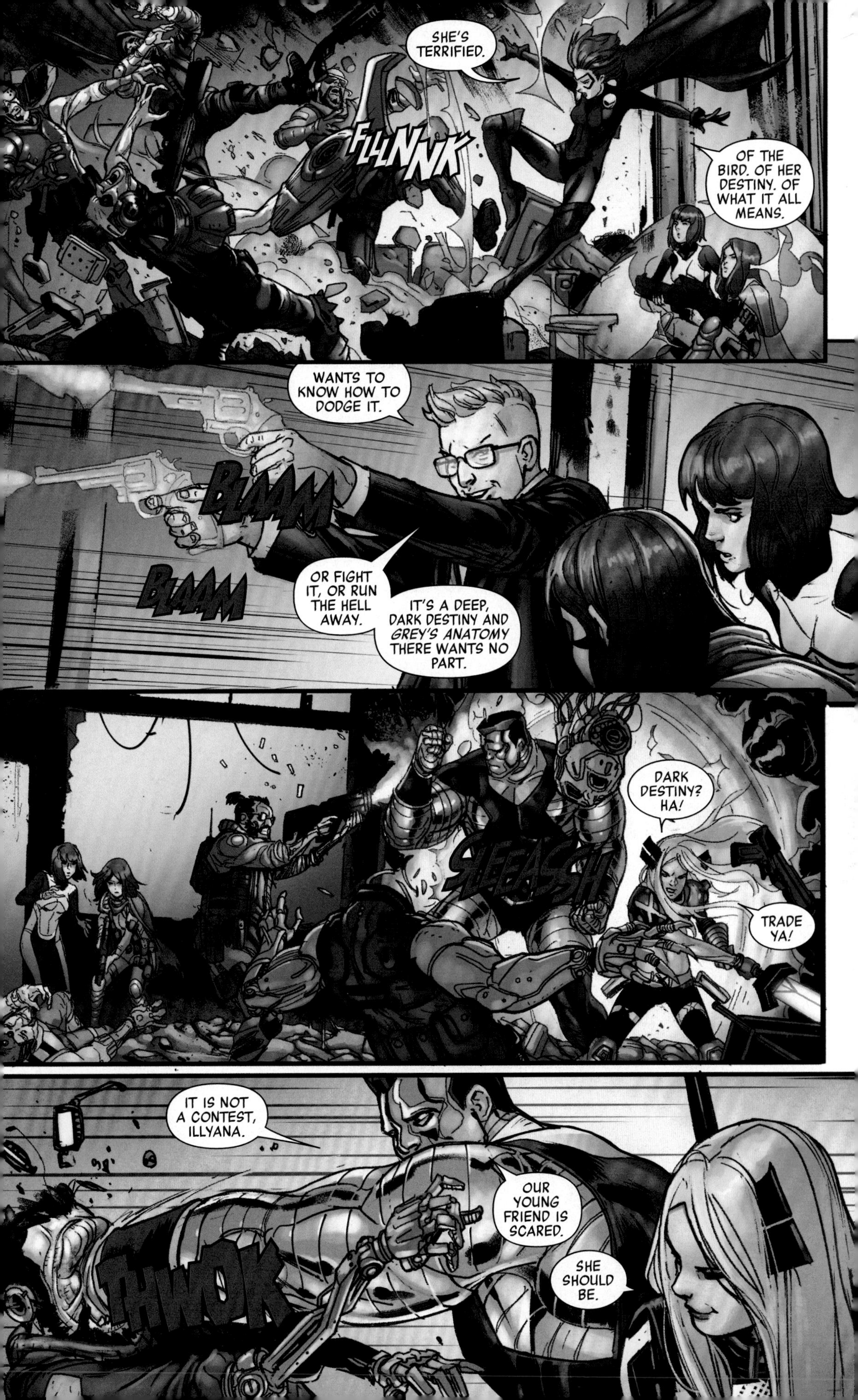
SHE'S TERRIFIED.
FLLNNNK
OF THE BIRD. OF HER DESTINY. OF WHAT IT ALL MEANS.
WANTS TO KNOW HOW TO DODGE IT.
BLAAM
BLAAM
OR FIGHT IT, OR RUN THE HELL AWAY.
IT'S A DEEP, DARK DESTINY AND *GREY'S ANATOMY* THERE WANTS NO PART.
DARK DESTINY? HA!
SLEEASH
TRADE YA!
IT IS NOT A CONTEST, ILLYANA.
OUR YOUNG FRIEND IS SCARED.
SHE SHOULD BE.
THWOK

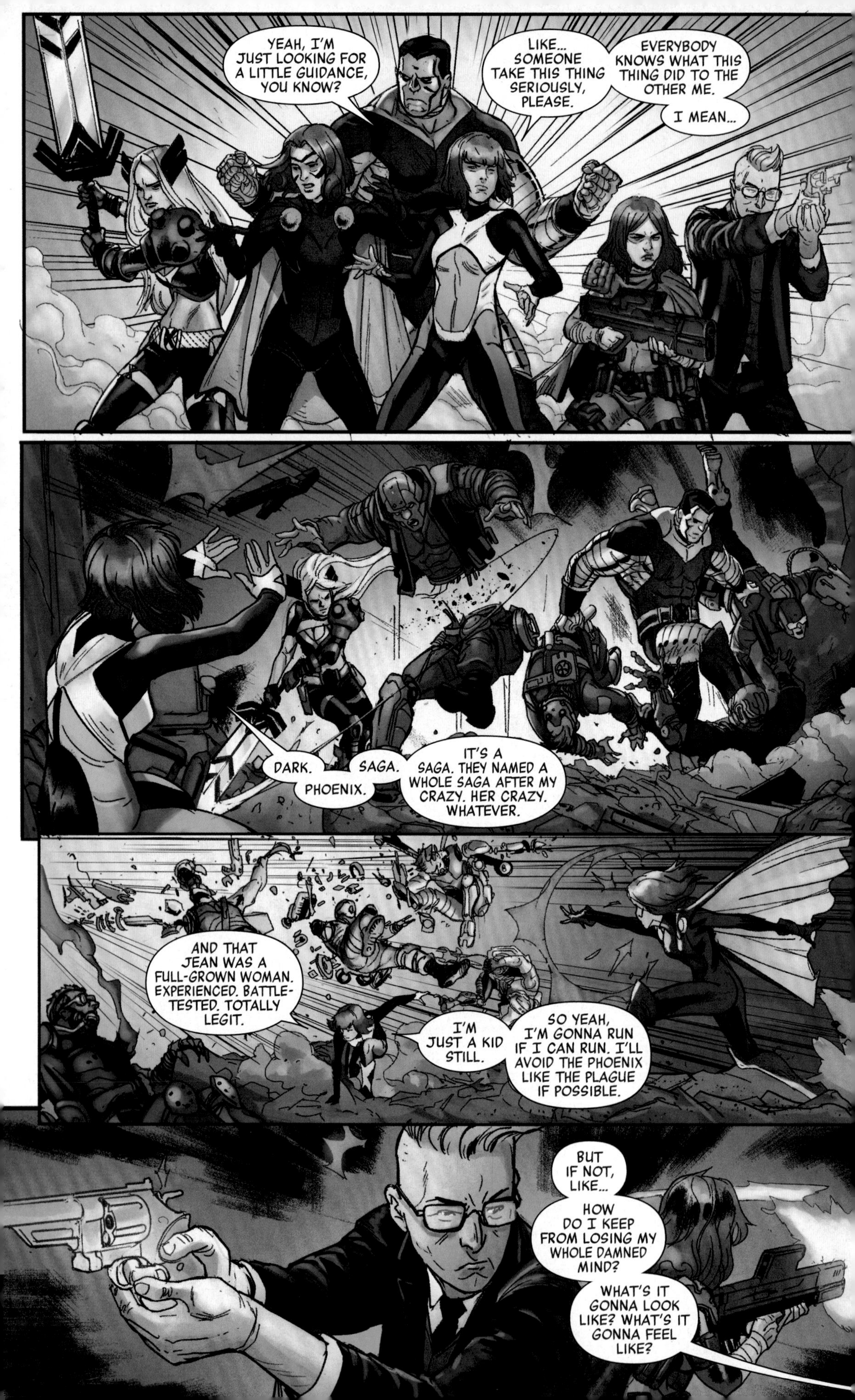
YEAH, I'M JUST LOOKING FOR A LITTLE GUIDANCE, YOU KNOW?
LIKE... SOMEONE TAKE THIS THING SERIOUSLY, PLEASE.
EVERYBODY KNOWS WHAT THIS THING DID TO THE OTHER ME.
I MEAN...
DARK.
PHOENIX.
SAGA.
IT'S A SAGA. THEY NAMED A WHOLE SAGA AFTER MY CRAZY. HER CRAZY. WHATEVER.
AND THAT JEAN WAS A FULL-GROWN WOMAN. EXPERIENCED. BATTLE-TESTED. TOTALLY LEGIT.
I'M JUST A KID STILL.
SO YEAH, I'M GONNA RUN IF I CAN RUN. I'LL AVOID THE PHOENIX LIKE THE PLAGUE IF POSSIBLE.
BUT IF NOT, LIKE...
HOW DO I KEEP FROM LOSING MY WHOLE DAMNED MIND?
WHAT'S IT GONNA LOOK LIKE? WHAT'S IT GONNA FEEL LIKE?

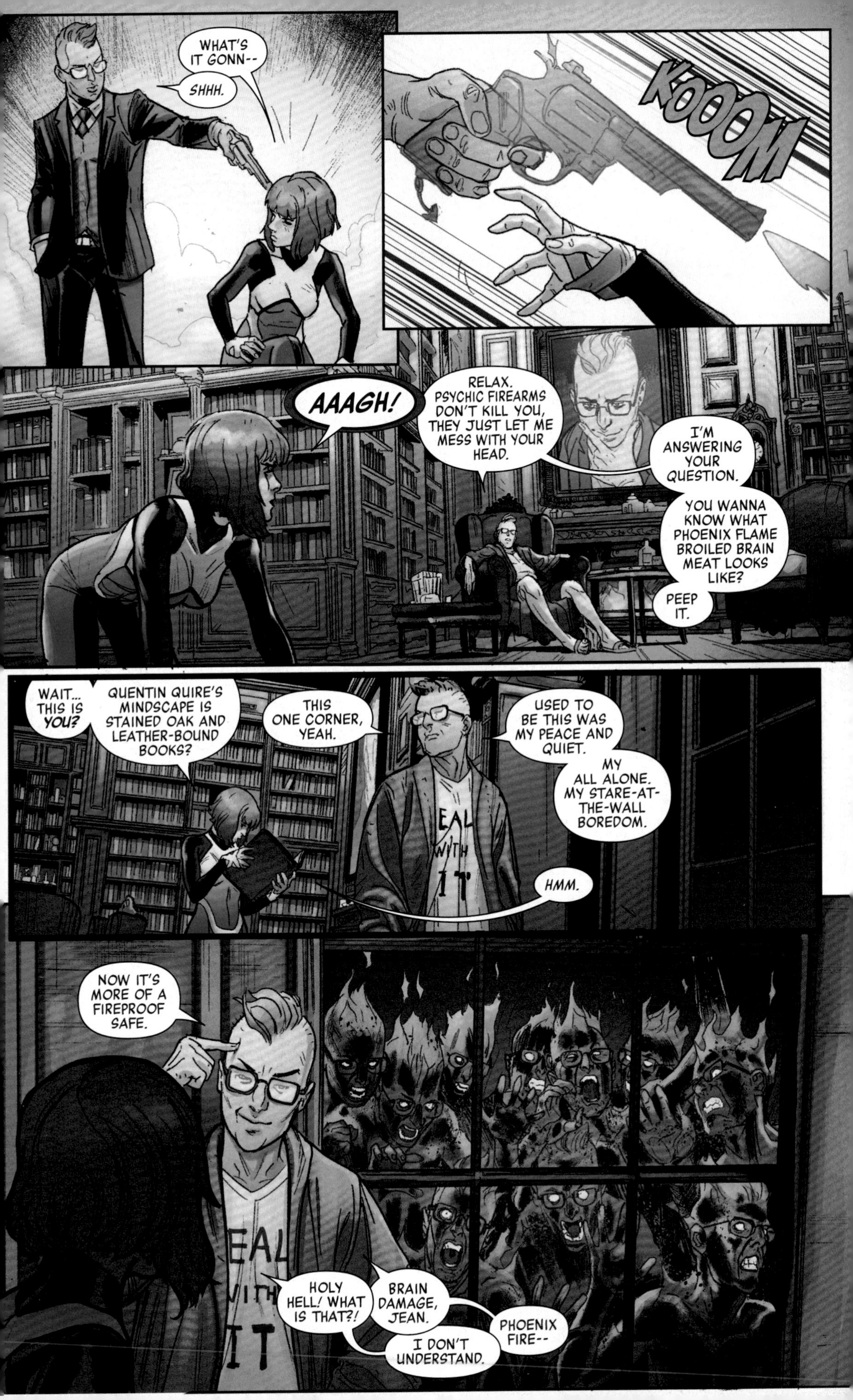
WHAT'S IT GONN--
SHHH.
KOOOM
AAAGH!
RELAX. PSYCHIC FIREARMS DON'T KILL YOU, THEY JUST LET ME MESS WITH YOUR HEAD.
I'M ANSWERING YOUR QUESTION.
YOU WANNA KNOW WHAT PHOENIX FLAME BROILED BRAIN MEAT LOOKS LIKE?
PEEP IT.
WAIT... THIS IS *YOU?*
QUENTIN QUIRE'S MINDSCAPE IS STAINED OAK AND LEATHER-BOUND BOOKS?
THIS ONE CORNER, YEAH.
USED TO BE THIS WAS MY PEACE AND QUIET.
MY ALL ALONE. MY STARE-AT-THE-WALL BOREDOM.
HMM.
NOW IT'S MORE OF A FIREPROOF SAFE.
HOLY HELL! WHAT IS THAT?!
BRAIN DAMAGE, JEAN.
I DON'T UNDERSTAND.
PHOENIX FIRE--

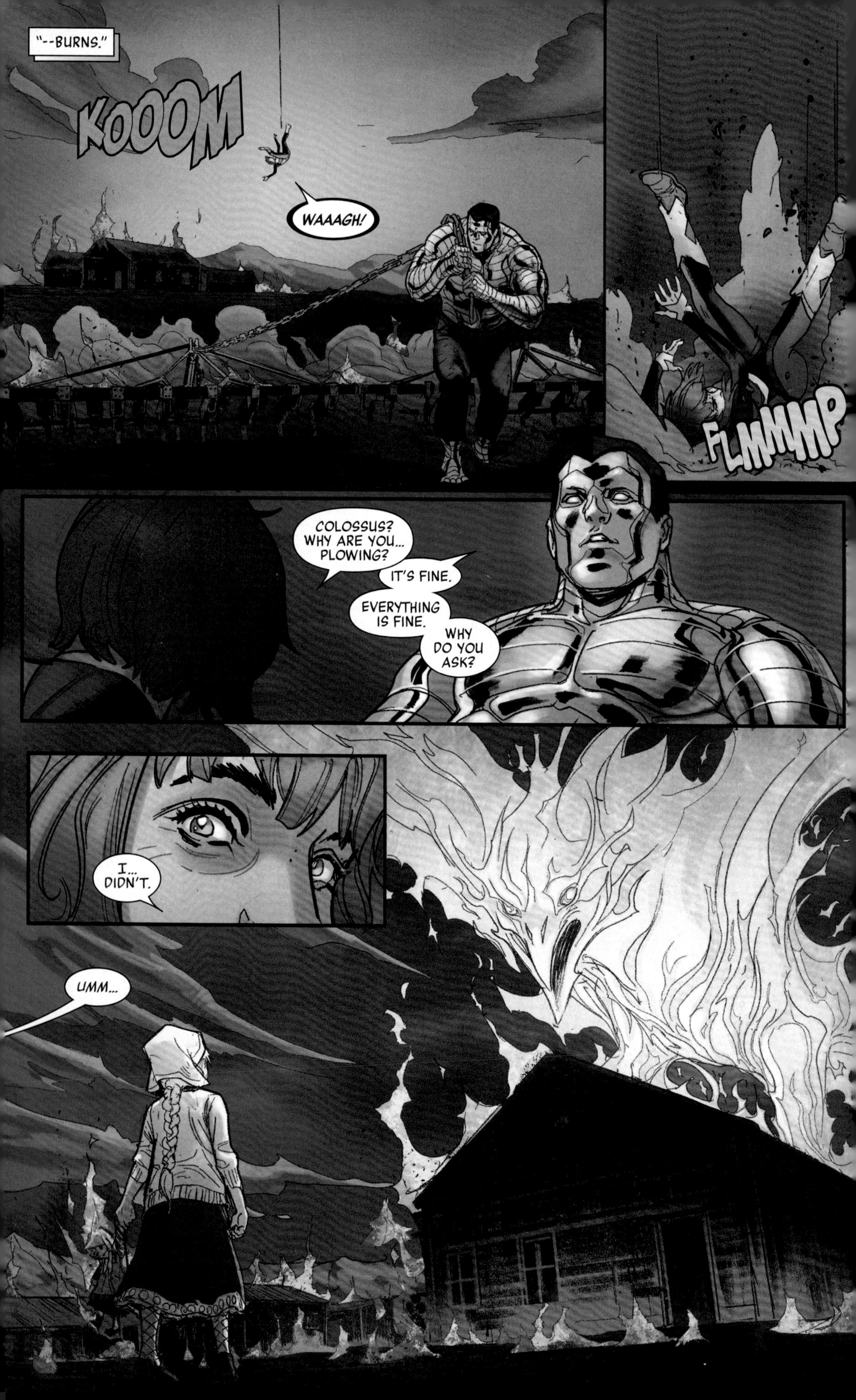
"--BURNS."
KOOOM
WAAAGH!
FLMMMP
COLOSSUS? WHY ARE YOU... PLOWING?
IT'S FINE.
EVERYTHING IS FINE.
WHY DO YOU ASK?
I... DIDN'T.
UMM...

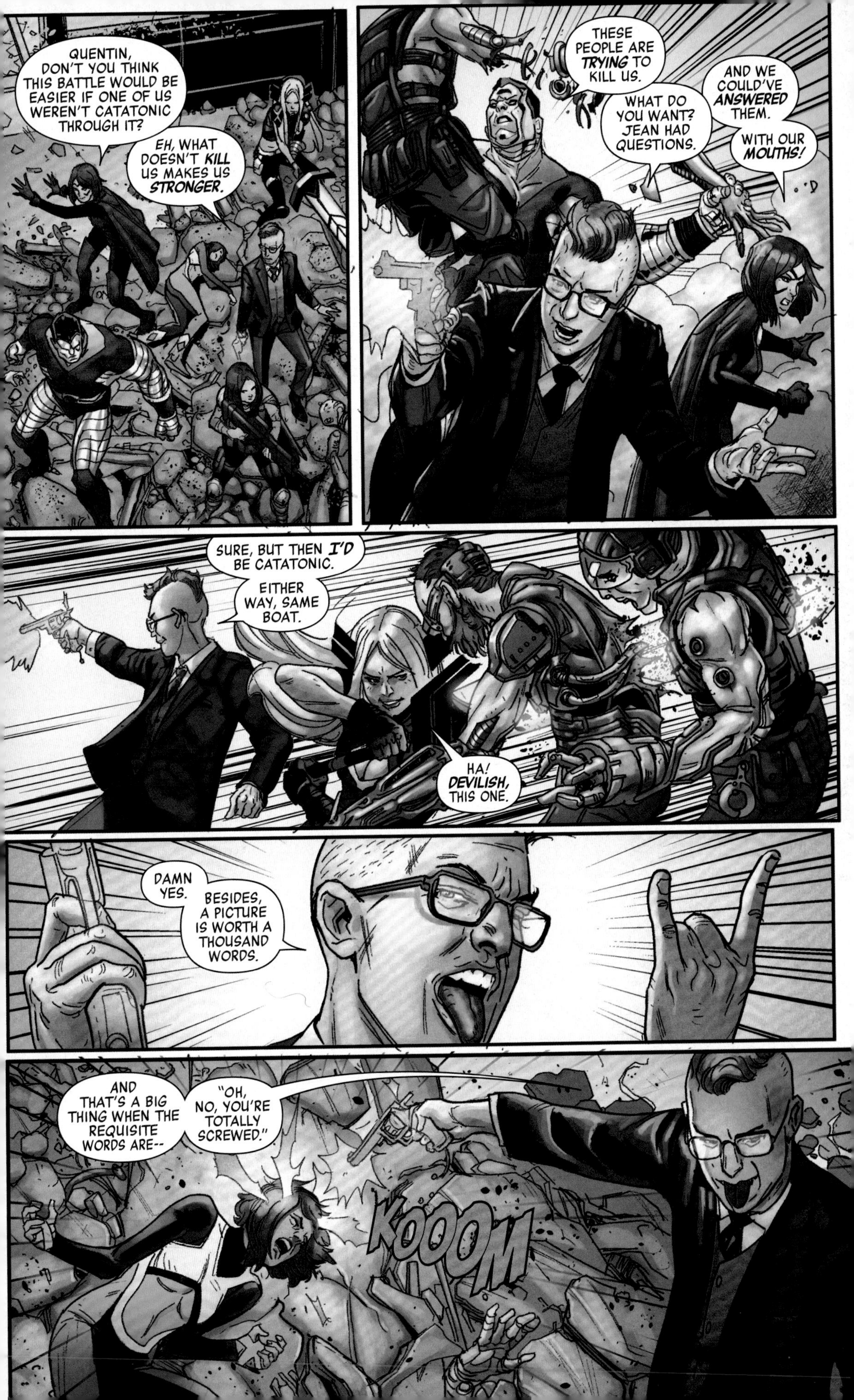
QUENTIN, DON'T YOU THINK THIS BATTLE WOULD BE EASIER IF ONE OF US WEREN'T CATATONIC THROUGH IT?
EH, WHAT DOESN'T KILL US MAKES US STRONGER.
THESE PEOPLE ARE TRYING TO KILL US.
WHAT DO YOU WANT? JEAN HAD QUESTIONS.
AND WE COULD'VE ANSWERED THEM.
WITH OUR MOUTHS!
SURE, BUT THEN I'D BE CATATONIC.
EITHER WAY, SAME BOAT.
HA! DEVILISH, THIS ONE.
DAMN YES.
BESIDES, A PICTURE IS WORTH A THOUSAND WORDS.
AND THAT'S A BIG THING WHEN THE REQUISITE WORDS ARE--
"OH, NO, YOU'RE TOTALLY SCREWED."
KOOOM

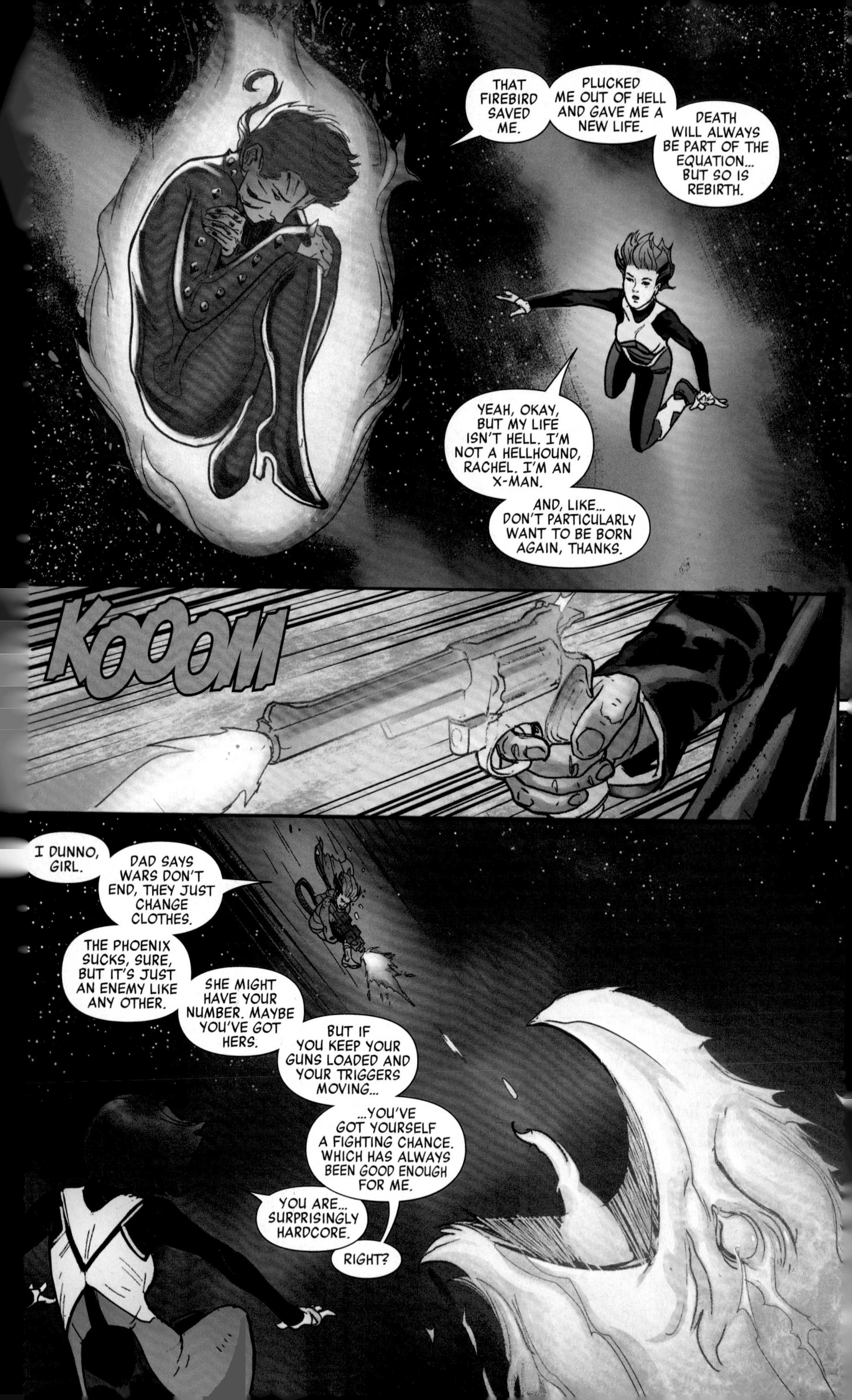
THAT FIREBIRD SAVED ME.
PLUCKED ME OUT OF HELL AND GAVE ME A NEW LIFE.
DEATH WILL ALWAYS BE PART OF THE EQUATION... BUT SO IS REBIRTH.
YEAH, OKAY, BUT MY LIFE ISN'T HELL. I'M NOT A HELLHOUND, RACHEL. I'M AN X-MAN.
AND, LIKE... DON'T PARTICULARLY WANT TO BE BORN AGAIN, THANKS.
KOOOM
I DUNNO, GIRL.
DAD SAYS WARS DON'T END, THEY JUST CHANGE CLOTHES.
THE PHOENIX SUCKS, SURE, BUT IT'S JUST AN ENEMY LIKE ANY OTHER.
SHE MIGHT HAVE YOUR NUMBER. MAYBE YOU'VE GOT HERS.
BUT IF YOU KEEP YOUR GUNS LOADED AND YOUR TRIGGERS MOVING...
...YOU'VE GOT YOURSELF A FIGHTING CHANCE. WHICH HAS ALWAYS BEEN GOOD ENOUGH FOR ME.
YOU ARE... SURPRISINGLY HARDCORE.
RIGHT?

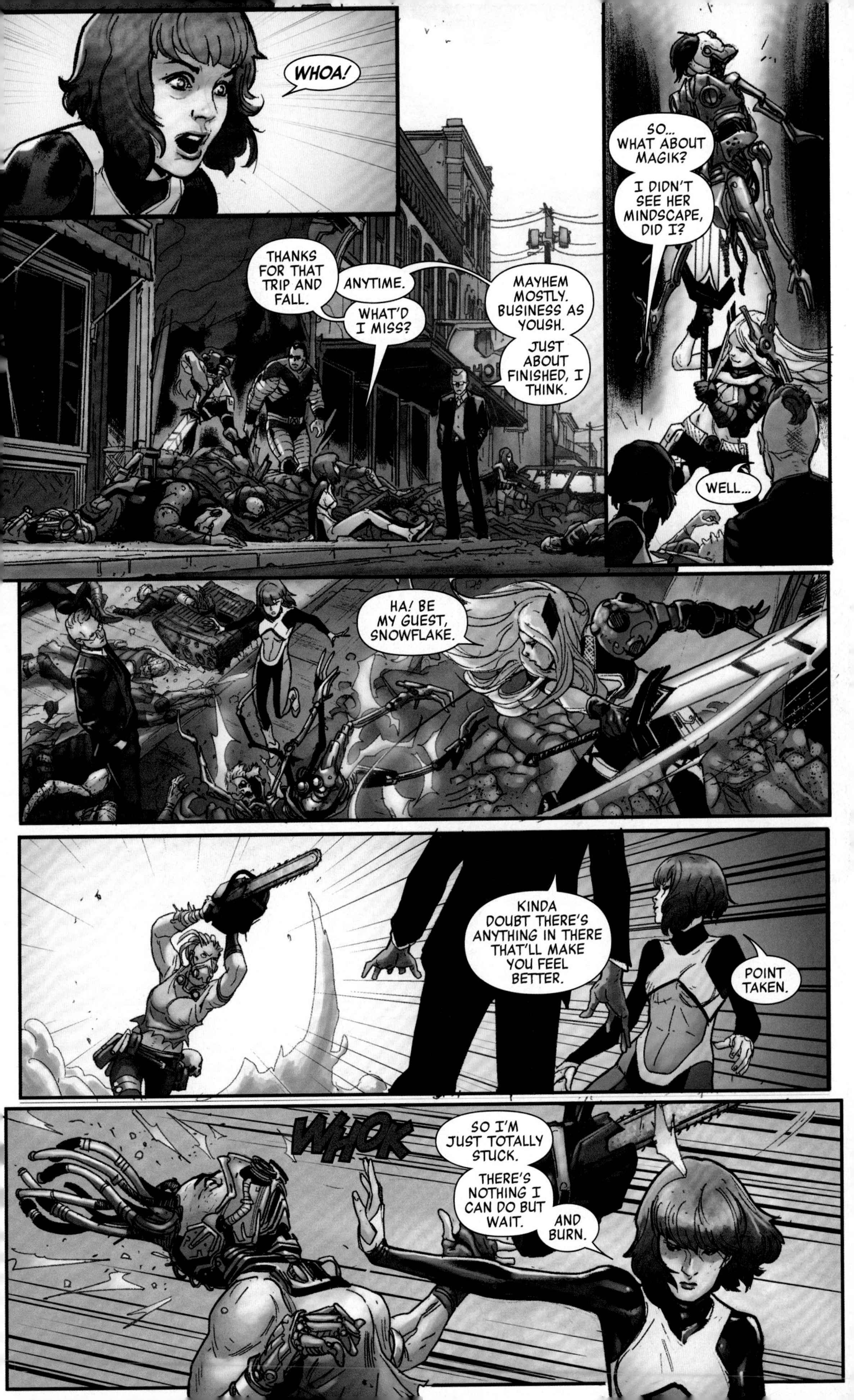
WHOA!
THANKS FOR THAT TRIP AND FALL.
ANYTIME.
WHAT'D I MISS?
MAYHEM MOSTLY. BUSINESS AS YOUSH.
JUST ABOUT FINISHED, I THINK.
SO... WHAT ABOUT MAGIK?
I DIDN'T SEE HER MINDSCAPE, DID I?
WELL...
HA! BE MY GUEST, SNOWFLAKE.
KINDA DOUBT THERE'S ANYTHING IN THERE THAT'LL MAKE YOU FEEL BETTER.
POINT TAKEN.
WHOK
SO I'M JUST TOTALLY STUCK.
THERE'S NOTHING I CAN DO BUT WAIT.
AND BURN.

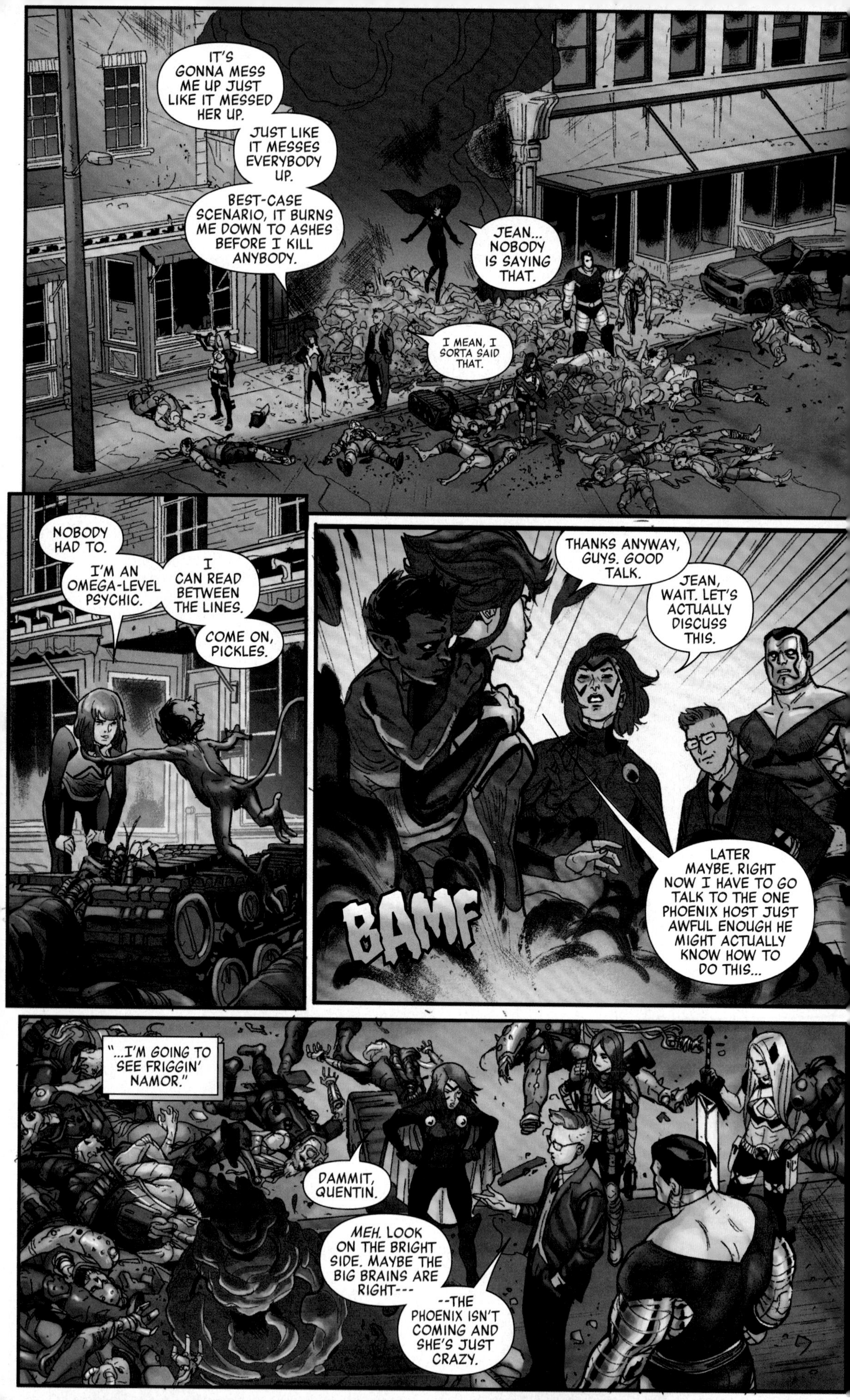

IT'S GONNA MESS ME UP JUST LIKE IT MESSED HER UP.
JUST LIKE IT MESSES EVERYBODY UP.
BEST-CASE SCENARIO, IT BURNS ME DOWN TO ASHES BEFORE I KILL ANYBODY.
JEAN... NOBODY IS SAYING THAT.
I MEAN, I SORTA SAID THAT.
NOBODY HAD TO.
I'M AN OMEGA-LEVEL PSYCHIC.
I CAN READ BETWEEN THE LINES.
COME ON, PICKLES.
THANKS ANYWAY, GUYS. GOOD TALK.
JEAN, WAIT. LET'S ACTUALLY DISCUSS THIS.
LATER MAYBE. RIGHT NOW I HAVE TO GO TALK TO THE ONE PHOENIX HOST JUST AWFUL ENOUGH HE MIGHT ACTUALLY KNOW HOW TO DO THIS...
BAMF
"...I'M GOING TO SEE FRIGGIN' NAMOR."
DAMMIT, QUENTIN.
MEH. LOOK ON THE BRIGHT SIDE. MAYBE THE BIG BRAINS ARE RIGHT---
--THE PHOENIX ISN'T COMING AND SHE'S JUST CRAZY.

3

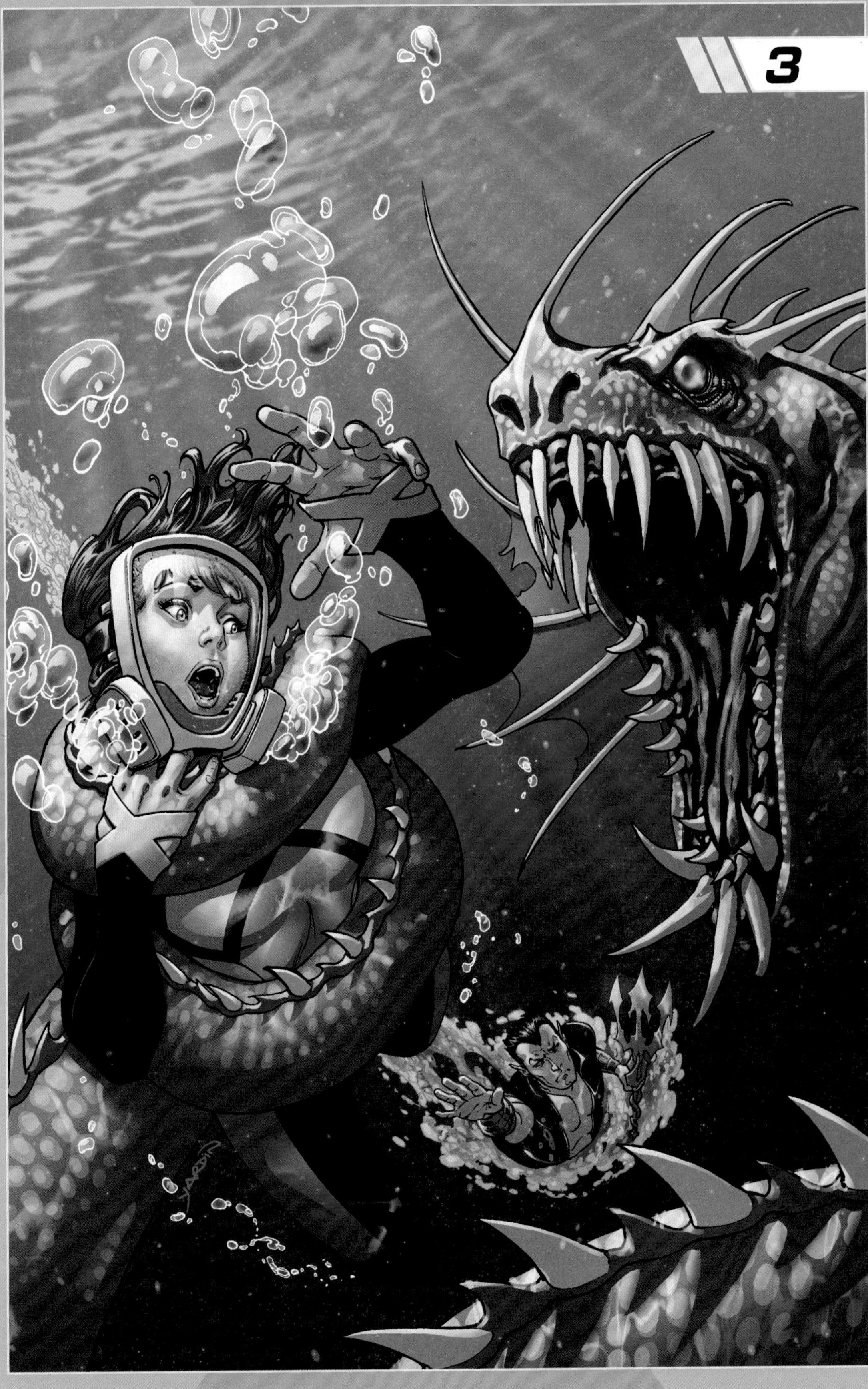

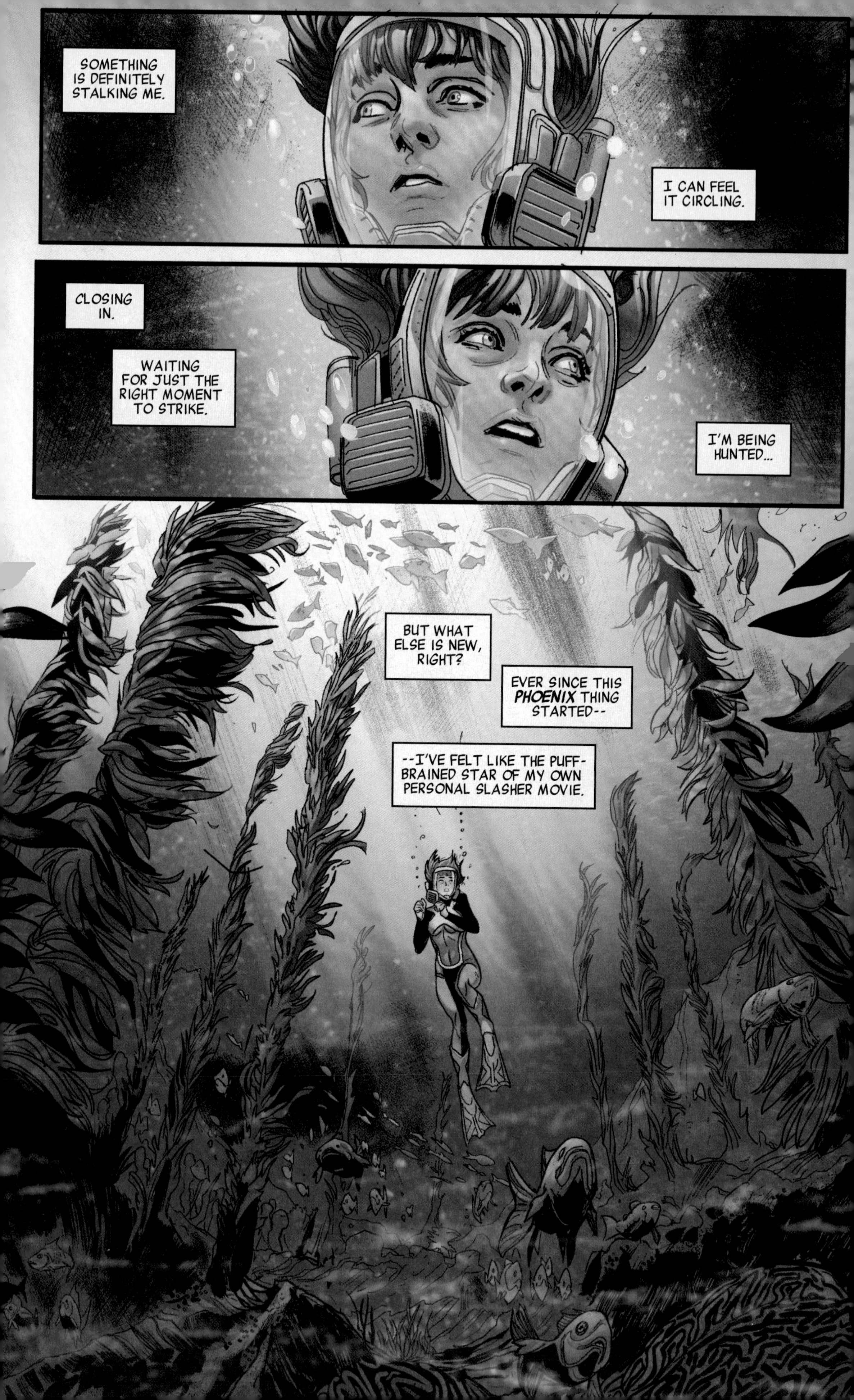

SOMETHING IS DEFINITELY STALKING ME.
I CAN FEEL IT CIRCLING.
CLOSING IN.
WAITING FOR JUST THE RIGHT MOMENT TO STRIKE.
I'M BEING HUNTED...
BUT WHAT ELSE IS NEW, RIGHT?
EVER SINCE THIS PHOENIX THING STARTED--
--I'VE FELT LIKE THE PUFF-BRAINED STAR OF MY OWN PERSONAL SLASHER MOVIE.

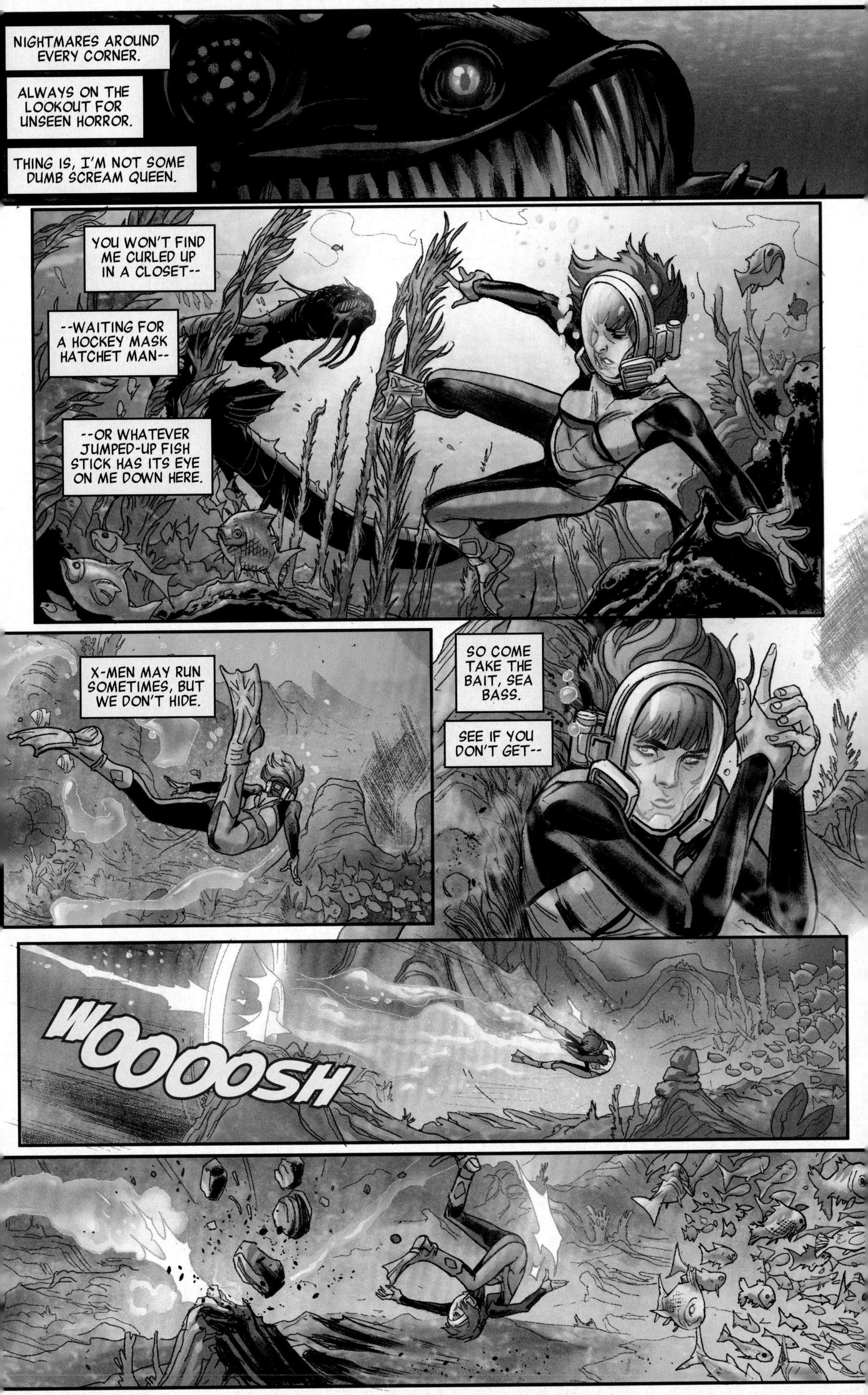
NIGHTMARES AROUND EVERY CORNER.
ALWAYS ON THE LOOKOUT FOR UNSEEN HORROR.
THING IS, I'M NOT SOME DUMB SCREAM QUEEN.
YOU WON'T FIND ME CURLED UP IN A CLOSET--
--WAITING FOR A HOCKEY MASK HATCHET MAN--
--OR WHATEVER JUMPED-UP FISH STICK HAS ITS EYE ON ME DOWN HERE.
X-MEN MAY RUN SOMETIMES, BUT WE DON'T HIDE.
SO COME TAKE THE BAIT, SEA BASS.
SEE IF YOU DON'T GET--
WOOOOSH

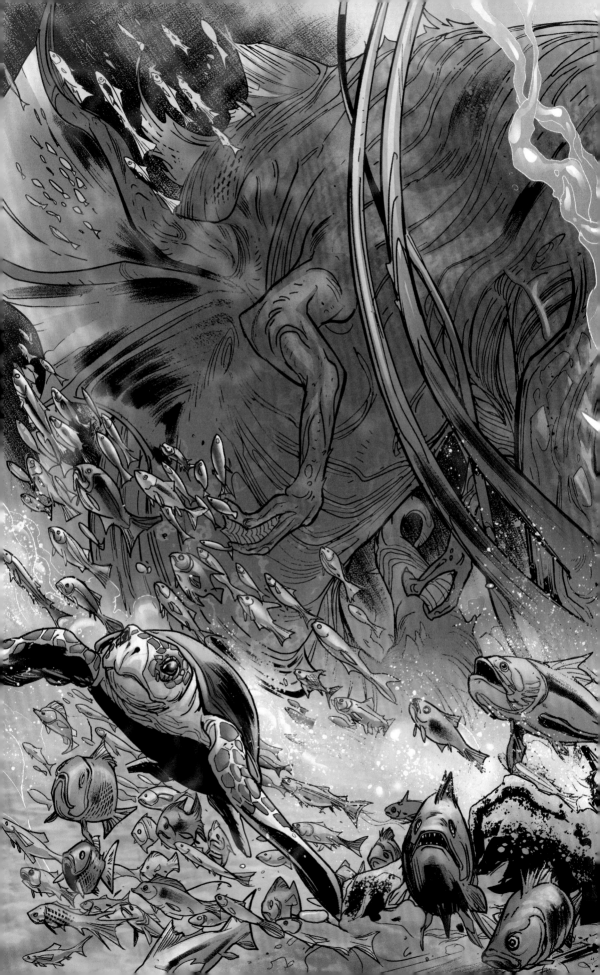

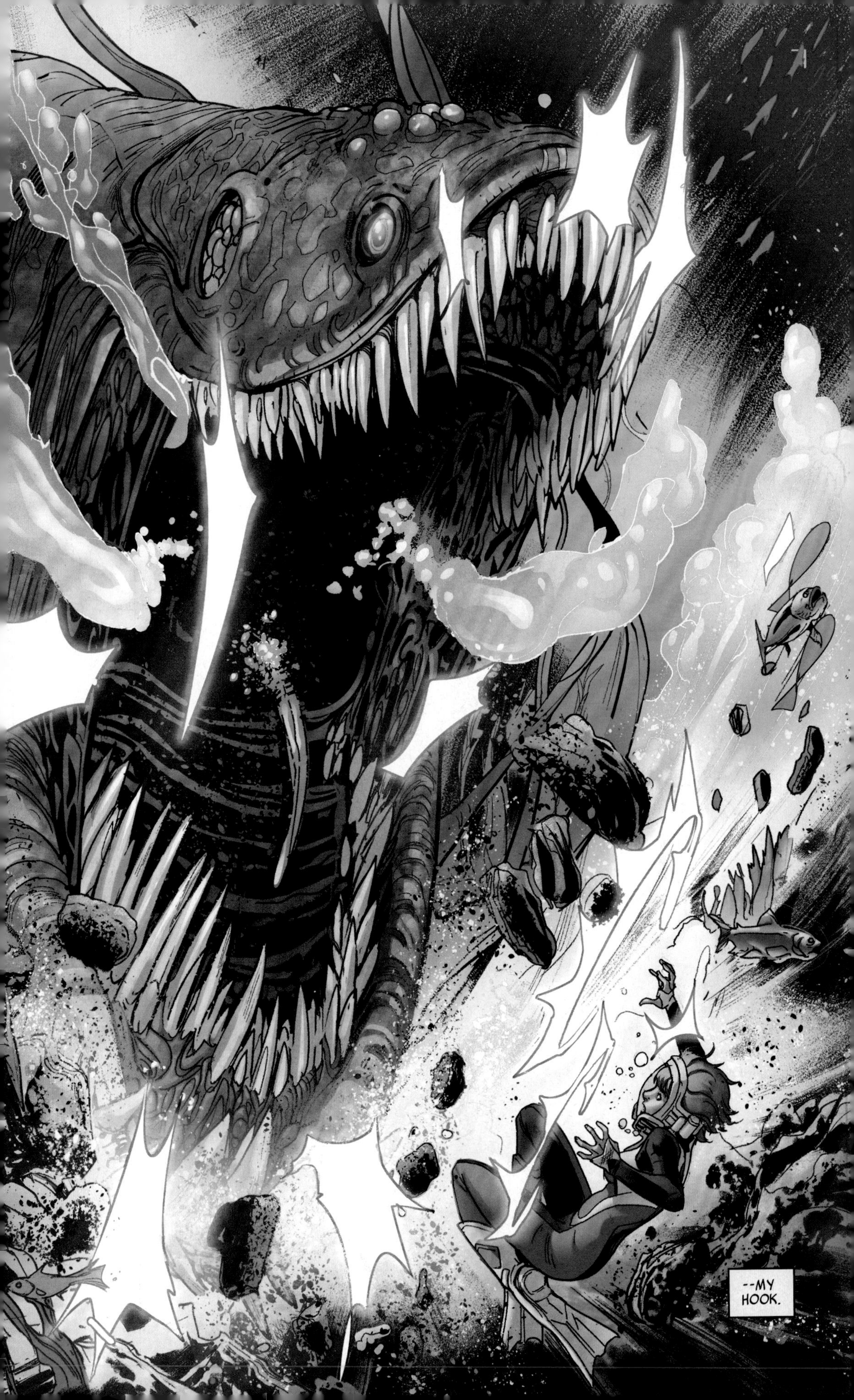
--MY HOOK.

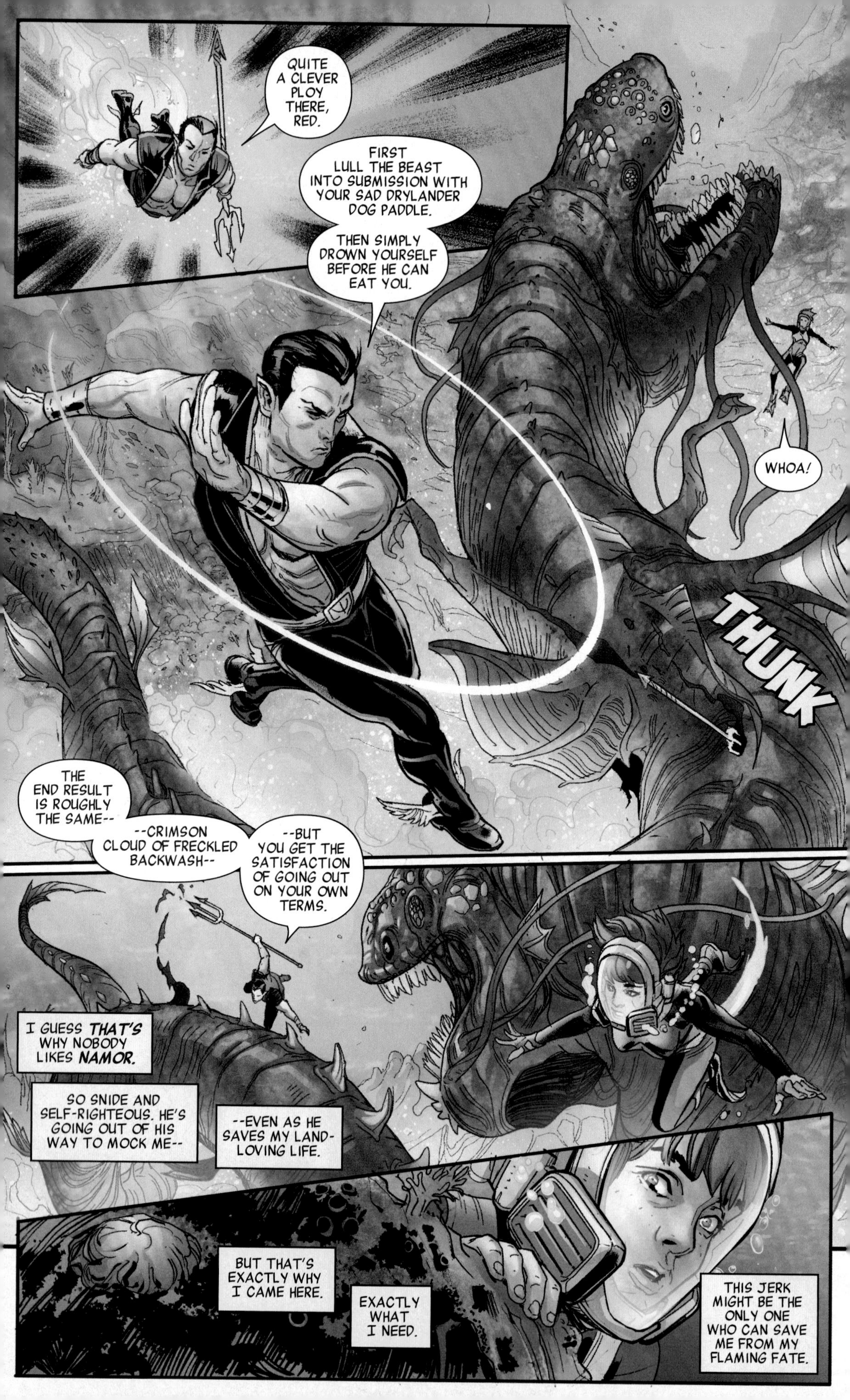
QUITE A CLEVER PLOY THERE, RED.
FIRST LULL THE BEAST INTO SUBMISSION WITH YOUR SAD DRYLANDER DOG PADDLE.
THEN SIMPLY DROWN YOURSELF BEFORE HE CAN EAT YOU.
WHOA!
THUNK
THE END RESULT IS ROUGHLY THE SAME--
--CRIMSON CLOUD OF FRECKLED BACKWASH--
--BUT YOU GET THE SATISFACTION OF GOING OUT ON YOUR OWN TERMS.
I GUESS THAT'S WHY NOBODY LIKES NAMOR.
SO SNIDE AND SELF-RIGHTEOUS. HE'S GOING OUT OF HIS WAY TO MOCK ME--
--EVEN AS HE SAVES MY LAND-LOVING LIFE.
BUT THAT'S EXACTLY WHY I CAME HERE.
EXACTLY WHAT I NEED.
THIS JERK MIGHT BE THE ONLY ONE WHO CAN SAVE ME FROM MY FLAMING FATE.

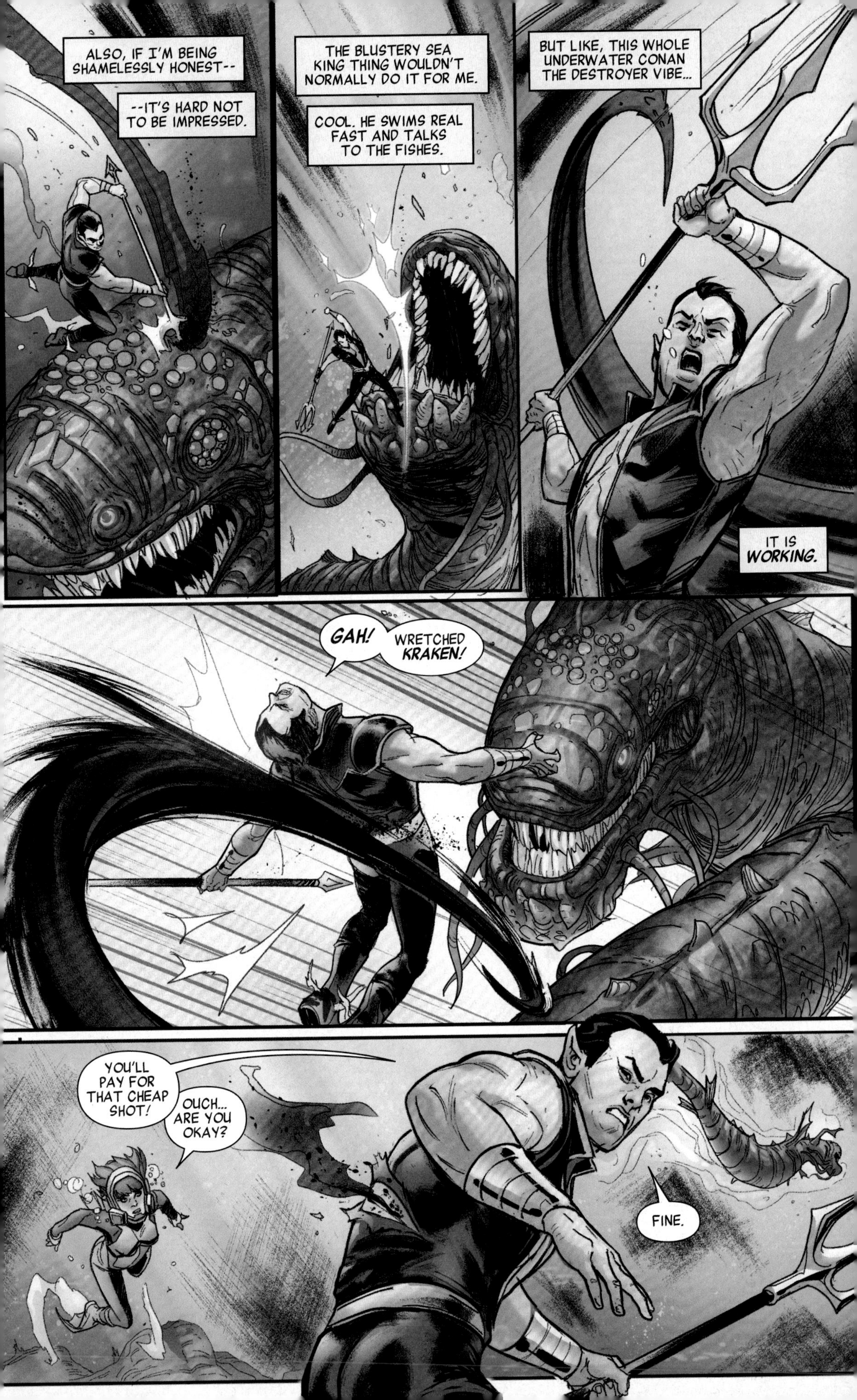
ALSO, IF I'M BEING SHAMELESSLY HONEST--
--IT'S HARD NOT TO BE IMPRESSED.
THE BLUSTERY SEA KING THING WOULDN'T NORMALLY DO IT FOR ME.
COOL. HE SWIMS REAL FAST AND TALKS TO THE FISHES.
BUT LIKE, THIS WHOLE UNDERWATER CONAN THE DESTROYER VIBE...
IT IS WORKING.
GAH!
WRETCHED KRAKEN!
YOU'LL PAY FOR THAT CHEAP SHOT!
OUCH... ARE YOU OKAY?
FINE.

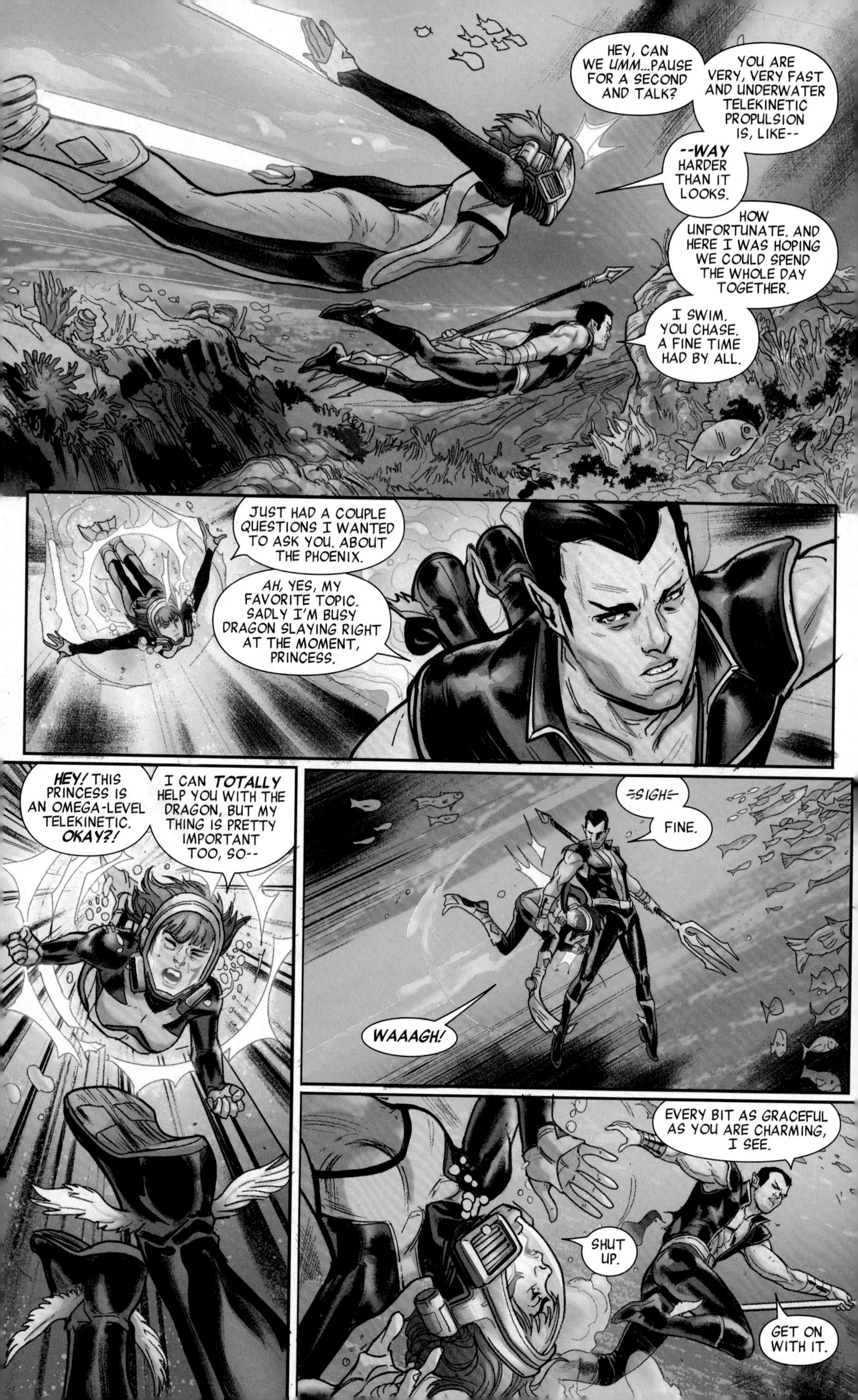
HEY, CAN WE UMM...PAUSE FOR A SECOND AND TALK?
YOU ARE VERY, VERY FAST AND UNDERWATER TELEKINETIC PROPULSION IS, LIKE--
--WAY HARDER THAN IT LOOKS.
HOW UNFORTUNATE. AND HERE I WAS HOPING WE COULD SPEND THE WHOLE DAY TOGETHER.
I SWIM. YOU CHASE. A FINE TIME HAD BY ALL.
JUST HAD A COUPLE QUESTIONS I WANTED TO ASK YOU. ABOUT THE PHOENIX.
AH, YES, MY FAVORITE TOPIC. SADLY I'M BUSY DRAGON SLAYING RIGHT AT THE MOMENT, PRINCESS.
HEY! THIS PRINCESS IS AN OMEGA-LEVEL TELEKINETIC. OKAY?!
I CAN TOTALLY HELP YOU WITH THE DRAGON, BUT MY THING IS PRETTY IMPORTANT TOO, SO--
=SIGH=
FINE.
WAAAGH!
EVERY BIT AS GRACEFUL AS YOU ARE CHARMING, I SEE.
SHUT UP.
GET ON WITH IT.

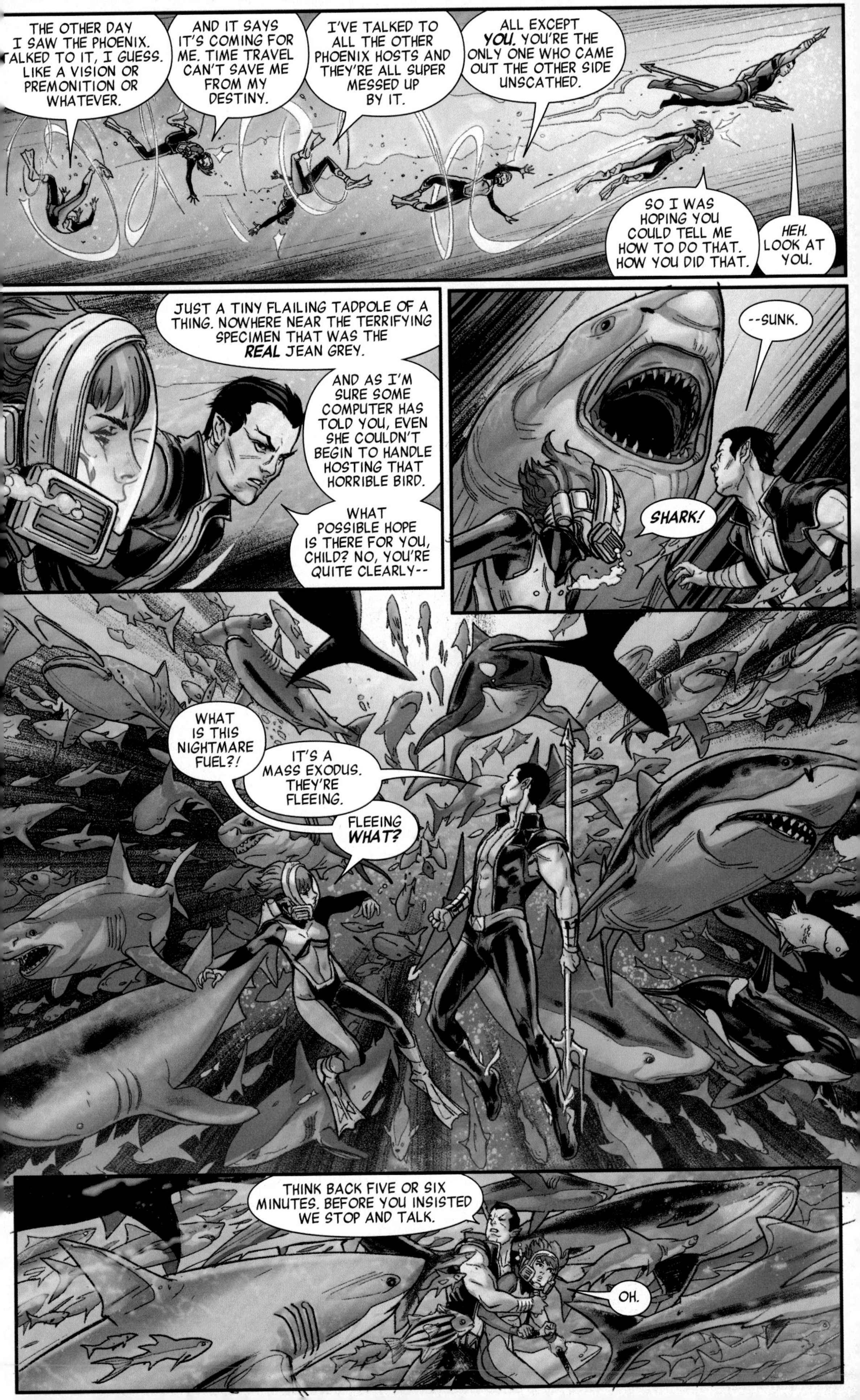

THE OTHER DAY I SAW THE PHOENIX. TALKED TO IT, I GUESS. LIKE A VISION OR PREMONITION OR WHATEVER.
AND IT SAYS IT'S COMING FOR ME. TIME TRAVEL CAN'T SAVE ME FROM MY DESTINY.
I'VE TALKED TO ALL THE OTHER PHOENIX HOSTS AND THEY'RE ALL SUPER MESSED UP BY IT.
ALL EXCEPT YOU. YOU'RE THE ONLY ONE WHO CAME OUT THE OTHER SIDE UNSCATHED.
SO I WAS HOPING YOU COULD TELL ME HOW TO DO THAT. HOW YOU DID THAT.
HEH. LOOK AT YOU.
JUST A TINY FLAILING TADPOLE OF A THING. NOWHERE NEAR THE TERRIFYING SPECIMEN THAT WAS THE REAL JEAN GREY.
AND AS I'M SURE SOME COMPUTER HAS TOLD YOU, EVEN SHE COULDN'T BEGIN TO HANDLE HOSTING THAT HORRIBLE BIRD.
WHAT POSSIBLE HOPE IS THERE FOR YOU, CHILD? NO, YOU'RE QUITE CLEARLY--
--SUNK.
SHARK!
WHAT IS THIS NIGHTMARE FUEL?!
IT'S A MASS EXODUS. THEY'RE FLEEING.
FLEEING WHAT?
THINK BACK FIVE OR SIX MINUTES. BEFORE YOU INSISTED WE STOP AND TALK.
OH.

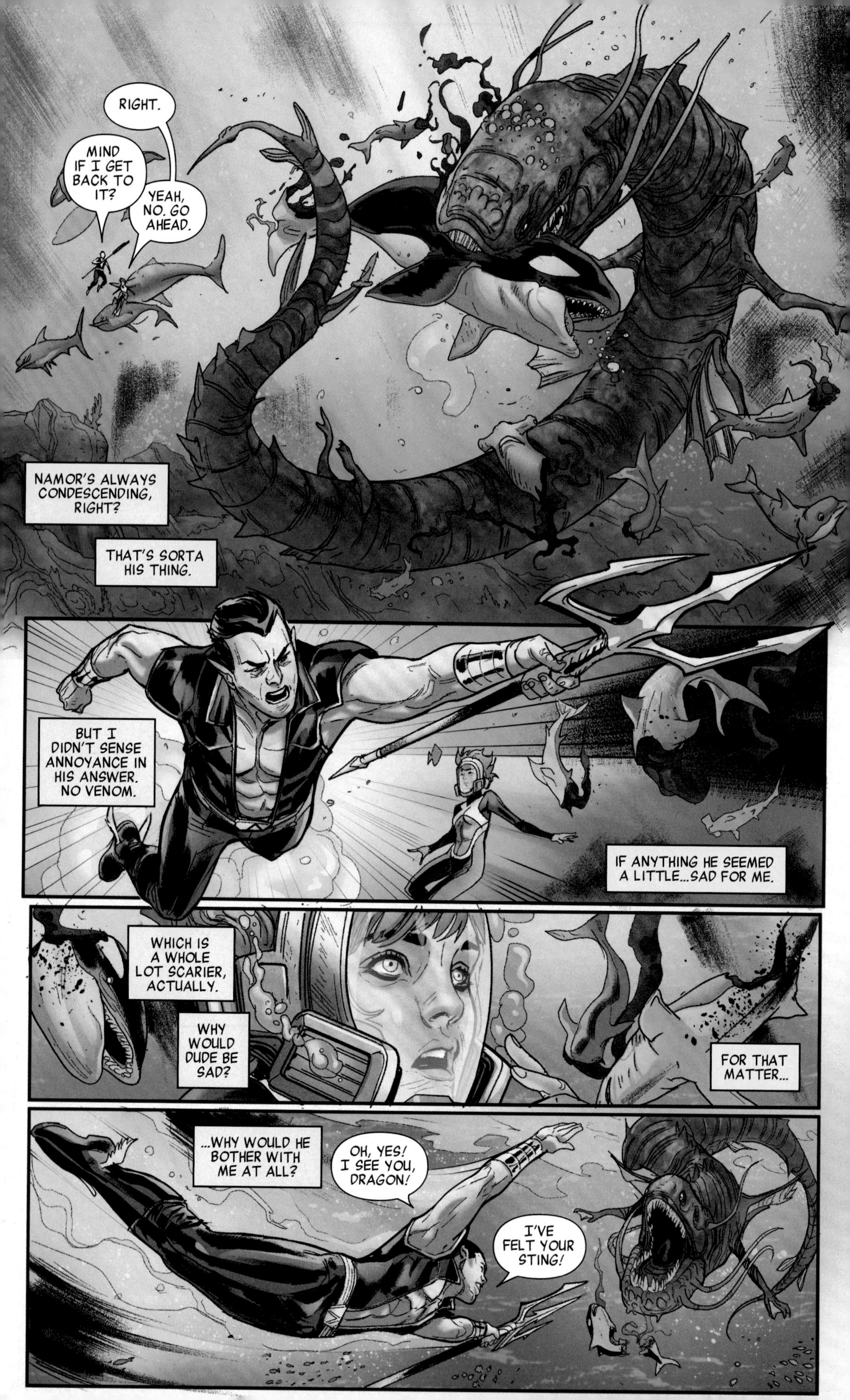
RIGHT.
MIND IF I GET BACK TO IT?
YEAH, NO. GO AHEAD.
NAMOR'S ALWAYS CONDESCENDING, RIGHT?
THAT'S SORTA HIS THING.
BUT I DIDN'T SENSE ANNOYANCE IN HIS ANSWER. NO VENOM.
IF ANYTHING HE SEEMED A LITTLE...SAD FOR ME.
WHICH IS A WHOLE LOT SCARIER, ACTUALLY.
WHY WOULD DUDE BE SAD?
FOR THAT MATTER...
...WHY WOULD HE BOTHER WITH ME AT ALL?
OH, YES! I SEE YOU, DRAGON!
I'VE FELT YOUR STING!

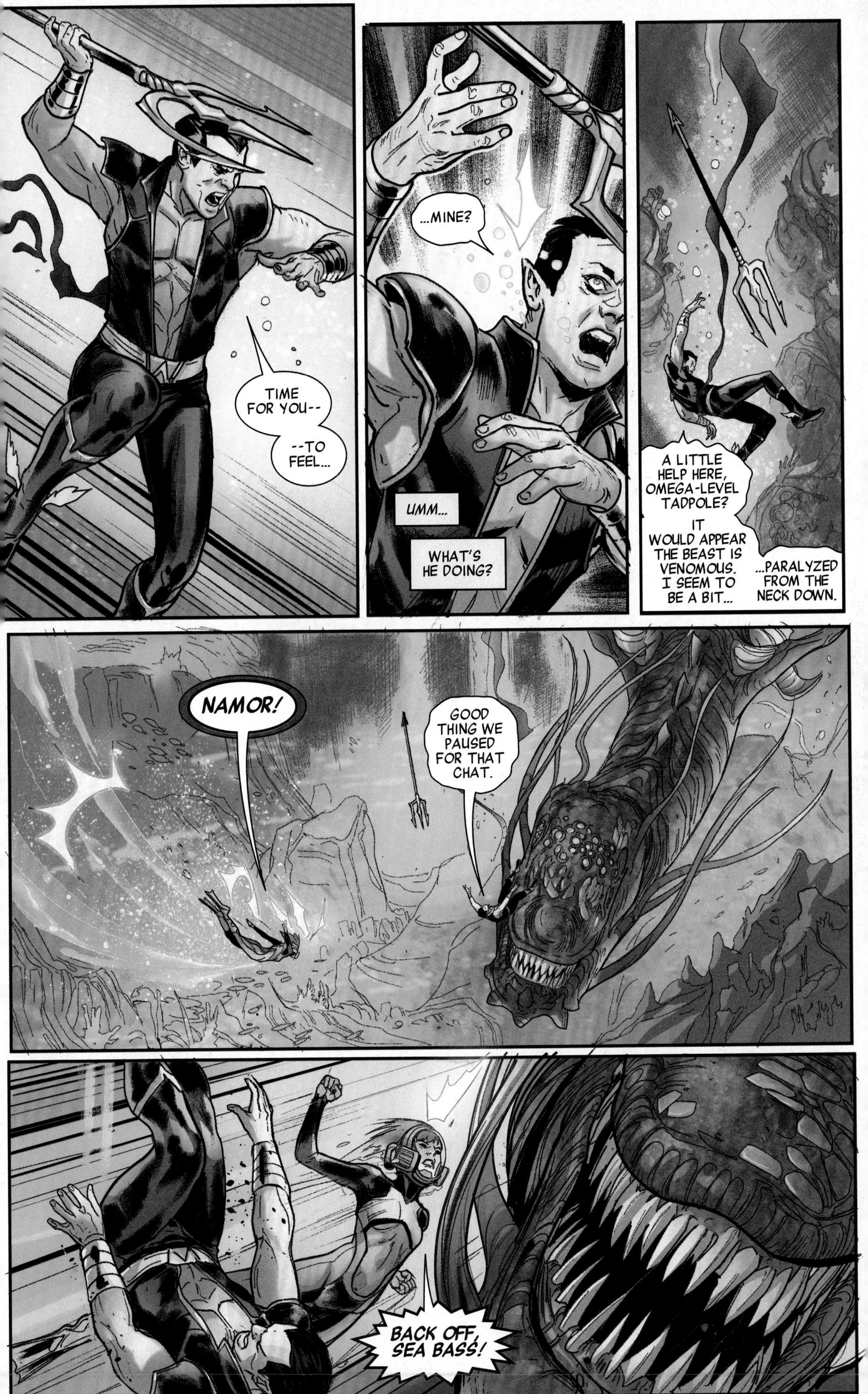
TIME FOR YOU--
--TO FEEL...
...MINE?
UMM...
WHAT'S HE DOING?
A LITTLE HELP HERE, OMEGA-LEVEL TADPOLE?
IT WOULD APPEAR THE BEAST IS VENOMOUS. I SEEM TO BE A BIT...
...PARALYZED FROM THE NECK DOWN.
NAMOR!
GOOD THING WE PAUSED FOR THAT CHAT.
BACK OFF, SEA BASS!

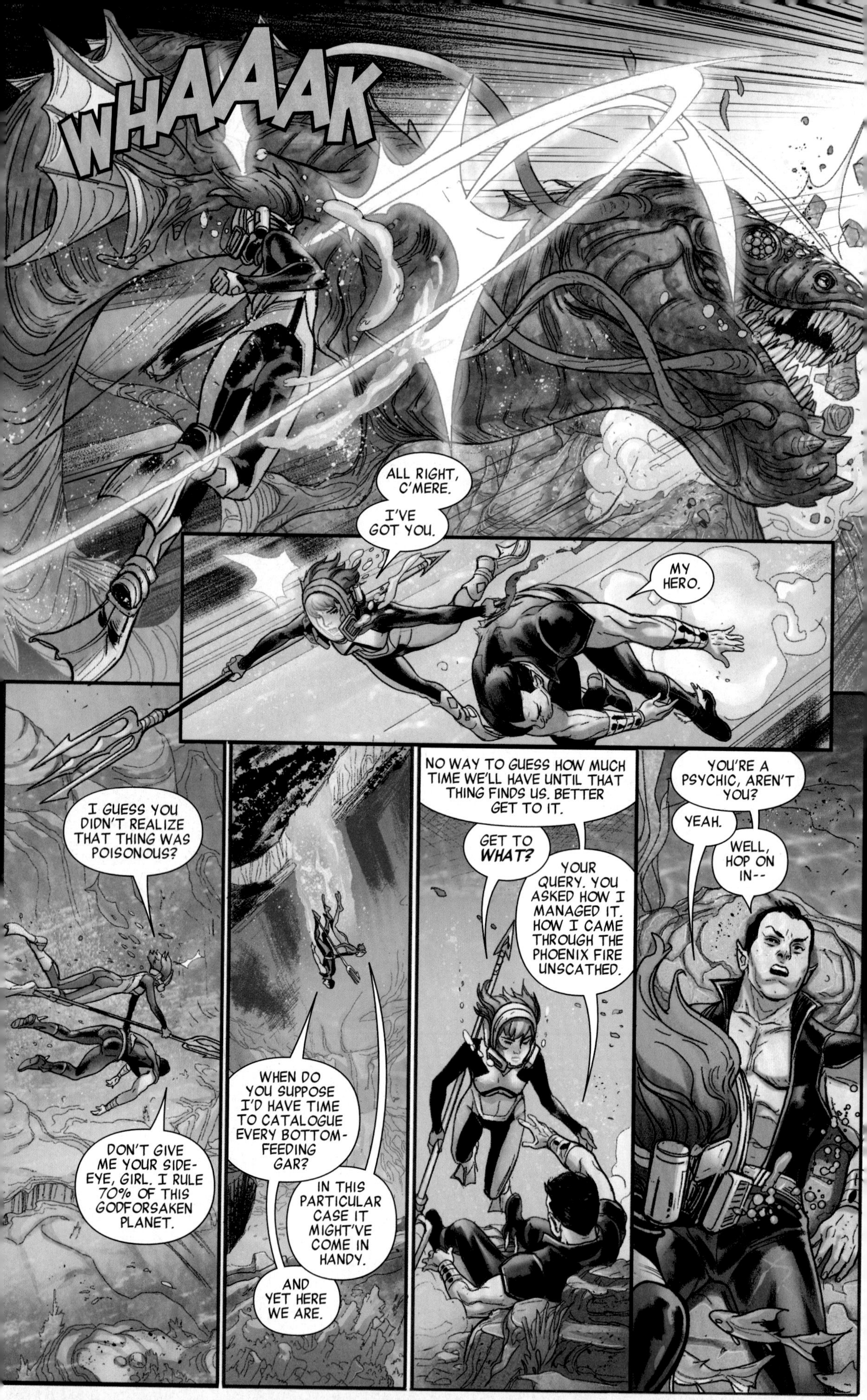
WHAAAK
ALL RIGHT, C'MERE.
I'VE GOT YOU.
MY HERO.
I GUESS YOU DIDN'T REALIZE THAT THING WAS POISONOUS?
DON'T GIVE ME YOUR SIDE-EYE, GIRL. I RULE 70% OF THIS GODFORSAKEN PLANET.
WHEN DO YOU SUPPOSE I'D HAVE TIME TO CATALOGUE EVERY BOTTOM-FEEDING GAR?
IN THIS PARTICULAR CASE IT MIGHT'VE COME IN HANDY.
AND YET HERE WE ARE.
NO WAY TO GUESS HOW MUCH TIME WE'LL HAVE UNTIL THAT THING FINDS US. BETTER GET TO IT.
GET TO ***WHAT?***
YOUR QUERY. YOU ASKED HOW I MANAGED IT. HOW I CAME THROUGH THE PHOENIX FIRE UNSCATHED.
YOU'RE A PSYCHIC, AREN'T YOU?
YEAH.
WELL, HOP ON IN--

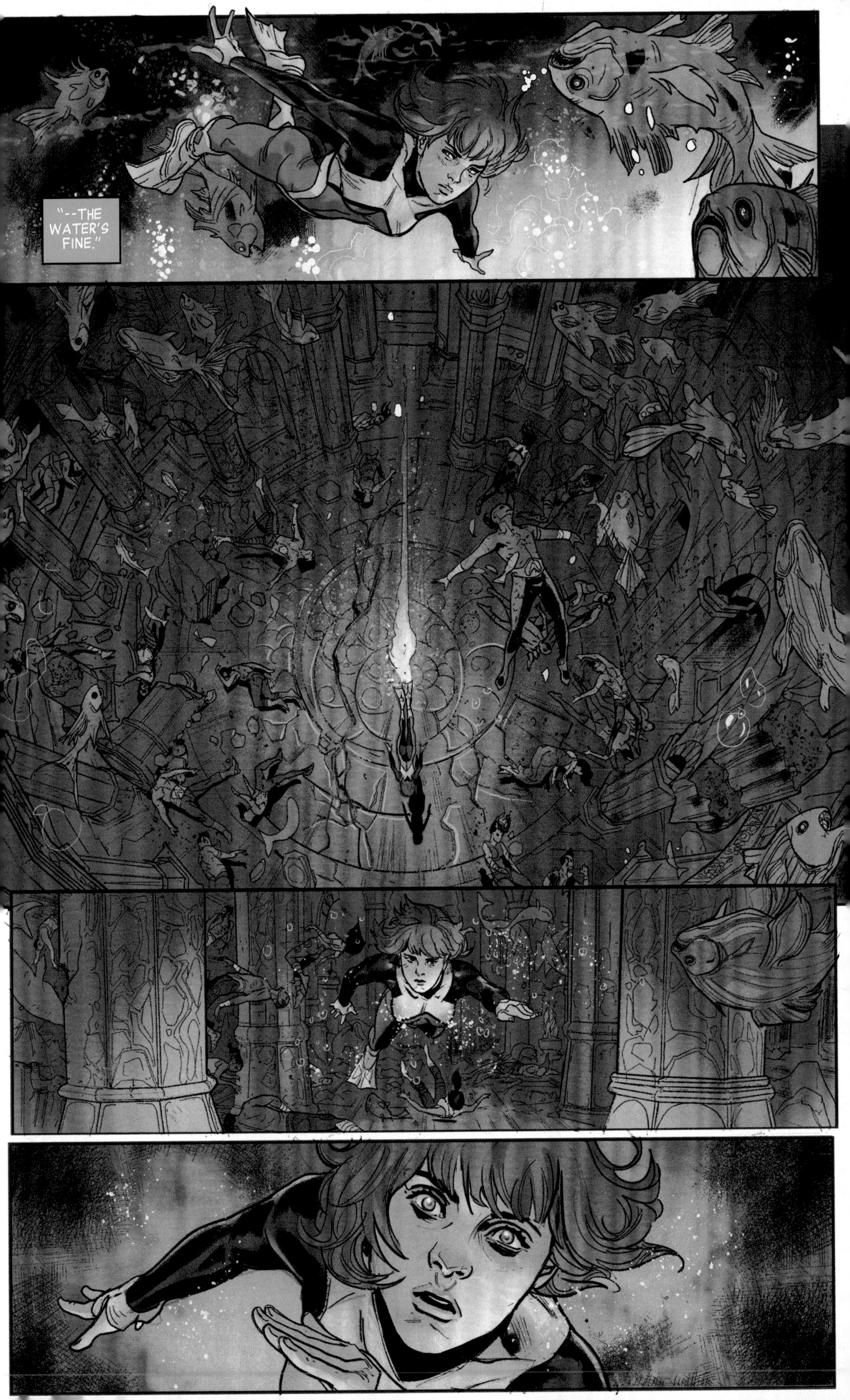
"--THE WATER'S FINE."

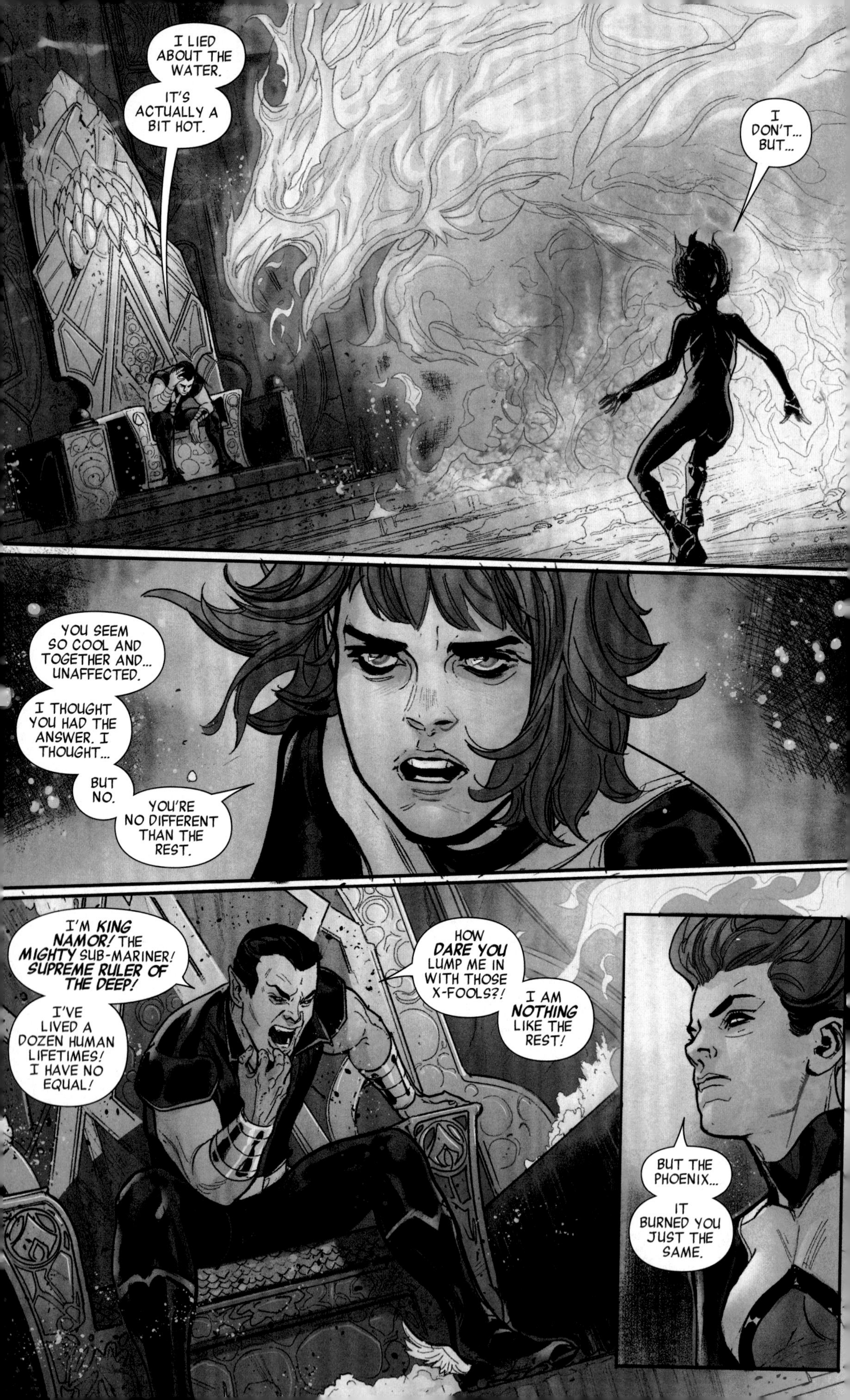
I LIED ABOUT THE WATER.
IT'S ACTUALLY A BIT HOT.
I DON'T... BUT...
YOU SEEM SO COOL AND TOGETHER AND... UNAFFECTED.
I THOUGHT YOU HAD THE ANSWER. I THOUGHT...
BUT NO.
YOU'RE NO DIFFERENT THAN THE REST.
I'M KING NAMOR! THE MIGHTY SUB-MARINER! SUPREME RULER OF THE DEEP!
I'VE LIVED A DOZEN HUMAN LIFETIMES! I HAVE NO EQUAL!
HOW DARE YOU LUMP ME IN WITH THOSE X-FOOLS?!
I AM NOTHING LIKE THE REST!
BUT THE PHOENIX...
IT BURNED YOU JUST THE SAME.

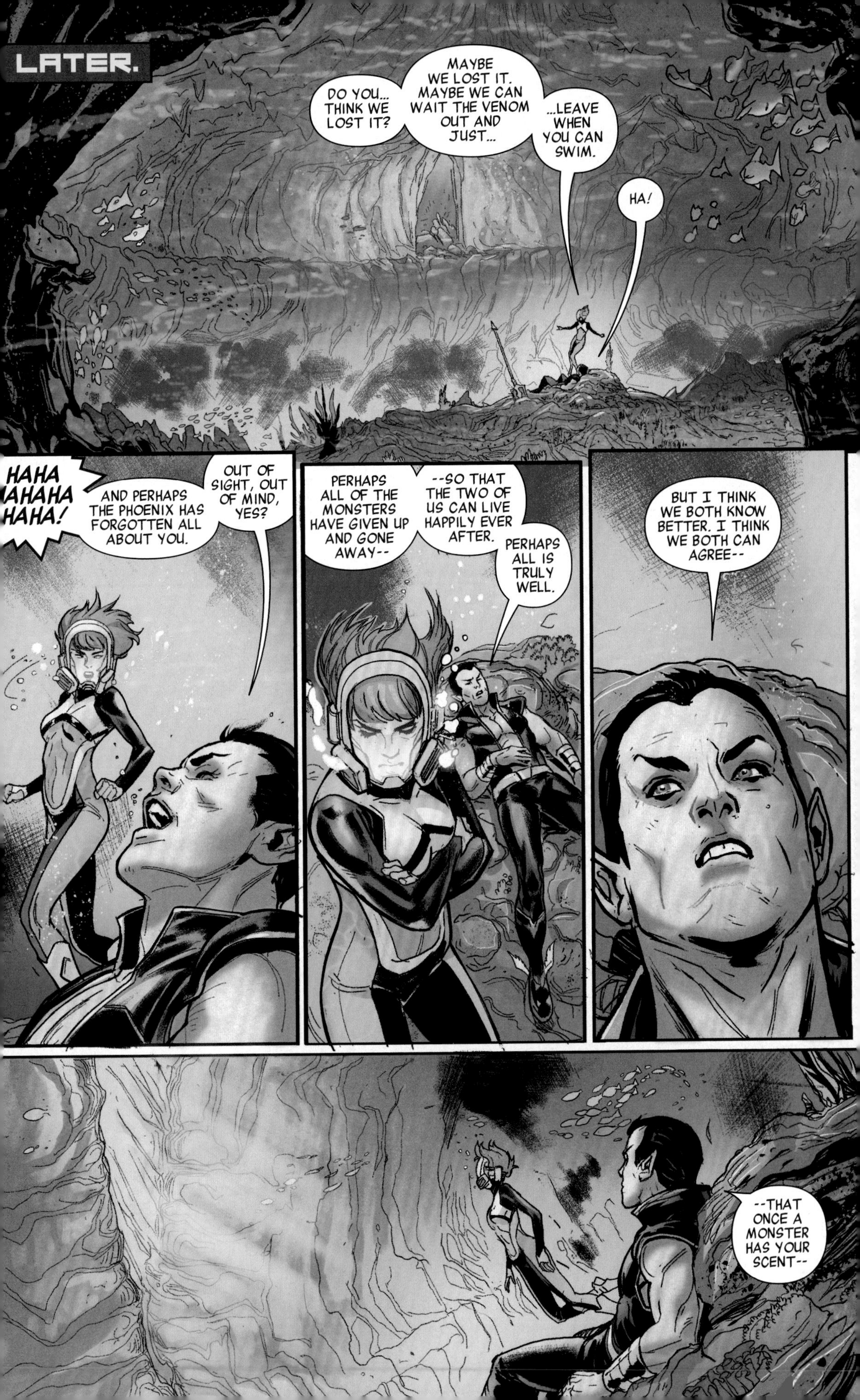
LATER.
DO YOU... THINK WE LOST IT?
MAYBE WE LOST IT. MAYBE WE CAN WAIT THE VENOM OUT AND JUST...
...LEAVE WHEN YOU CAN SWIM.
HA!
HAHA AHAHA HAHA!
AND PERHAPS THE PHOENIX HAS FORGOTTEN ALL ABOUT YOU.
OUT OF SIGHT, OUT OF MIND, YES?
PERHAPS ALL OF THE MONSTERS HAVE GIVEN UP AND GONE AWAY--
--SO THAT THE TWO OF US CAN LIVE HAPPILY EVER AFTER.
PERHAPS ALL IS TRULY WELL.
BUT I THINK WE BOTH KNOW BETTER. I THINK WE BOTH CAN AGREE--
--THAT ONCE A MONSTER HAS YOUR SCENT--

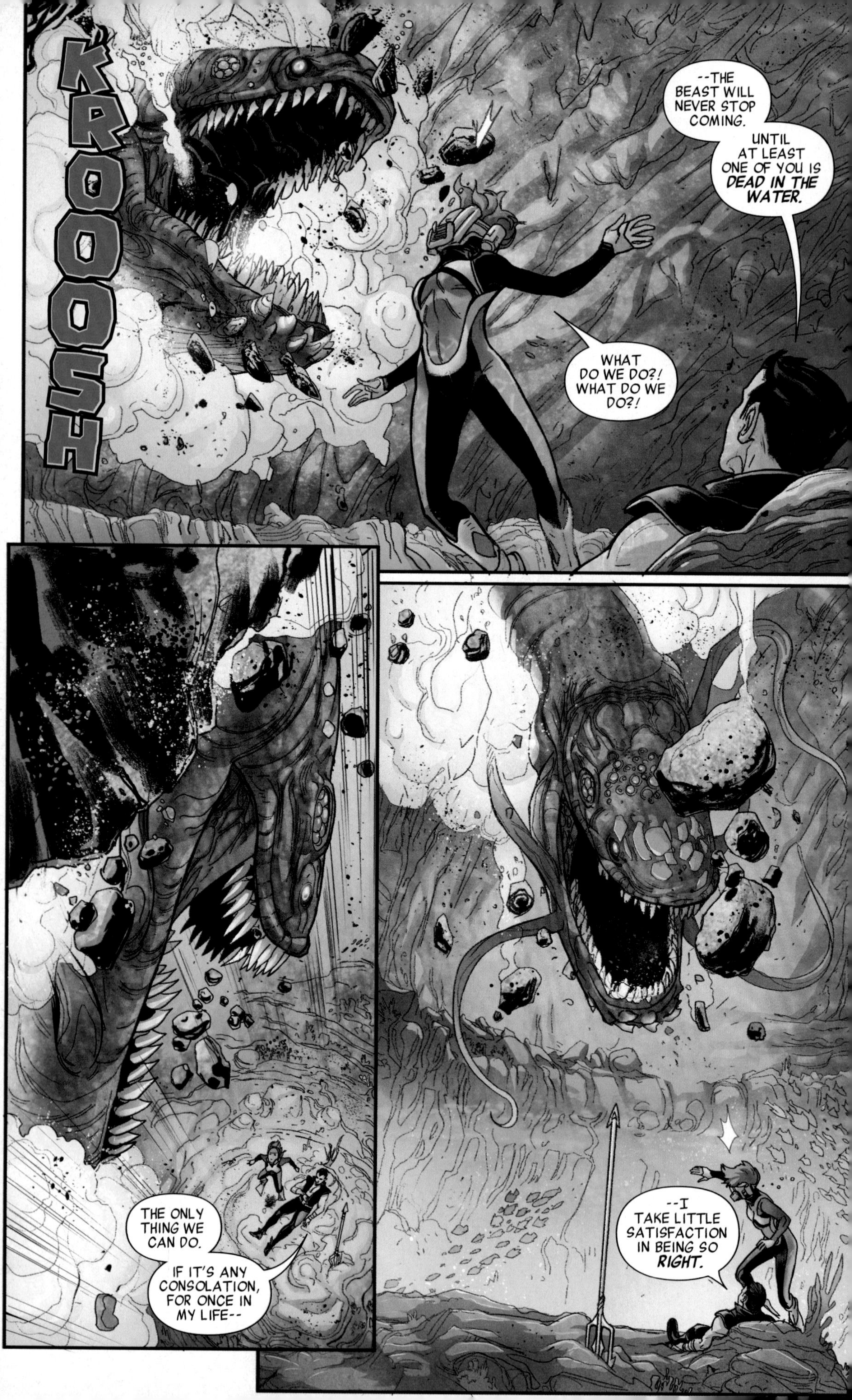
KROOOOSH
--THE BEAST WILL NEVER STOP COMING.
UNTIL AT LEAST ONE OF YOU IS DEAD IN THE WATER.
WHAT DO WE DO?! WHAT DO WE DO?!
THE ONLY THING WE CAN DO.
IF IT'S ANY CONSOLATION, FOR ONCE IN MY LIFE--
--I TAKE LITTLE SATISFACTION IN BEING SO RIGHT.

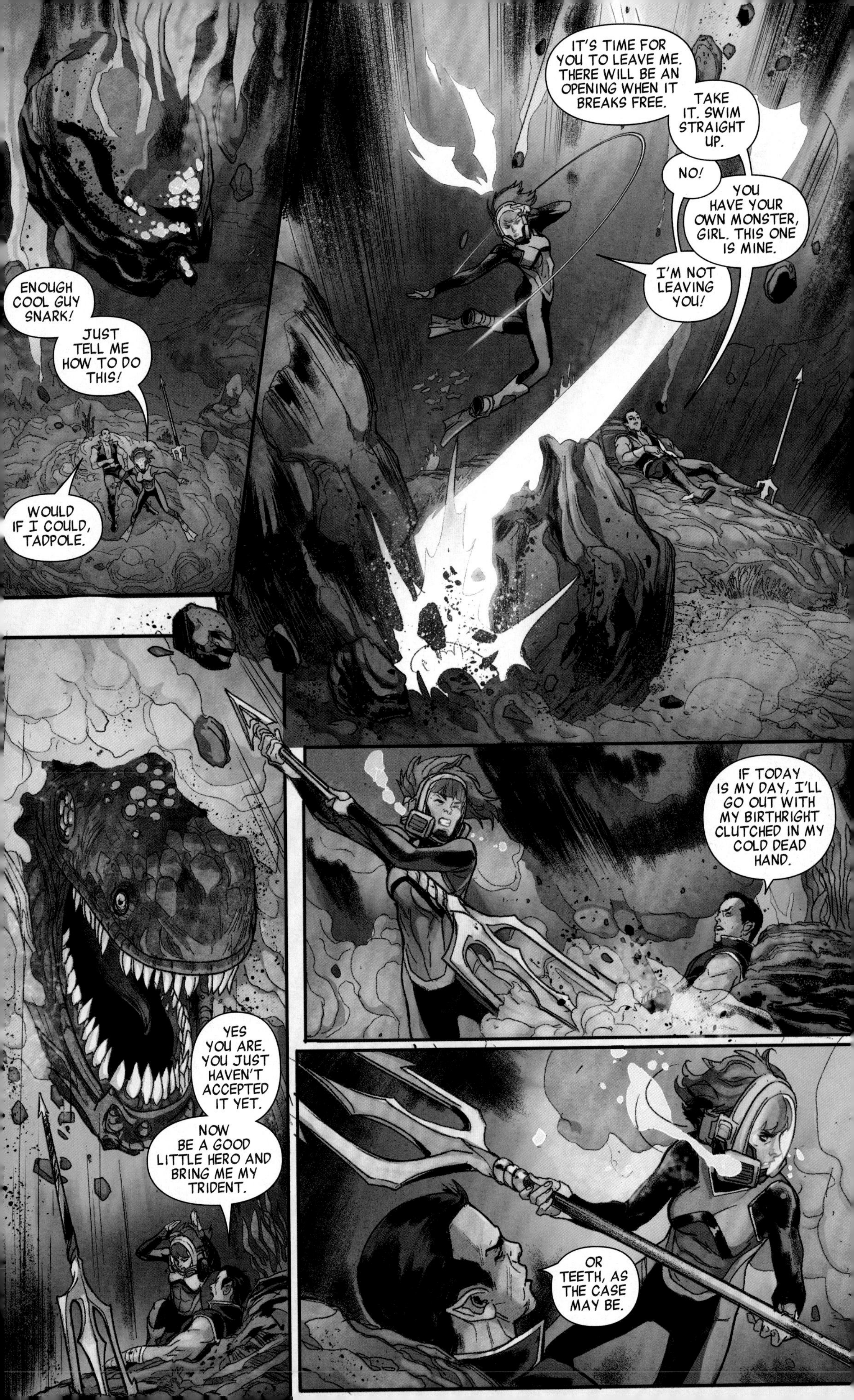
ENOUGH COOL GUY SNARK!
JUST TELL ME HOW TO DO THIS!
WOULD IF I COULD, TADPOLE.
IT'S TIME FOR YOU TO LEAVE ME. THERE WILL BE AN OPENING WHEN IT BREAKS FREE.
TAKE IT. SWIM STRAIGHT UP.
NO!
YOU HAVE YOUR OWN MONSTER, GIRL. THIS ONE IS MINE.
I'M NOT LEAVING YOU!
YES YOU ARE. YOU JUST HAVEN'T ACCEPTED IT YET.
NOW BE A GOOD LITTLE HERO AND BRING ME MY TRIDENT.
IF TODAY IS MY DAY, I'LL GO OUT WITH MY BIRTHRIGHT CLUTCHED IN MY COLD DEAD HAND.
OR TEETH, AS THE CASE MAY BE.

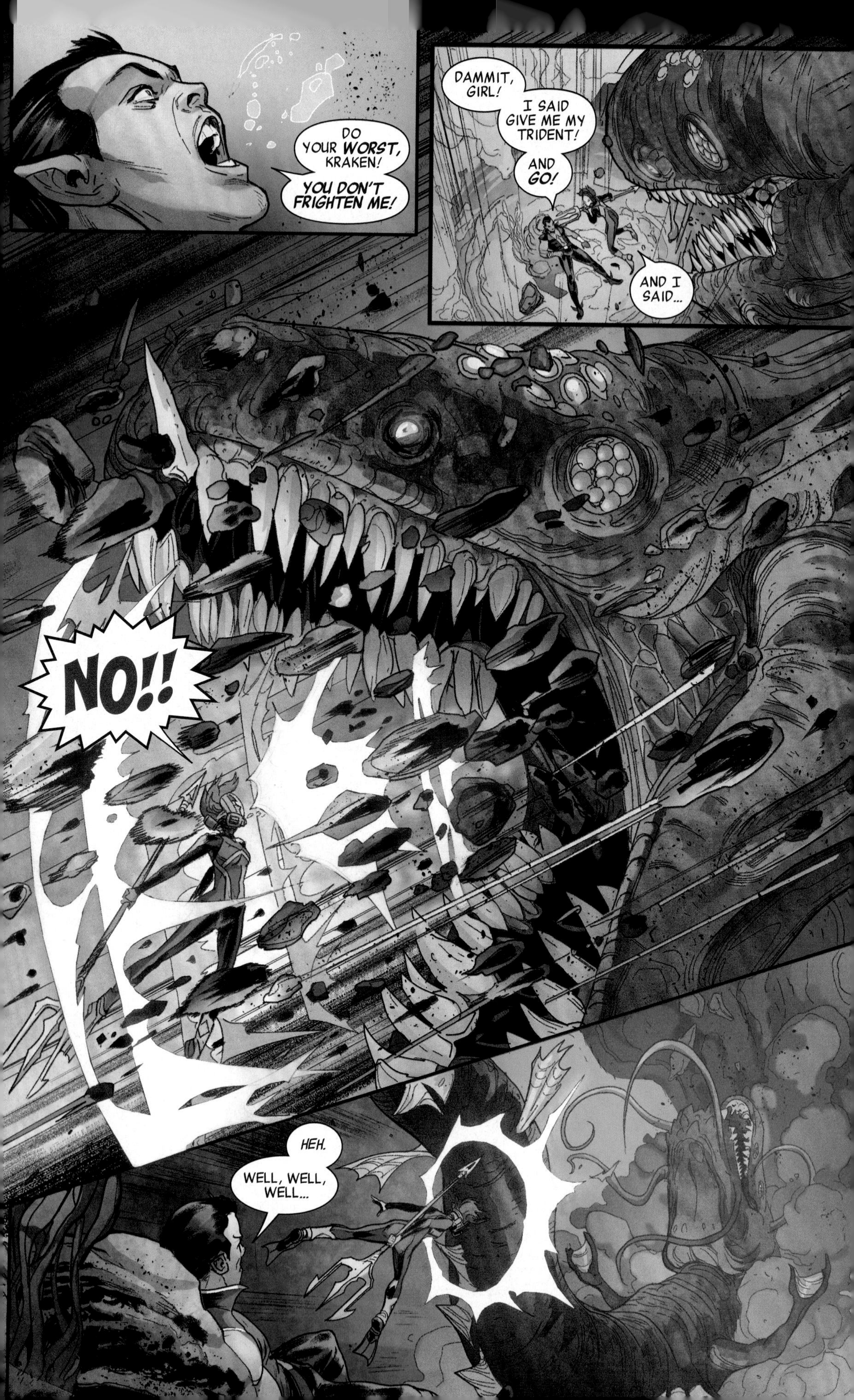
DO YOUR WORST, KRAKEN!
YOU DON'T FRIGHTEN ME!
DAMMIT, GIRL!
I SAID GIVE ME MY TRIDENT!
AND GO!
AND I SAID...
NO!!
HEH.
WELL, WELL, WELL...

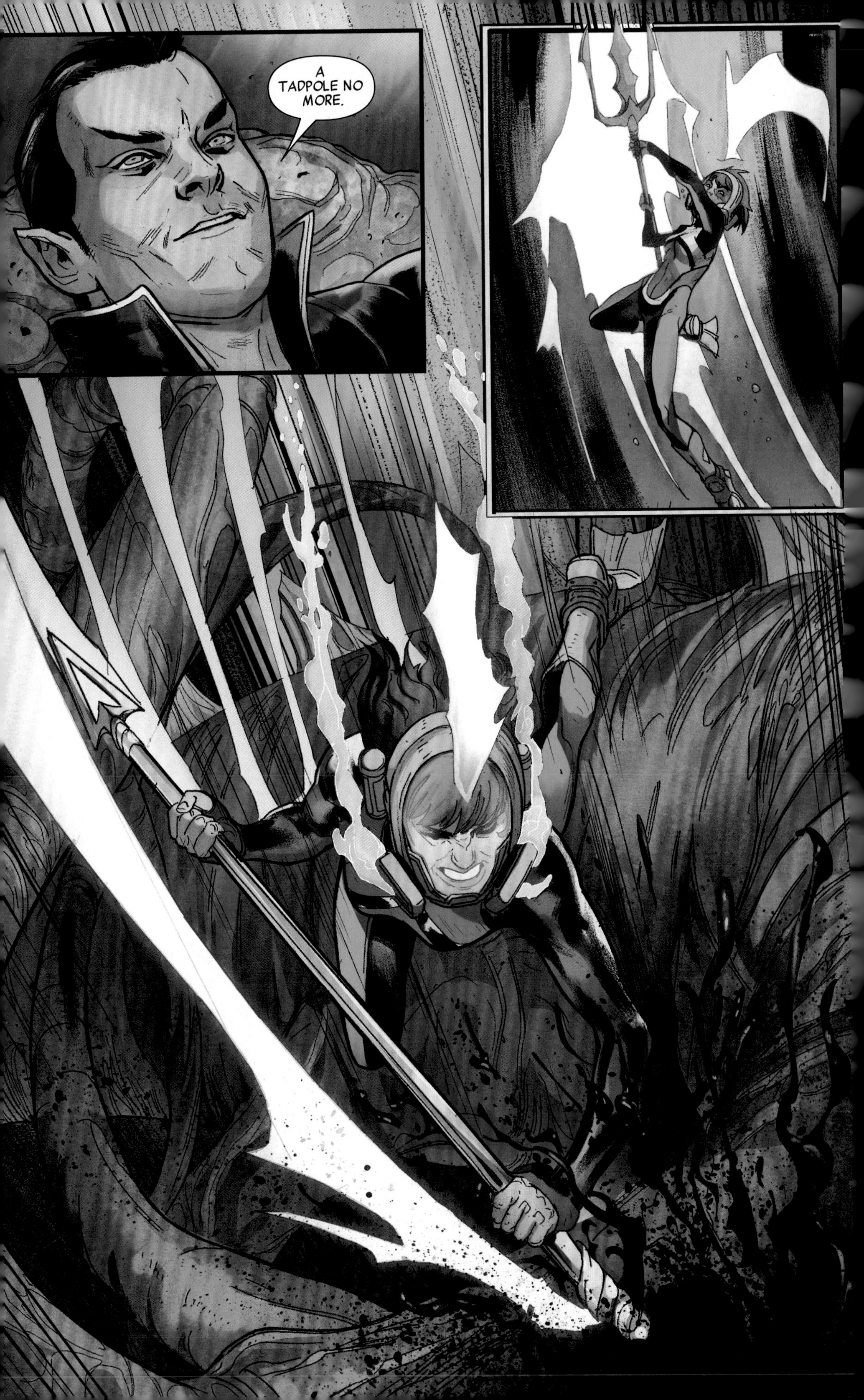
A TADPOLE NO MORE.

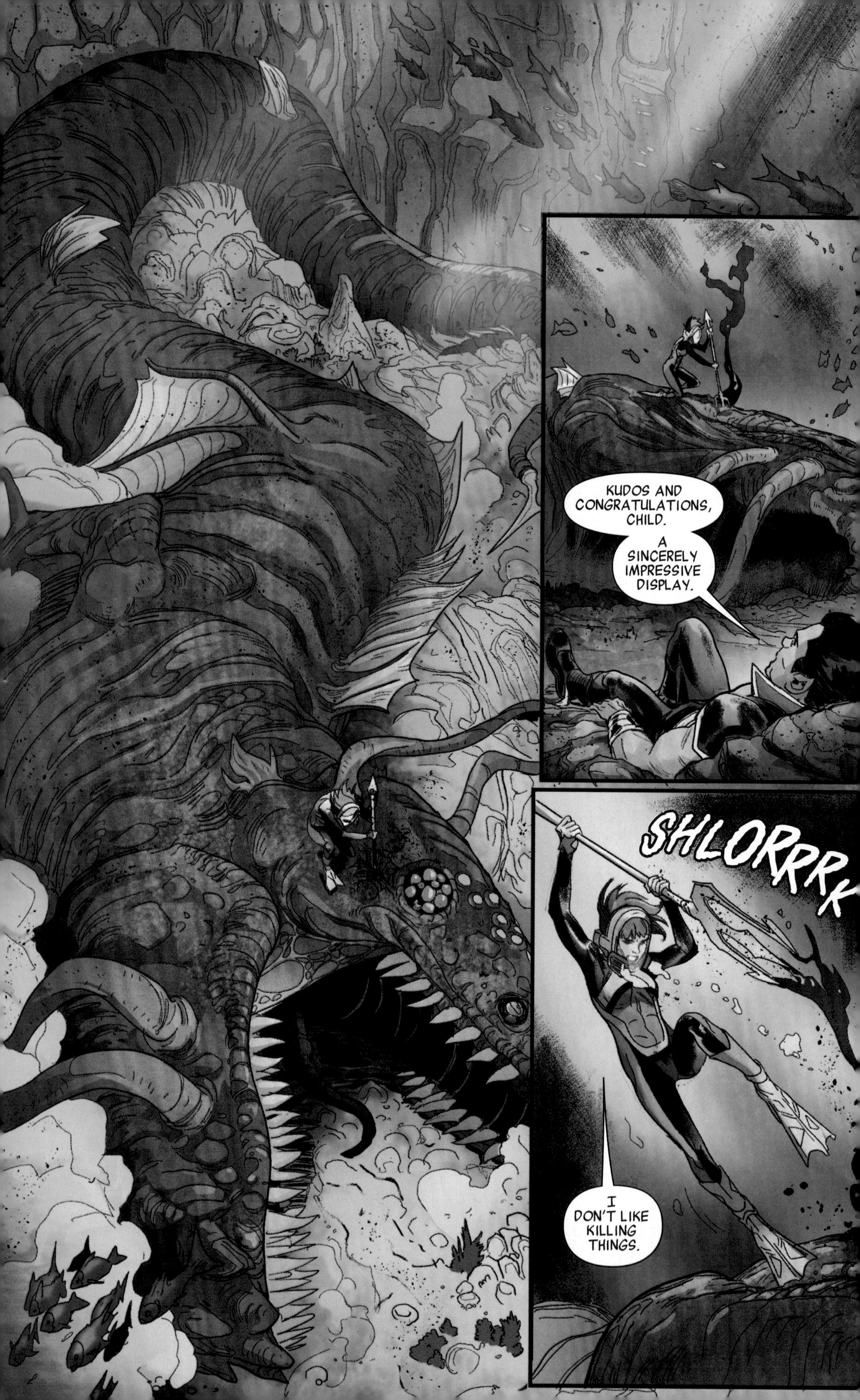
KUDOS AND CONGRATULATIONS, CHILD.
A SINCERELY IMPRESSIVE DISPLAY.
SHLORRRK
I DON'T LIKE KILLING THINGS.

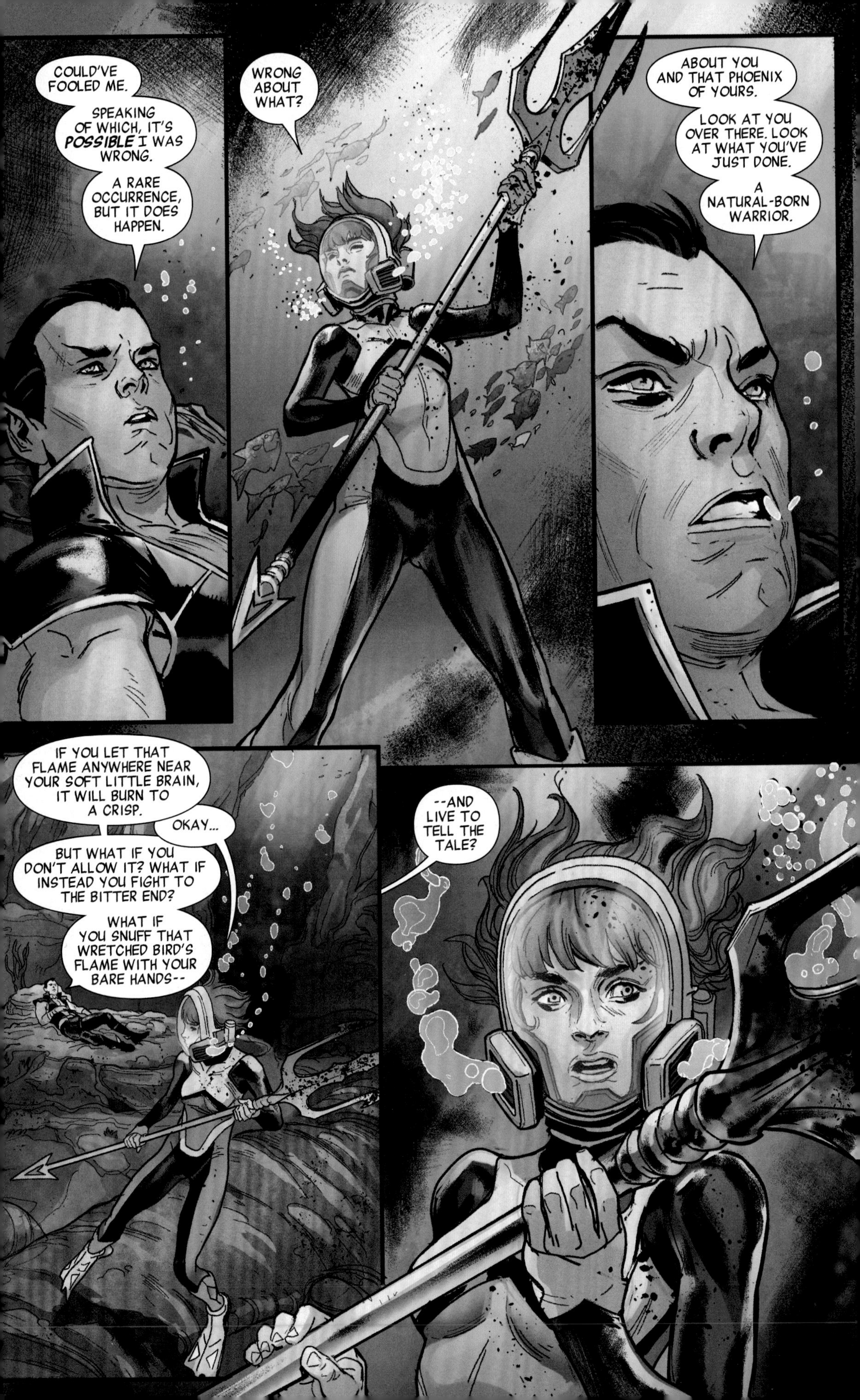
COULD'VE FOOLED ME.
SPEAKING OF WHICH, IT'S POSSIBLE I WAS WRONG.
A RARE OCCURRENCE, BUT IT DOES HAPPEN.
WRONG ABOUT WHAT?
ABOUT YOU AND THAT PHOENIX OF YOURS.
LOOK AT YOU OVER THERE. LOOK AT WHAT YOU'VE JUST DONE.
A NATURAL-BORN WARRIOR.
IF YOU LET THAT FLAME ANYWHERE NEAR YOUR SOFT LITTLE BRAIN, IT WILL BURN TO A CRISP.
OKAY...
BUT WHAT IF YOU DON'T ALLOW IT? WHAT IF INSTEAD YOU FIGHT TO THE BITTER END?
WHAT IF YOU SNUFF THAT WRETCHED BIRD'S FLAME WITH YOUR BARE HANDS--
--AND LIVE TO TELL THE TALE?

#1 VARIANT BY **MARGUERITE SAUVAGE**

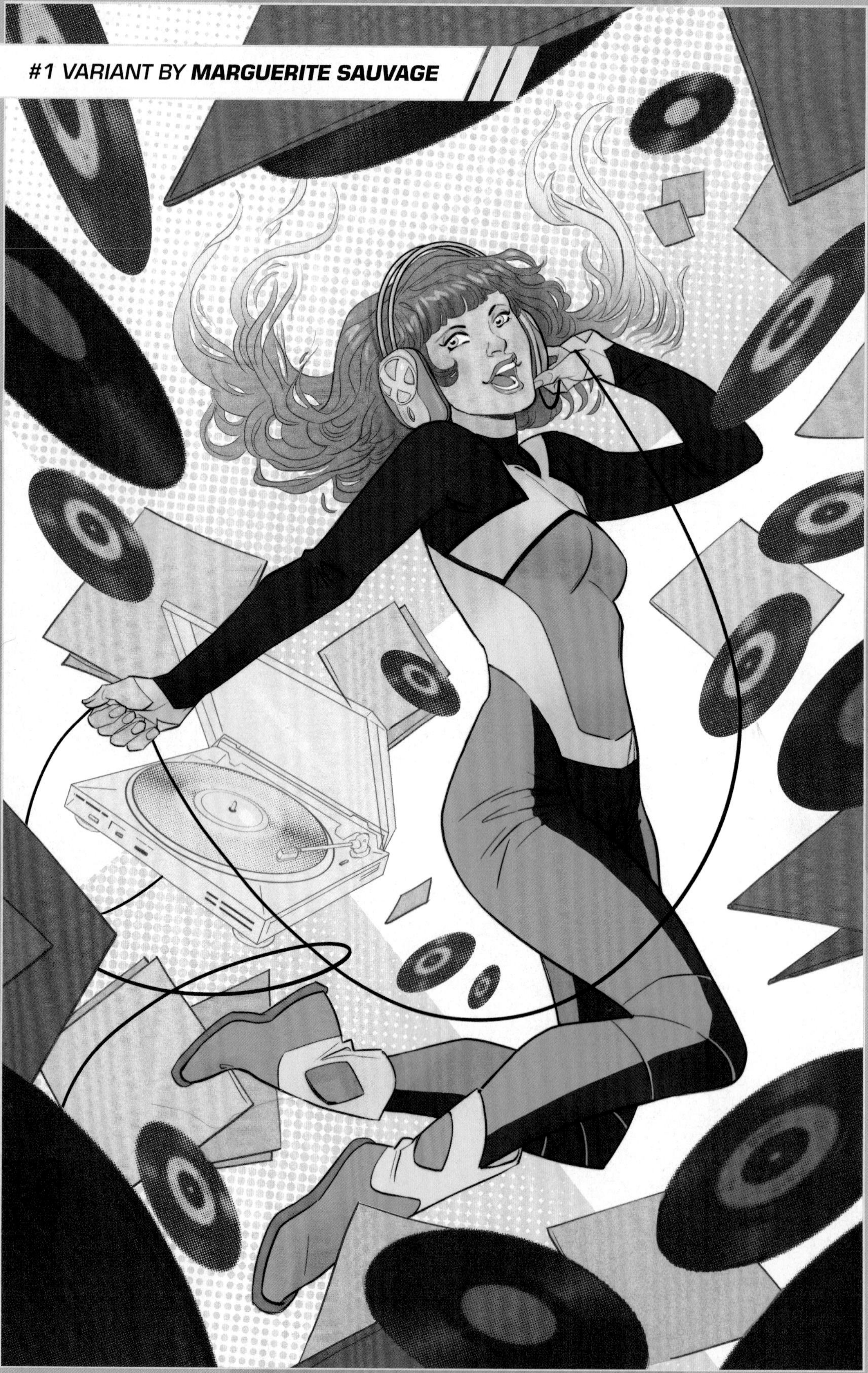

4

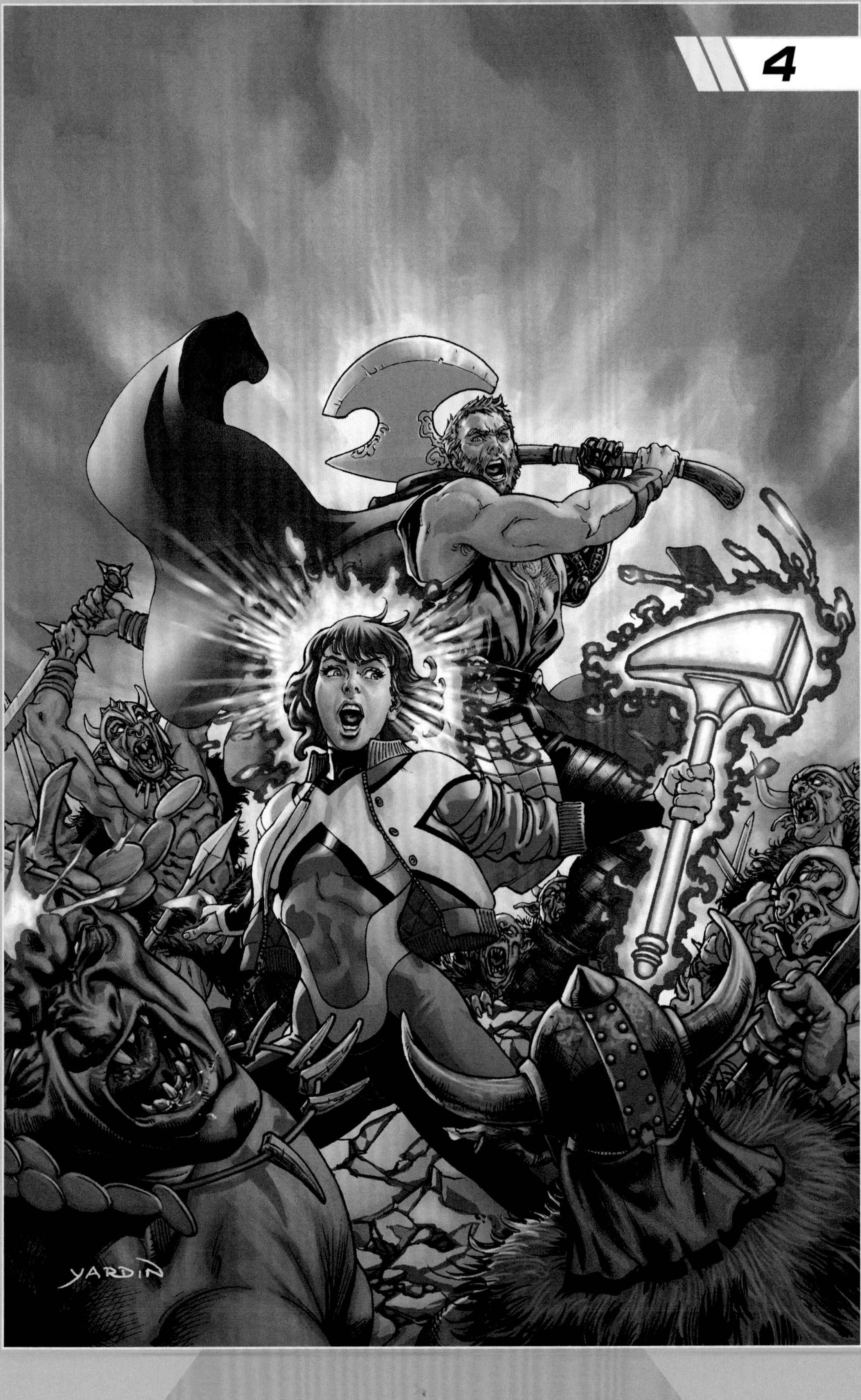
YARDIN

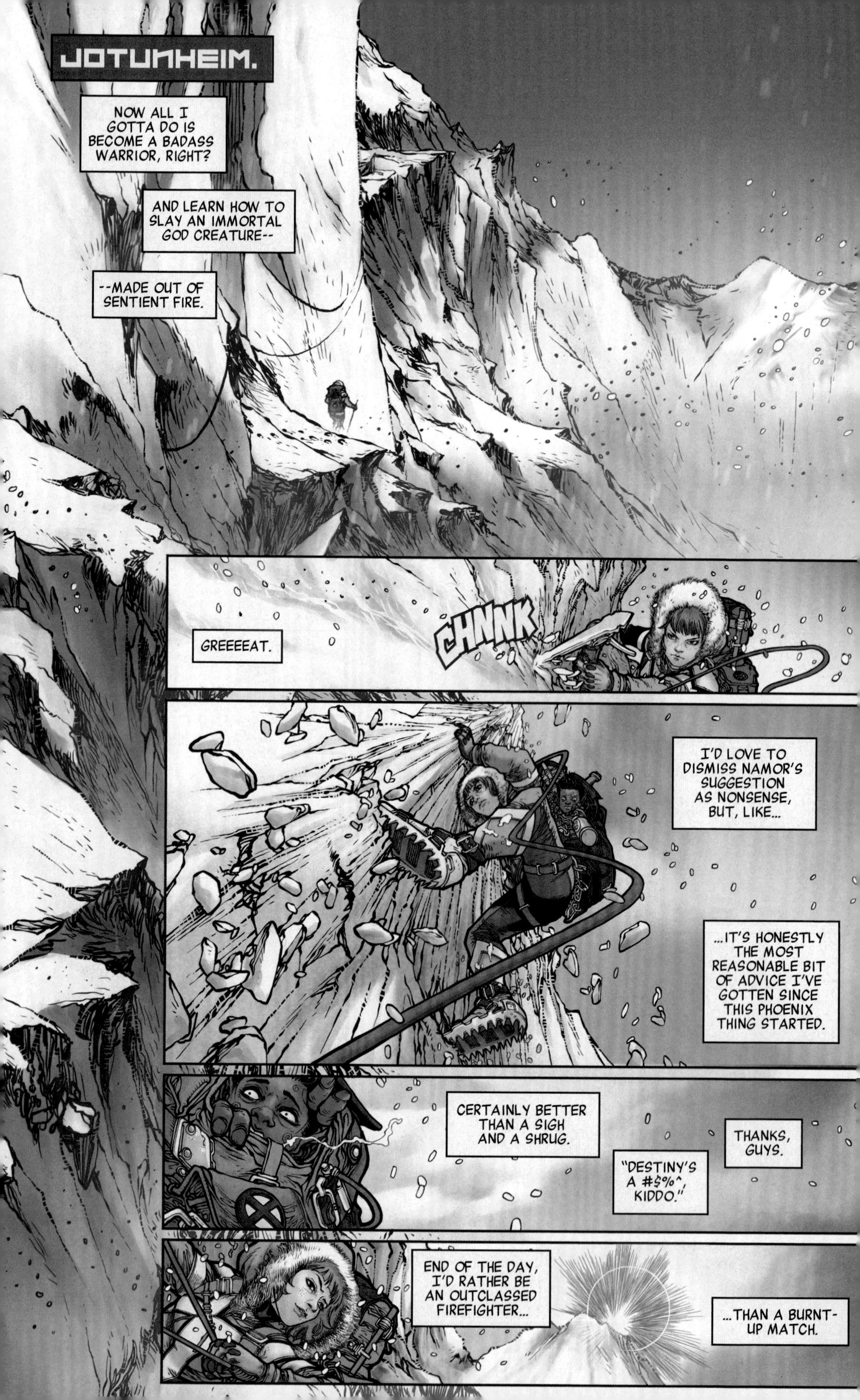
JOTUNHEIM.
NOW ALL I GOTTA DO IS BECOME A BADASS WARRIOR, RIGHT?
AND LEARN HOW TO SLAY AN IMMORTAL GOD CREATURE--
--MADE OUT OF SENTIENT FIRE.
GREEEEAT.
CHNNK
I'D LOVE TO DISMISS NAMOR'S SUGGESTION AS NONSENSE, BUT, LIKE...
...IT'S HONESTLY THE MOST REASONABLE BIT OF ADVICE I'VE GOTTEN SINCE THIS PHOENIX THING STARTED.
CERTAINLY BETTER THAN A SIGH AND A SHRUG.
"DESTINY'S A #$%^, KIDDO."
THANKS, GUYS.
END OF THE DAY, I'D RATHER BE AN OUTCLASSED FIREFIGHTER...
...THAN A BURNT-UP MATCH.

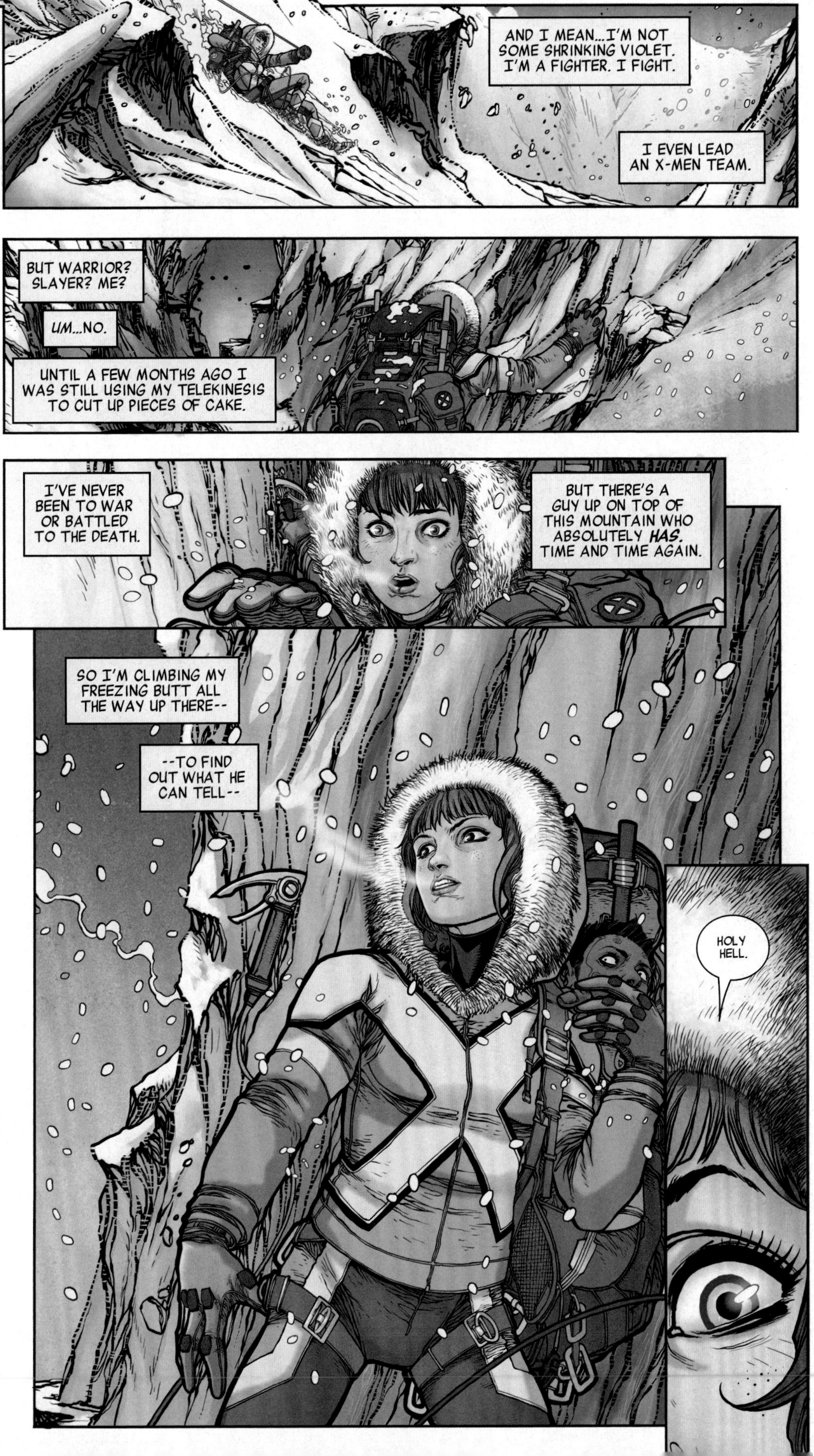
AND I MEAN...I'M NOT SOME SHRINKING VIOLET. I'M A FIGHTER. I FIGHT.
I EVEN LEAD AN X-MEN TEAM.
BUT WARRIOR? SLAYER? ME?
UM...NO.
UNTIL A FEW MONTHS AGO I WAS STILL USING MY TELEKINESIS TO CUT UP PIECES OF CAKE.
I'VE NEVER BEEN TO WAR OR BATTLED TO THE DEATH.
BUT THERE'S A GUY UP ON TOP OF THIS MOUNTAIN WHO ABSOLUTELY HAS. TIME AND TIME AGAIN.
SO I'M CLIMBING MY FREEZING BUTT ALL THE WAY UP THERE--
--TO FIND OUT WHAT HE CAN TELL--
HOLY HELL.

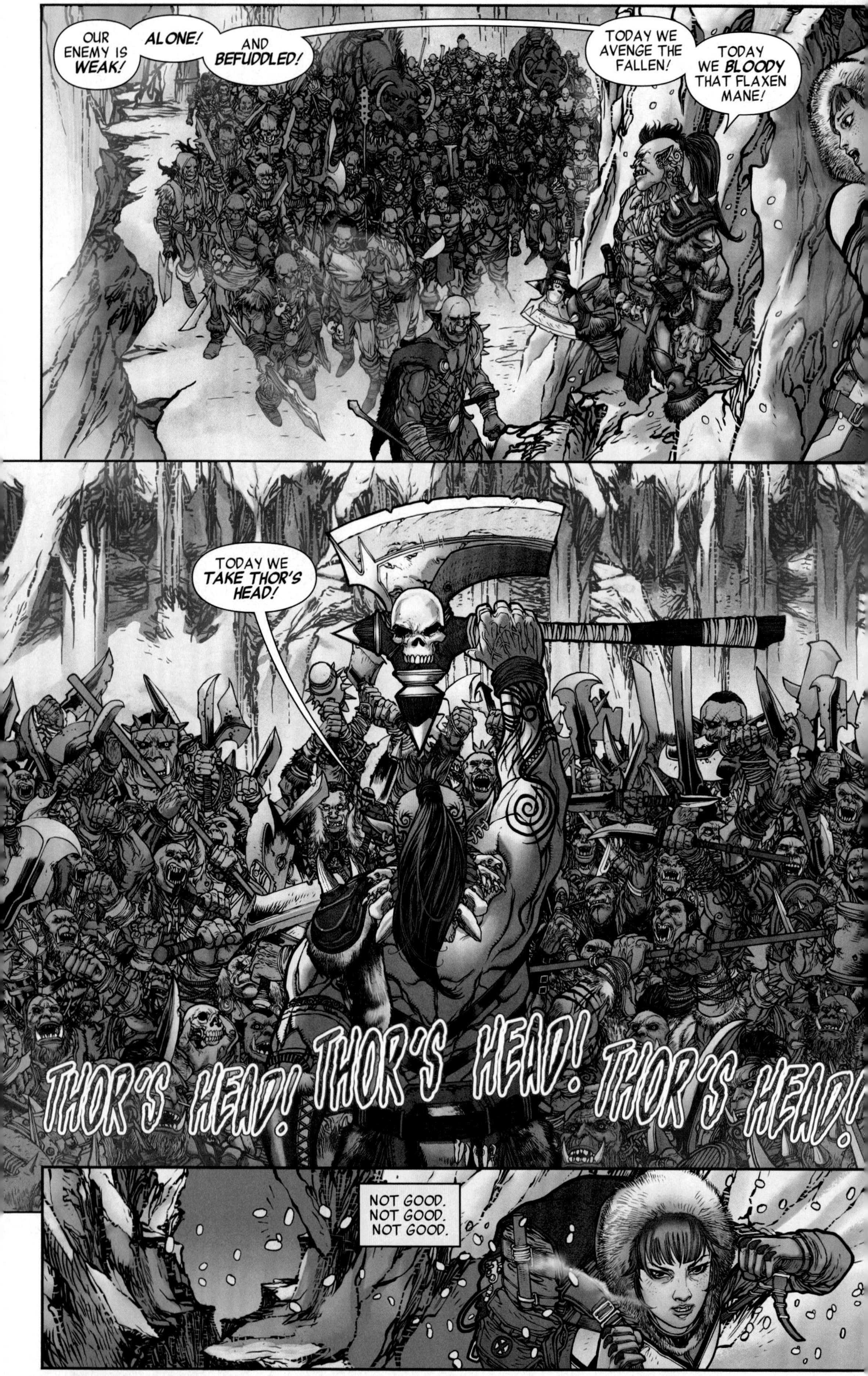
OUR ENEMY IS WEAK!
ALONE!
AND BEFUDDLED!
TODAY WE AVENGE THE FALLEN!
TODAY WE BLOODY THAT FLAXEN MANE!
TODAY WE TAKE THOR'S HEAD!
THOR'S HEAD! THOR'S HEAD! THOR'S HEAD!
NOT GOOD. NOT GOOD. NOT GOOD.

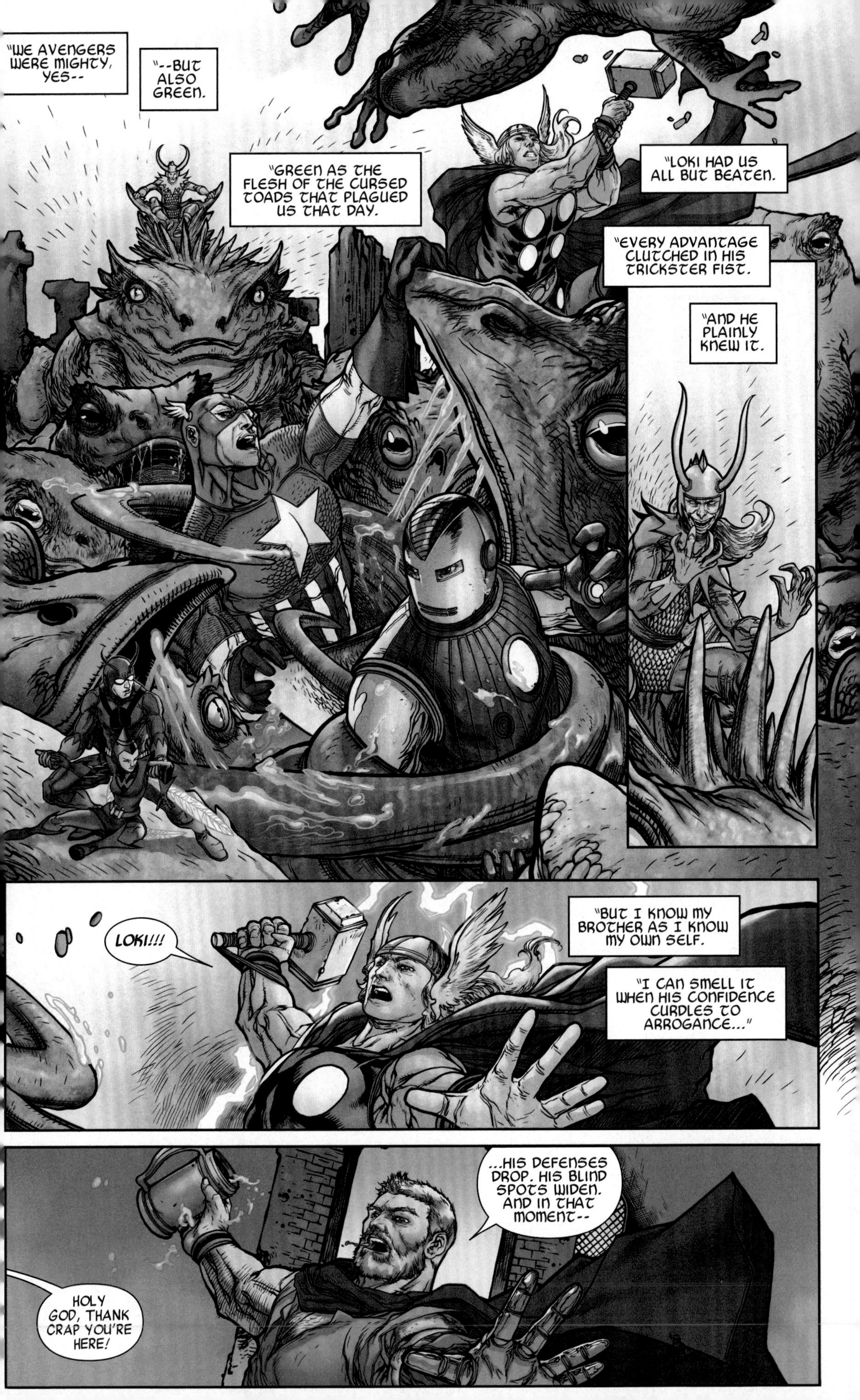
"WE AVENGERS WERE MIGHTY, YES--
"--BUT ALSO GREEN.
"GREEN AS THE FLESH OF THE CURSED TOADS THAT PLAGUED US THAT DAY.
"LOKI HAD US ALL BUT BEATEN.
"EVERY ADVANTAGE CLUTCHED IN HIS TRICKSTER FIST.
"AND HE PLAINLY KNEW IT.
LOKI!!!
"BUT I KNOW MY BROTHER AS I KNOW MY OWN SELF.
"I CAN SMELL IT WHEN HIS CONFIDENCE CURDLES TO ARROGANCE..."
...HIS DEFENSES DROP. HIS BLIND SPOTS WIDEN. AND IN THAT MOMENT--
HOLY GOD, THANK CRAP YOU'RE HERE!

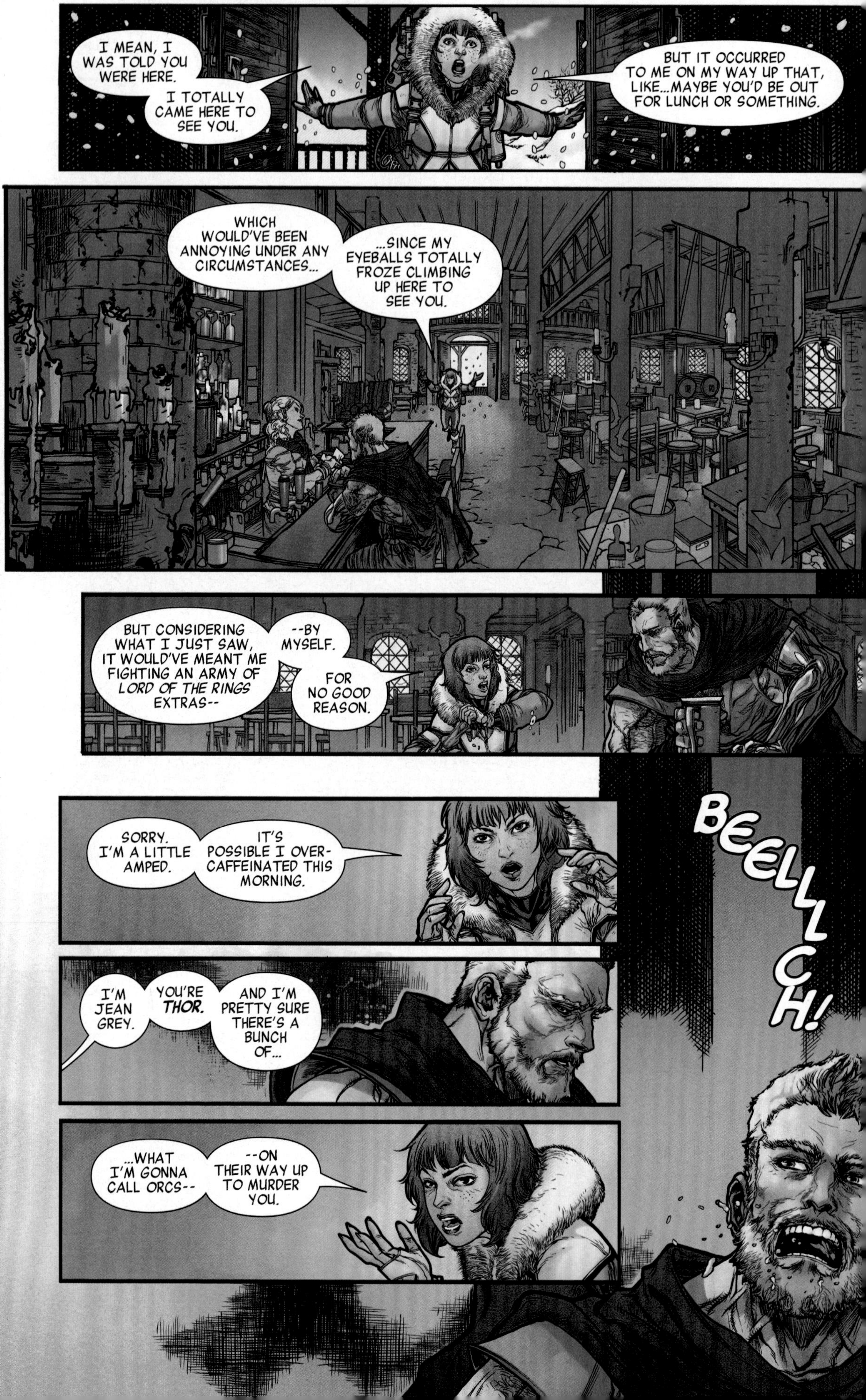
I MEAN, I WAS TOLD YOU WERE HERE.
I TOTALLY CAME HERE TO SEE YOU.
BUT IT OCCURRED TO ME ON MY WAY UP THAT, LIKE...MAYBE YOU'D BE OUT FOR LUNCH OR SOMETHING.
WHICH WOULD'VE BEEN ANNOYING UNDER ANY CIRCUMSTANCES...
...SINCE MY EYEBALLS TOTALLY FROZE CLIMBING UP HERE TO SEE YOU.
BUT CONSIDERING WHAT I JUST SAW, IT WOULD'VE MEANT ME FIGHTING AN ARMY OF *LORD OF THE RINGS* EXTRAS--
--BY MYSELF.
FOR NO GOOD REASON.
SORRY. I'M A LITTLE AMPED.
IT'S POSSIBLE I OVER-CAFFEINATED THIS MORNING.
BEELLLCH!
I'M JEAN GREY.
YOU'RE ***THOR.***
AND I'M PRETTY SURE THERE'S A BUNCH OF...
...WHAT I'M GONNA CALL ORCS--
--ON THEIR WAY UP TO MURDER YOU.

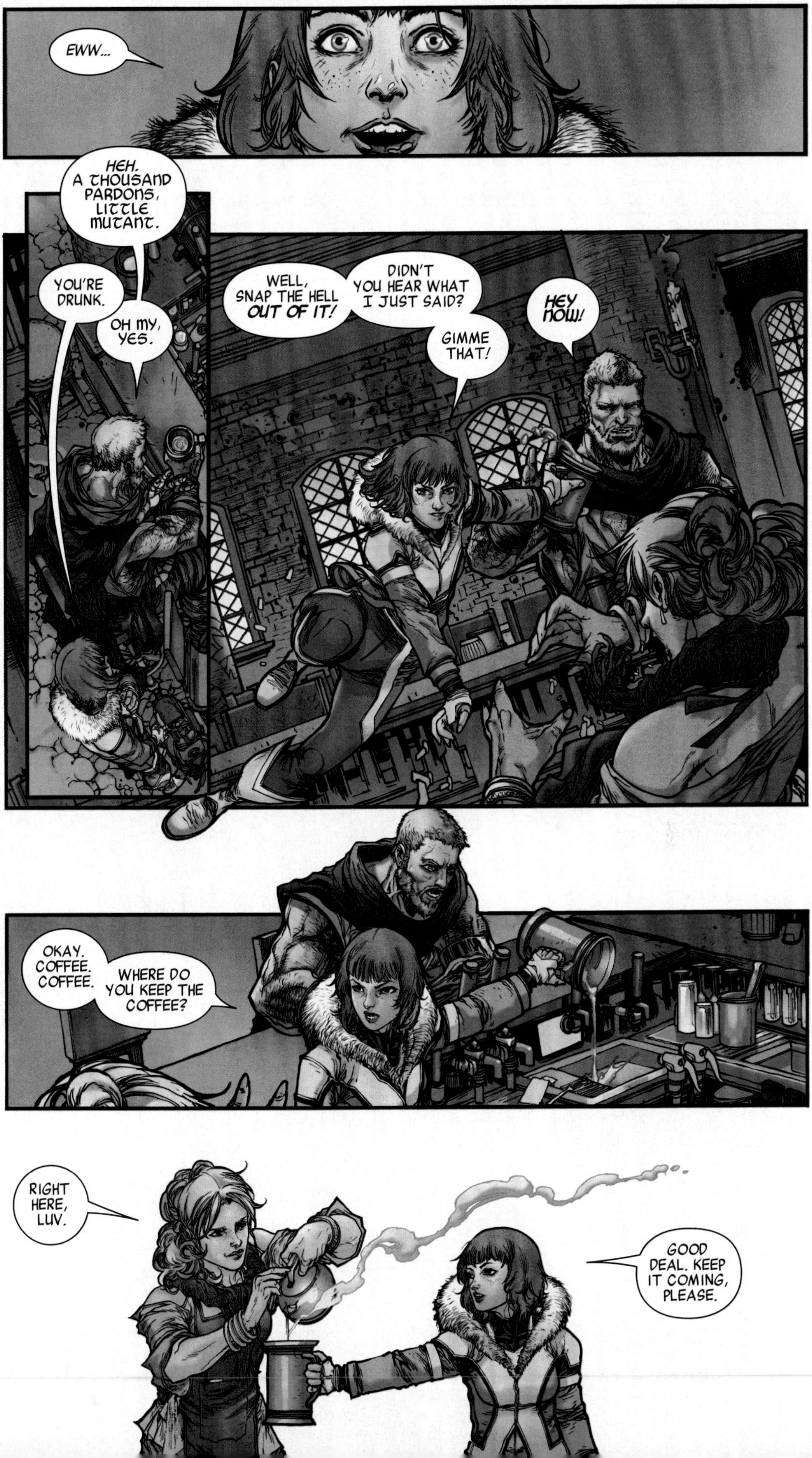
EWW...
HEH. A THOUSAND PARDONS, LITTLE MUTANT.
YOU'RE DRUNK.
OH MY, YES.
WELL, SNAP THE HELL OUT OF IT!
DIDN'T YOU HEAR WHAT I JUST SAID?
GIMME THAT!
HEY NOW!
OKAY. COFFEE. COFFEE.
WHERE DO YOU KEEP THE COFFEE?
RIGHT HERE, LUV.
GOOD DEAL. KEEP IT COMING, PLEASE.

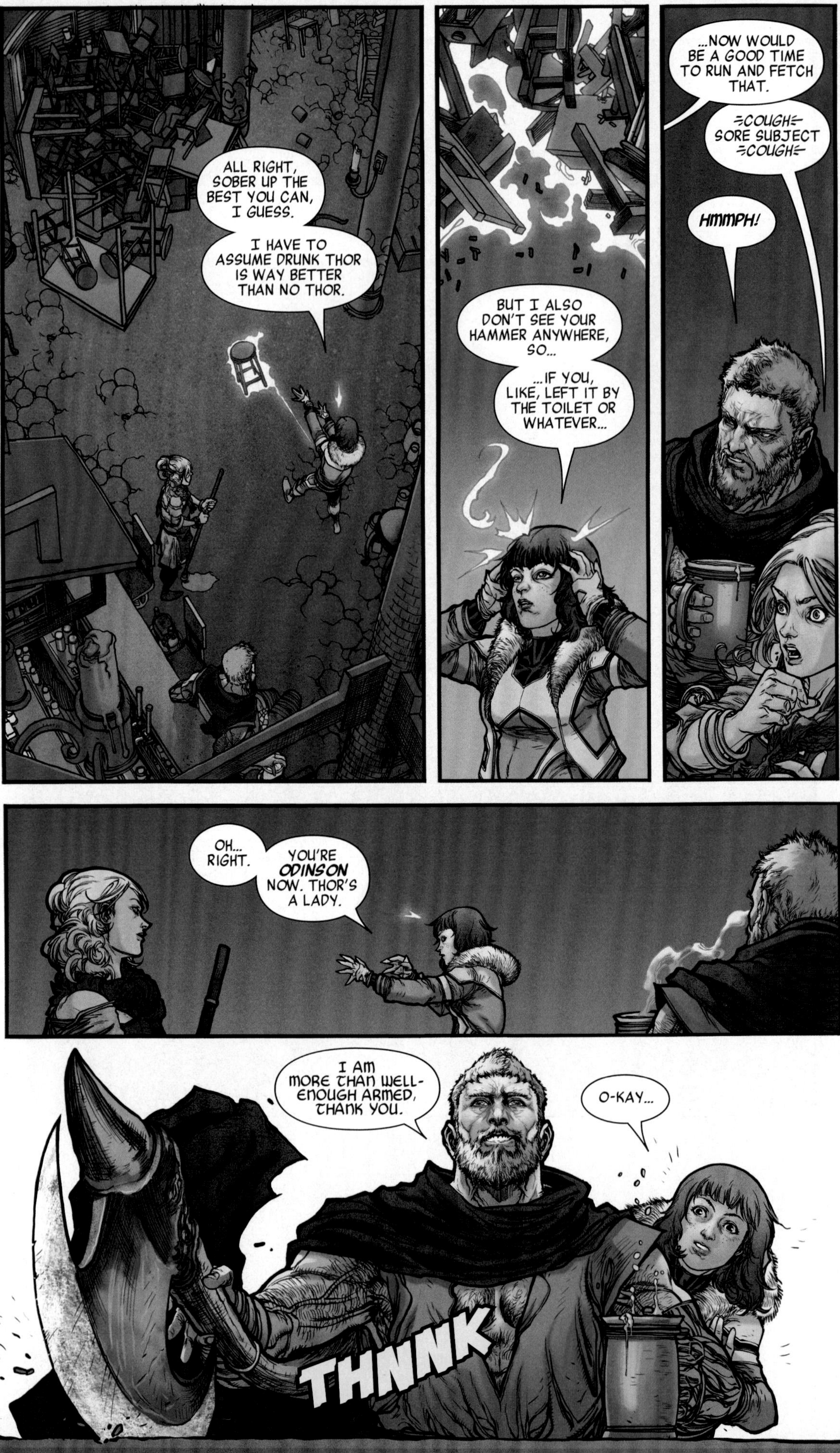
ALL RIGHT, SOBER UP THE BEST YOU CAN, I GUESS.
I HAVE TO ASSUME DRUNK THOR IS WAY BETTER THAN NO THOR.
BUT I ALSO DON'T SEE YOUR HAMMER ANYWHERE, SO...
...IF YOU, LIKE, LEFT IT BY THE TOILET OR WHATEVER...
...NOW WOULD BE A GOOD TIME TO RUN AND FETCH THAT.
=COUGH= SORE SUBJECT =COUGH=
HMMPH!
OH... RIGHT.
YOU'RE ODINSON NOW. THOR'S A LADY.
I AM MORE THAN WELL-ENOUGH ARMED, THANK YOU.
O-KAY...
THNNK

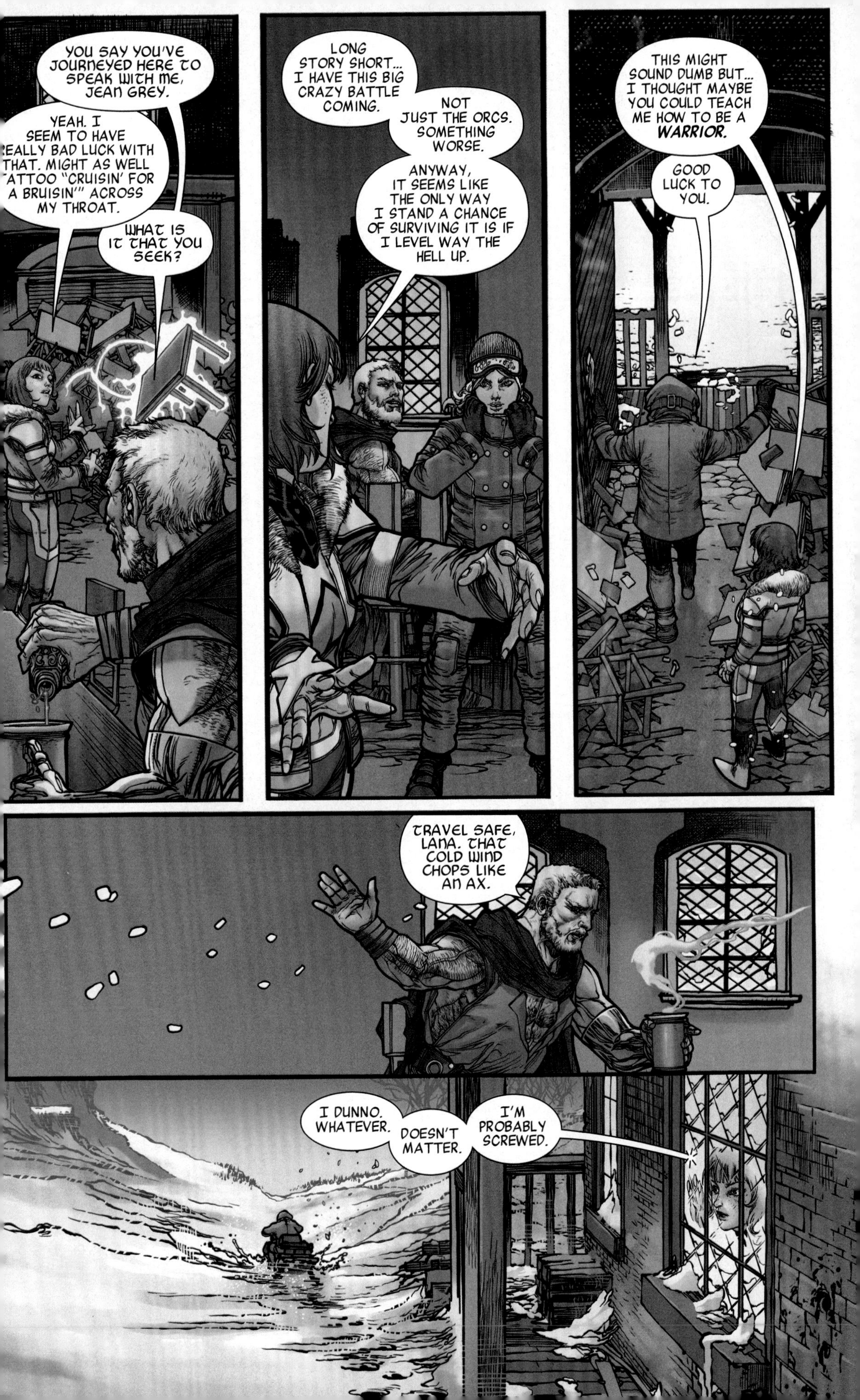
YOU SAY YOU'VE JOURNEYED HERE TO SPEAK WITH ME, JEAN GREY.
YEAH. I SEEM TO HAVE REALLY BAD LUCK WITH THAT. MIGHT AS WELL TATTOO "CRUISIN' FOR A BRUISIN'" ACROSS MY THROAT.
WHAT IS IT THAT YOU SEEK?
LONG STORY SHORT... I HAVE THIS BIG CRAZY BATTLE COMING.
NOT JUST THE ORCS. SOMETHING WORSE.
ANYWAY, IT SEEMS LIKE THE ONLY WAY I STAND A CHANCE OF SURVIVING IT IS IF I LEVEL WAY THE HELL UP.
THIS MIGHT SOUND DUMB BUT... I THOUGHT MAYBE YOU COULD TEACH ME HOW TO BE A WARRIOR.
GOOD LUCK TO YOU.
TRAVEL SAFE, LANA. THAT COLD WIND CHOPS LIKE AN AX.
I DUNNO. WHATEVER.
DOESN'T MATTER.
I'M PROBABLY SCREWED.

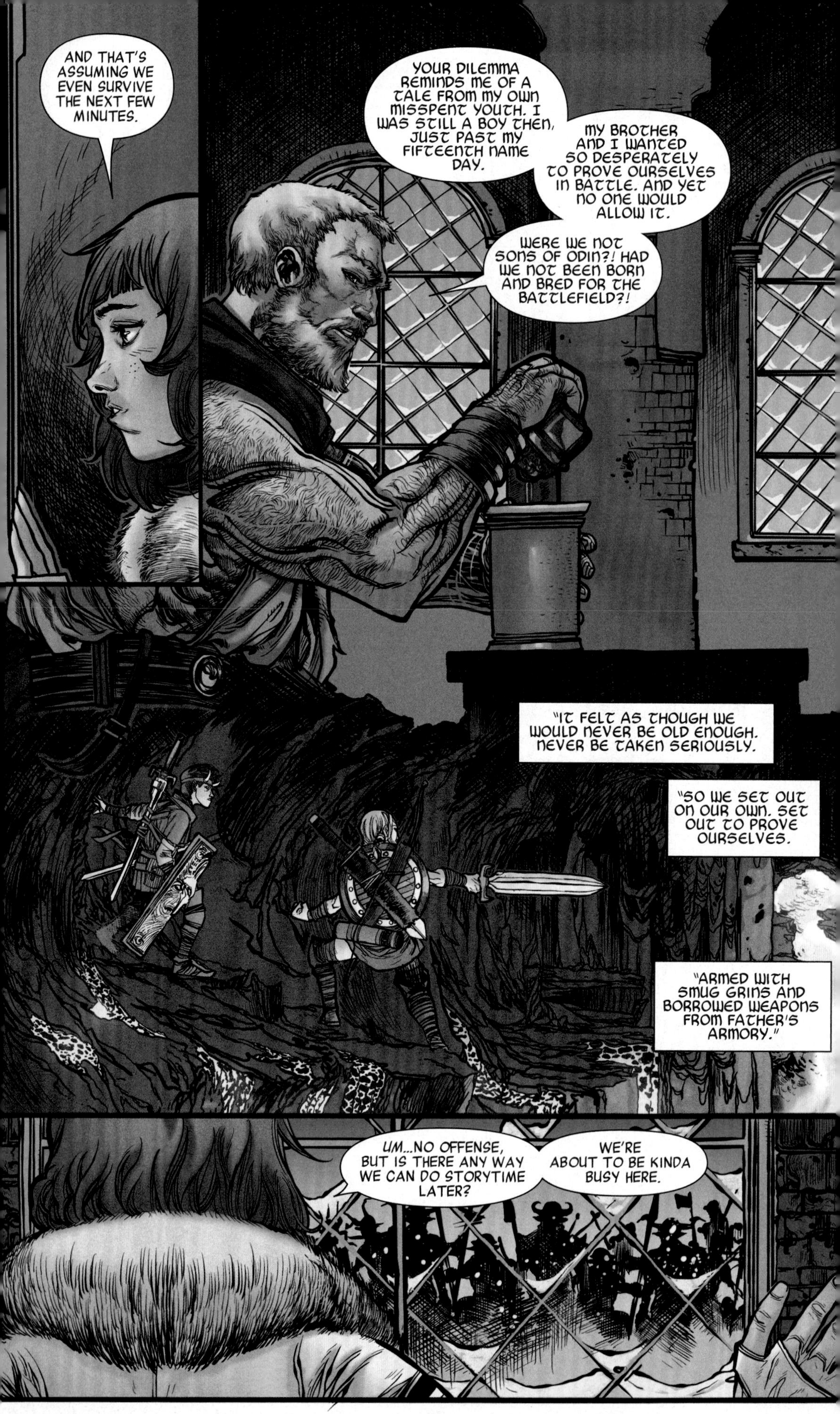
AND THAT'S ASSUMING WE EVEN SURVIVE THE NEXT FEW MINUTES.
YOUR DILEMMA REMINDS ME OF A TALE FROM MY OWN MISSPENT YOUTH. I WAS STILL A BOY THEN, JUST PAST MY FIFTEENTH NAME DAY.
MY BROTHER AND I WANTED SO DESPERATELY TO PROVE OURSELVES IN BATTLE. AND YET NO ONE WOULD ALLOW IT.
WERE WE NOT SONS OF ODIN?! HAD WE NOT BEEN BORN AND BRED FOR THE BATTLEFIELD?!
"IT FELT AS THOUGH WE WOULD NEVER BE OLD ENOUGH. NEVER BE TAKEN SERIOUSLY.
"SO WE SET OUT ON OUR OWN. SET OUT TO PROVE OURSELVES.
"ARMED WITH SMUG GRINS AND BORROWED WEAPONS FROM FATHER'S ARMORY."
UM...NO OFFENSE, BUT IS THERE ANY WAY WE CAN DO STORYTIME LATER?
WE'RE ABOUT TO BE KINDA BUSY HERE.

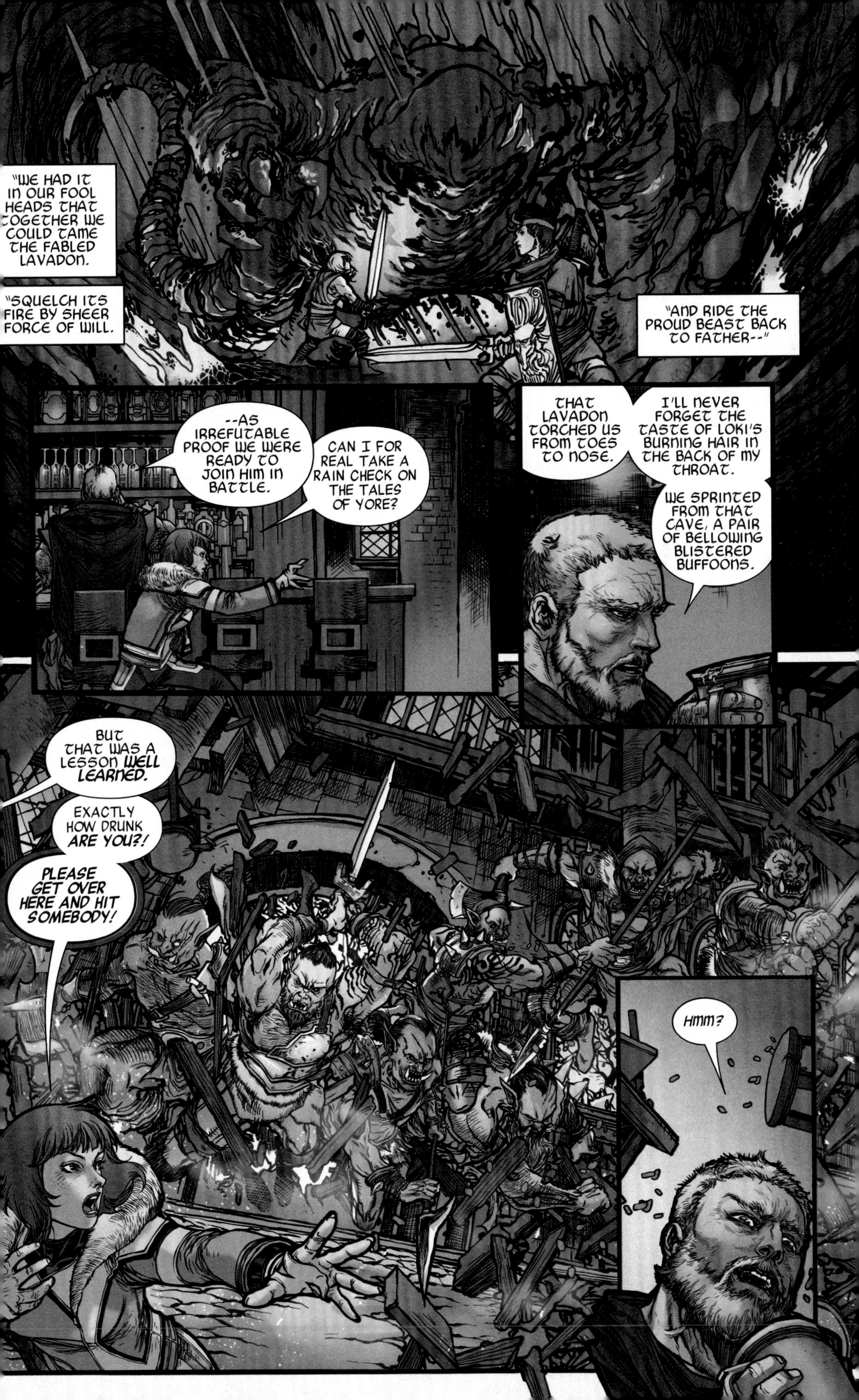

"WE HAD IT IN OUR FOOL HEADS THAT TOGETHER WE COULD TAME THE FABLED LAVADON.
"SQUELCH ITS FIRE BY SHEER FORCE OF WILL.
"AND RIDE THE PROUD BEAST BACK TO FATHER--"
--AS IRREFUTABLE PROOF WE WERE READY TO JOIN HIM IN BATTLE.
CAN I FOR REAL TAKE A RAIN CHECK ON THE TALES OF YORE?
THAT LAVADON TORCHED US FROM TOES TO NOSE.
I'LL NEVER FORGET THE TASTE OF LOKI'S BURNING HAIR IN THE BACK OF MY THROAT.
WE SPRINTED FROM THAT CAVE, A PAIR OF BELLOWING BLISTERED BUFFOONS.
BUT THAT WAS A LESSON WELL LEARNED.
EXACTLY HOW DRUNK ARE YOU?!
PLEASE GET OVER HERE AND HIT SOMEBODY!
HMM?

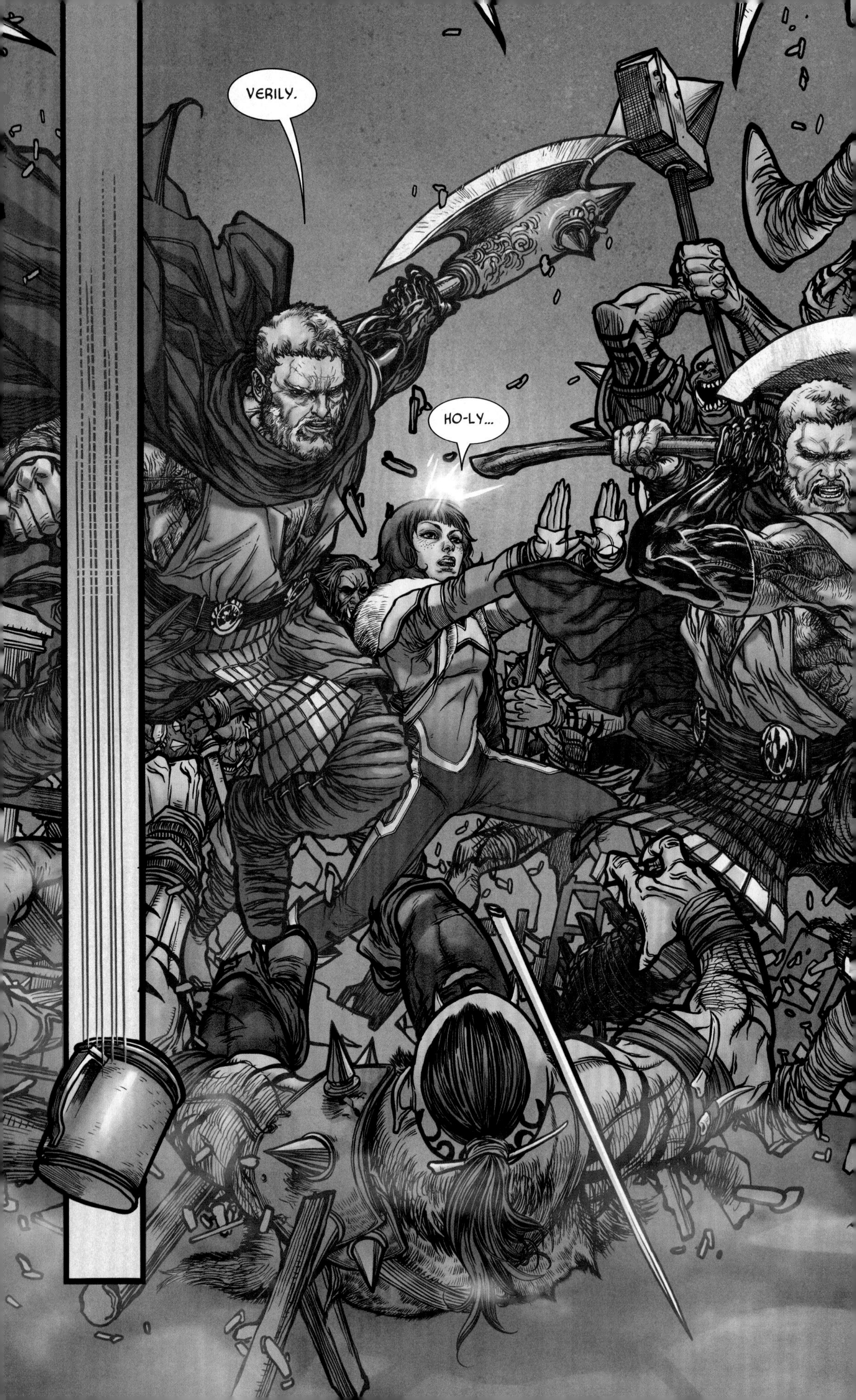
VERILY.
HO-LY...

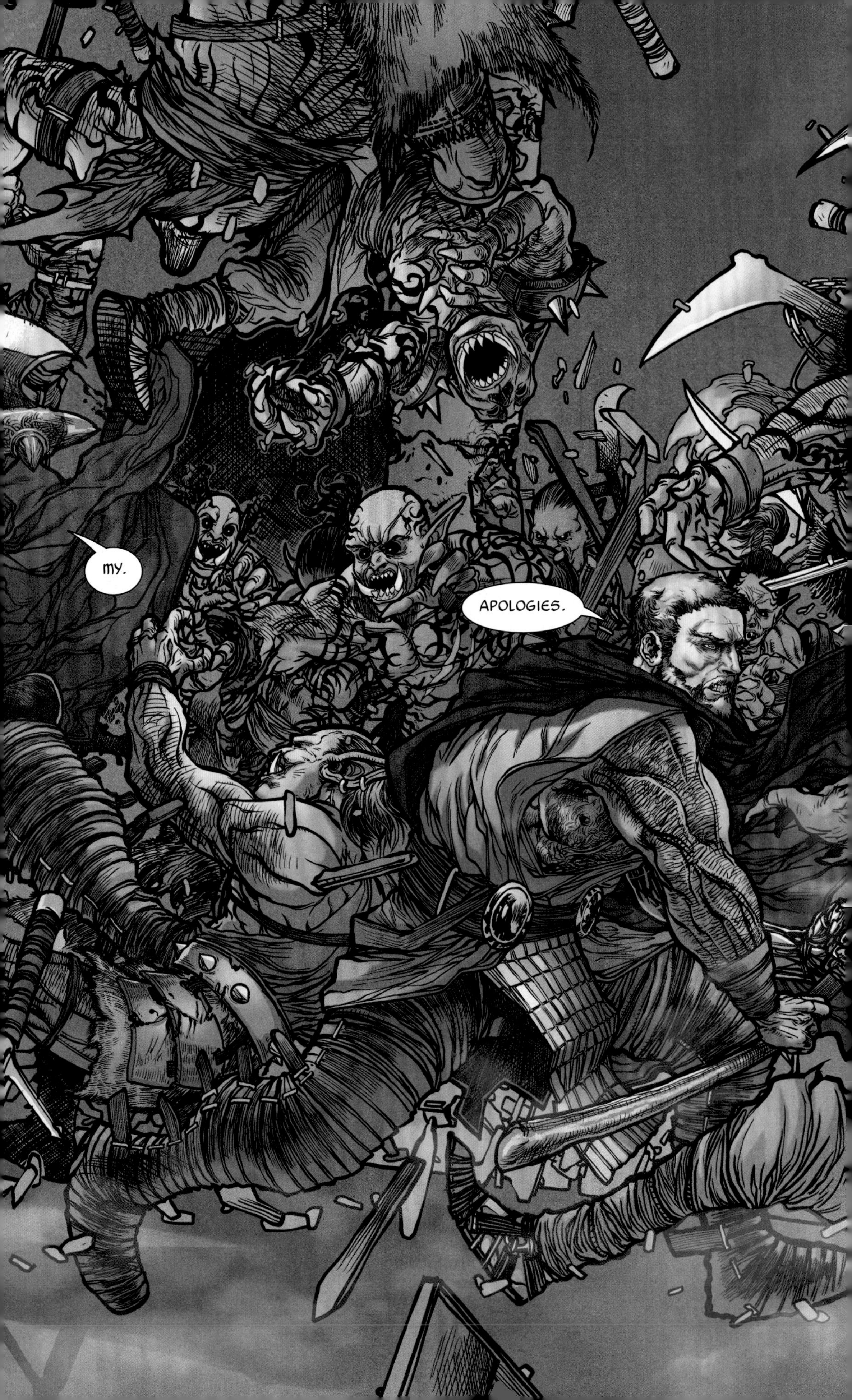
MY.
APOLOGIES.

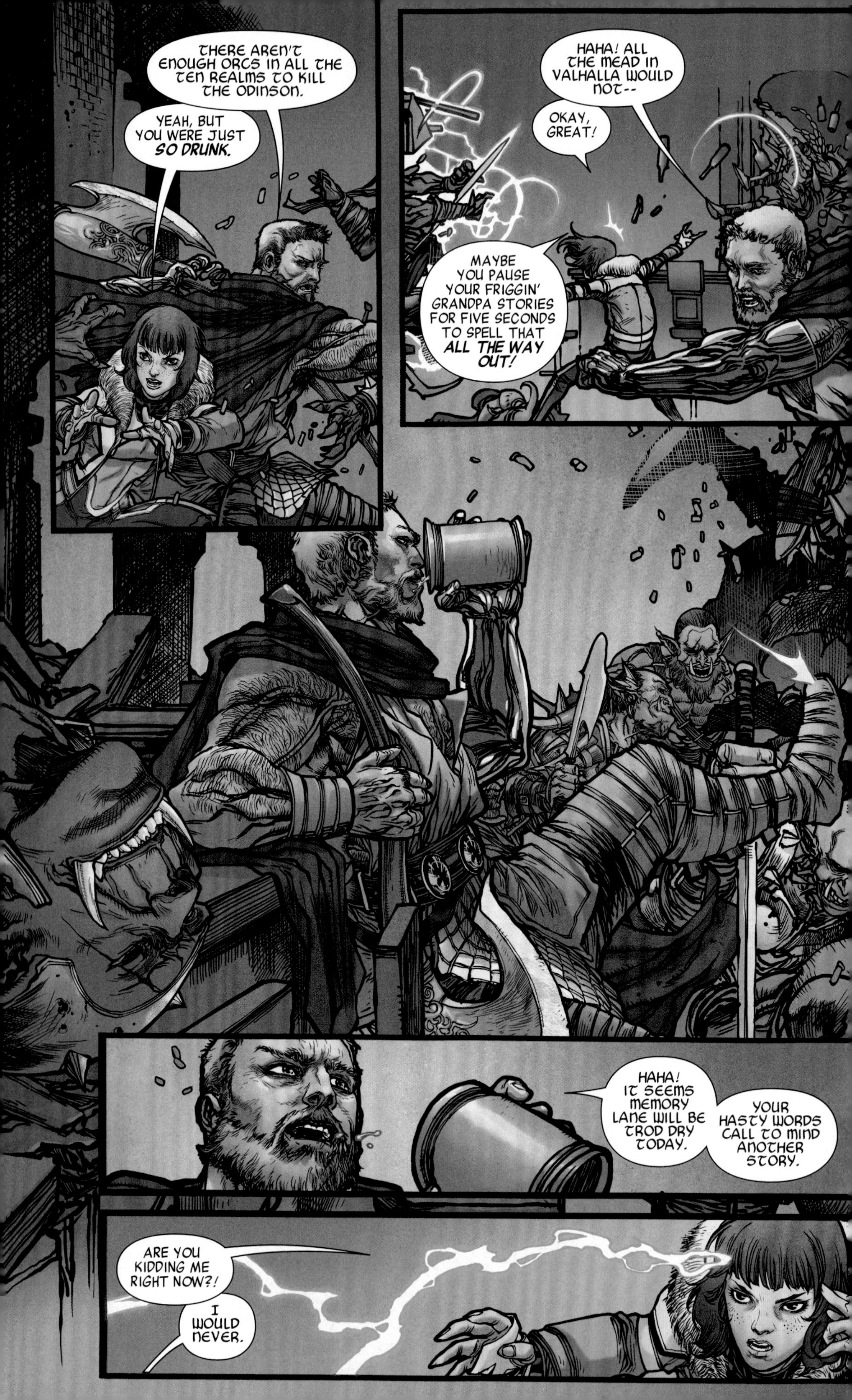
THERE AREN'T ENOUGH ORCS IN ALL THE TEN REALMS TO KILL THE ODINSON.
YEAH, BUT YOU WERE JUST **SO DRUNK.**
HAHA! ALL THE MEAD IN VALHALLA WOULD NOT--
OKAY, GREAT!
MAYBE YOU PAUSE YOUR FRIGGIN' GRANDPA STORIES FOR FIVE SECONDS TO SPELL THAT **ALL THE WAY OUT!**
HAHA! IT SEEMS MEMORY LANE WILL BE TROD DRY TODAY.
YOUR HASTY WORDS CALL TO MIND ANOTHER STORY.
ARE YOU KIDDING ME RIGHT NOW?!
I WOULD NEVER.

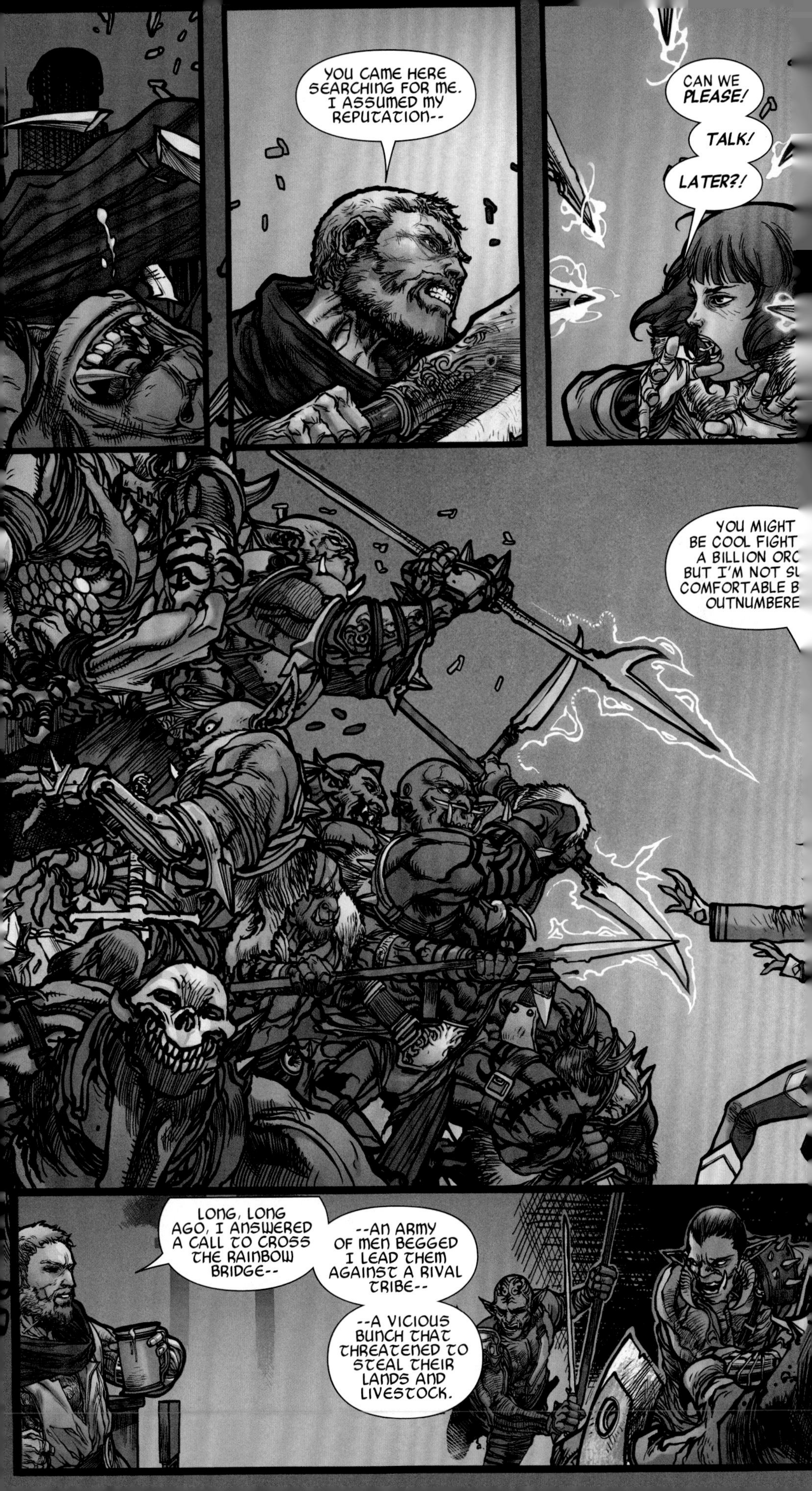
YOU CAME HERE SEARCHING FOR ME. I ASSUMED MY REPUTATION--
CAN WE PLEASE!
TALK!
LATER?!
YOU MIGHT BE COOL FIGHT A BILLION ORC BUT I'M NOT SU COMFORTABLE B OUTNUMBERE
LONG, LONG AGO, I ANSWERED A CALL TO CROSS THE RAINBOW BRIDGE--
--AN ARMY OF MEN BEGGED I LEAD THEM AGAINST A RIVAL TRIBE--
--A VICIOUS BUNCH THAT THREATENED TO STEAL THEIR LANDS AND LIVESTOCK.

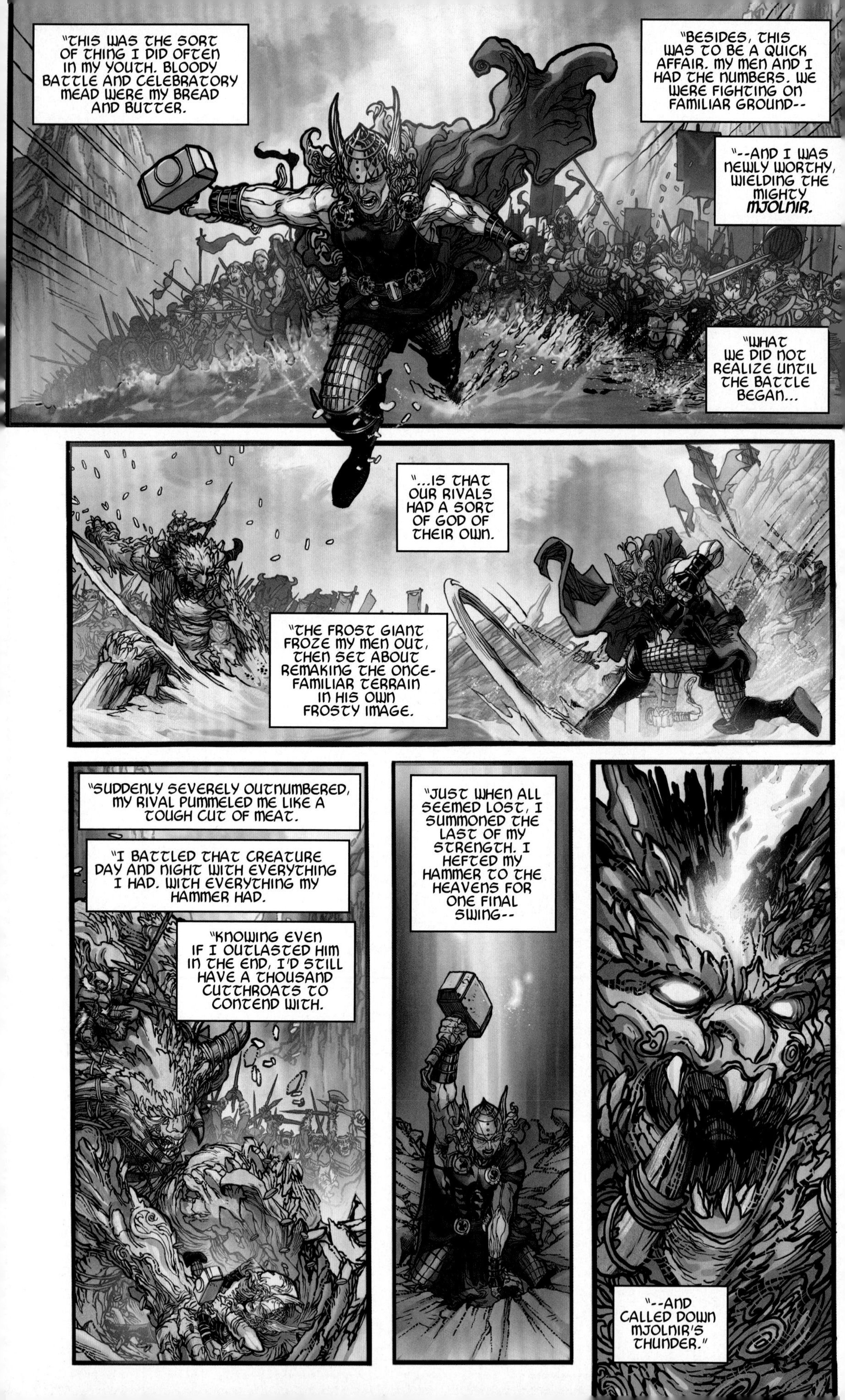

"THIS WAS THE SORT OF THING I DID OFTEN IN MY YOUTH. BLOODY BATTLE AND CELEBRATORY MEAD WERE MY BREAD AND BUTTER.
"BESIDES, THIS WAS TO BE A QUICK AFFAIR. MY MEN AND I HAD THE NUMBERS. WE WERE FIGHTING ON FAMILIAR GROUND--
"--AND I WAS NEWLY WORTHY, WIELDING THE MIGHTY MJOLNIR.
"WHAT WE DID NOT REALIZE UNTIL THE BATTLE BEGAN...
"...IS THAT OUR RIVALS HAD A SORT OF GOD OF THEIR OWN.
"THE FROST GIANT FROZE MY MEN OUT, THEN SET ABOUT REMAKING THE ONCE-FAMILIAR TERRAIN IN HIS OWN FROSTY IMAGE.
"SUDDENLY SEVERELY OUTNUMBERED, MY RIVAL PUMMELED ME LIKE A TOUGH CUT OF MEAT.
"I BATTLED THAT CREATURE DAY AND NIGHT WITH EVERYTHING I HAD. WITH EVERYTHING MY HAMMER HAD.
"KNOWING EVEN IF I OUTLASTED HIM IN THE END, I'D STILL HAVE A THOUSAND CUTTHROATS TO CONTEND WITH.
"JUST WHEN ALL SEEMED LOST, I SUMMONED THE LAST OF MY STRENGTH. I HEFTED MY HAMMER TO THE HEAVENS FOR ONE FINAL SWING--
"--AND CALLED DOWN MJOLNIR'S THUNDER."

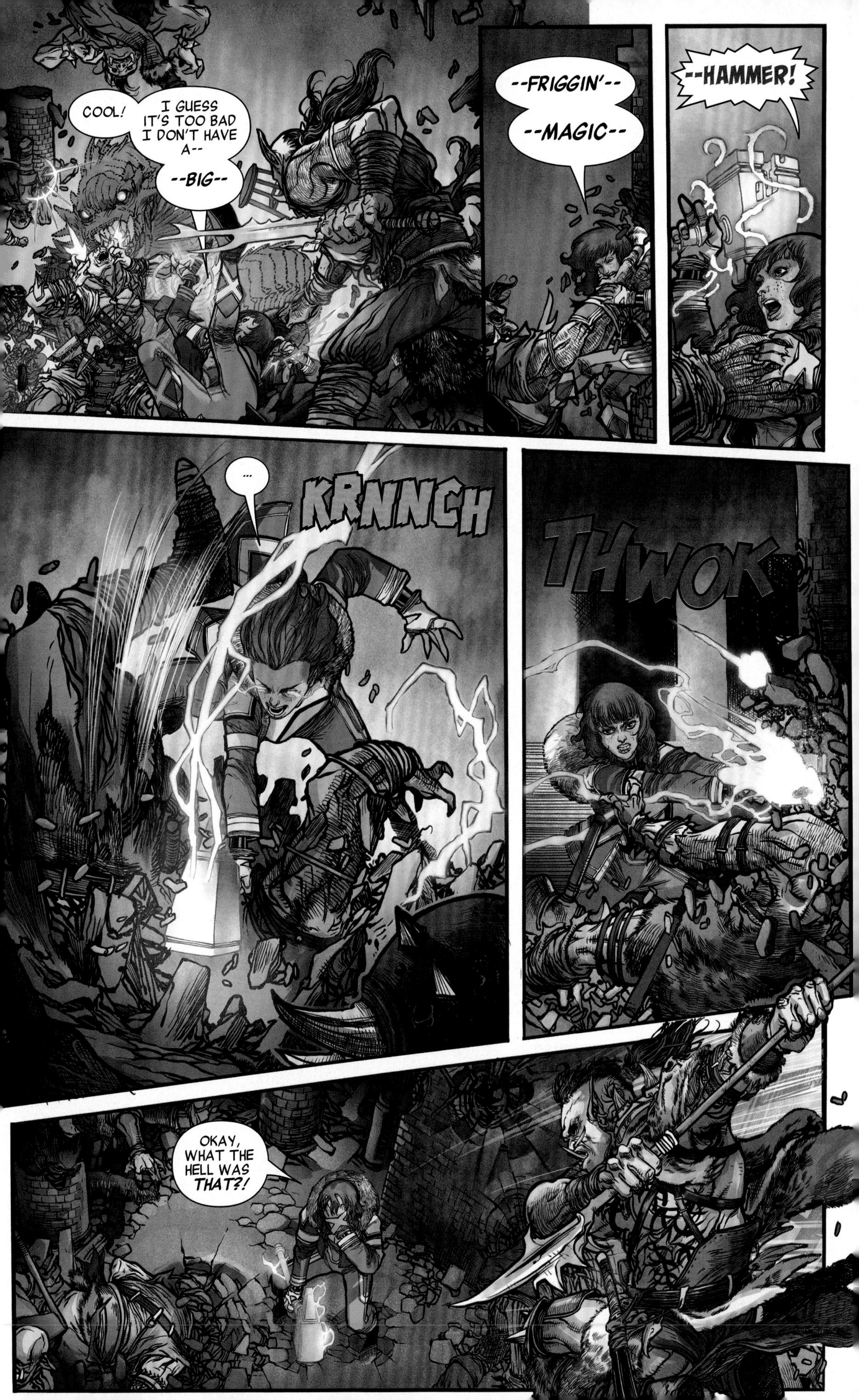
COOL!
I GUESS IT'S TOO BAD I DON'T HAVE A--
--BIG--
--FRIGGIN'--
--MAGIC--
--HAMMER!
...
KRNNCH
THWOK
OKAY, WHAT THE HELL WAS THAT?!

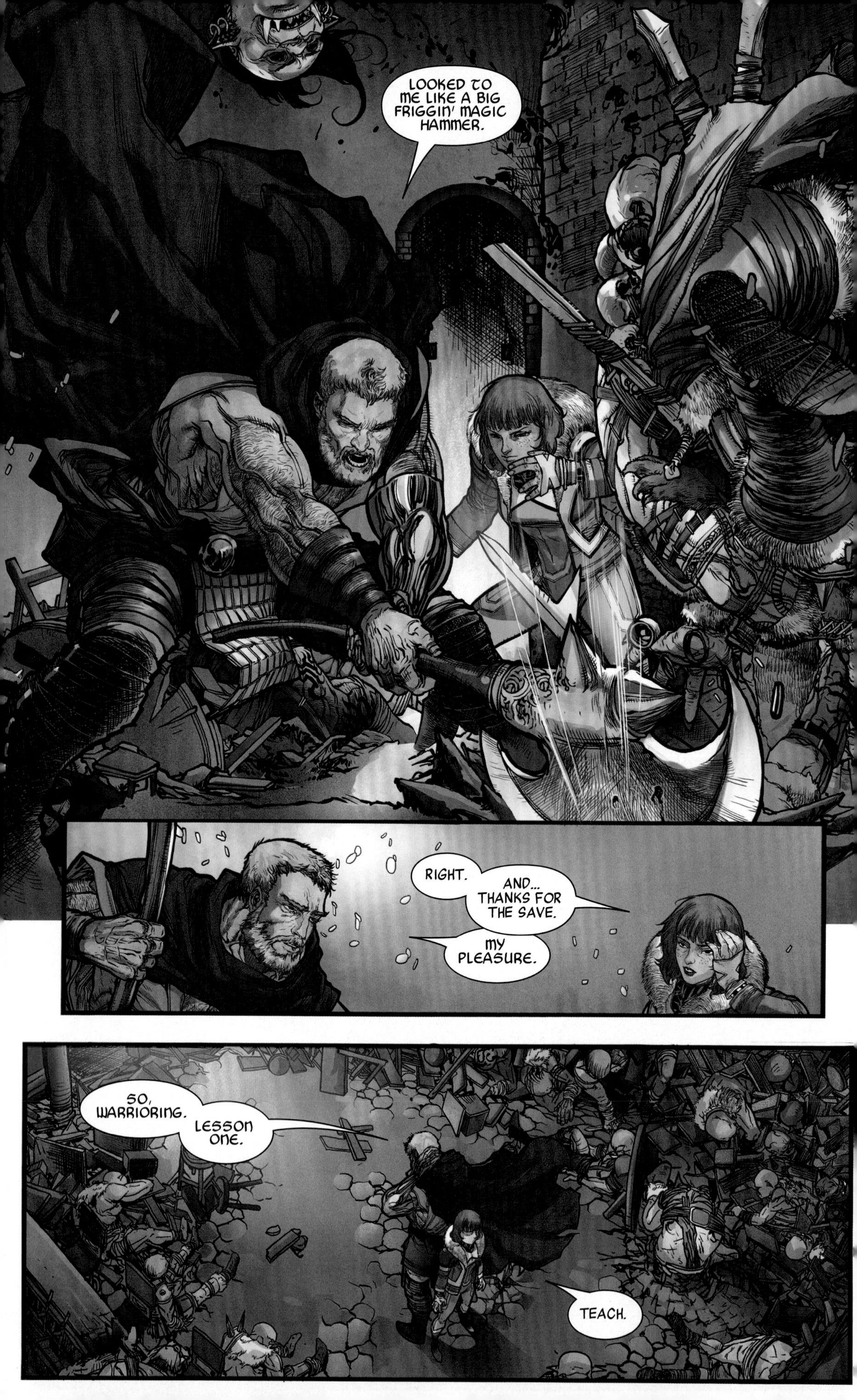

LOOKED TO ME LIKE A BIG FRIGGIN' MAGIC HAMMER.
RIGHT.
AND... THANKS FOR THE SAVE.
MY PLEASURE.
SO, WARRIORING.
LESSON ONE.
TEACH.

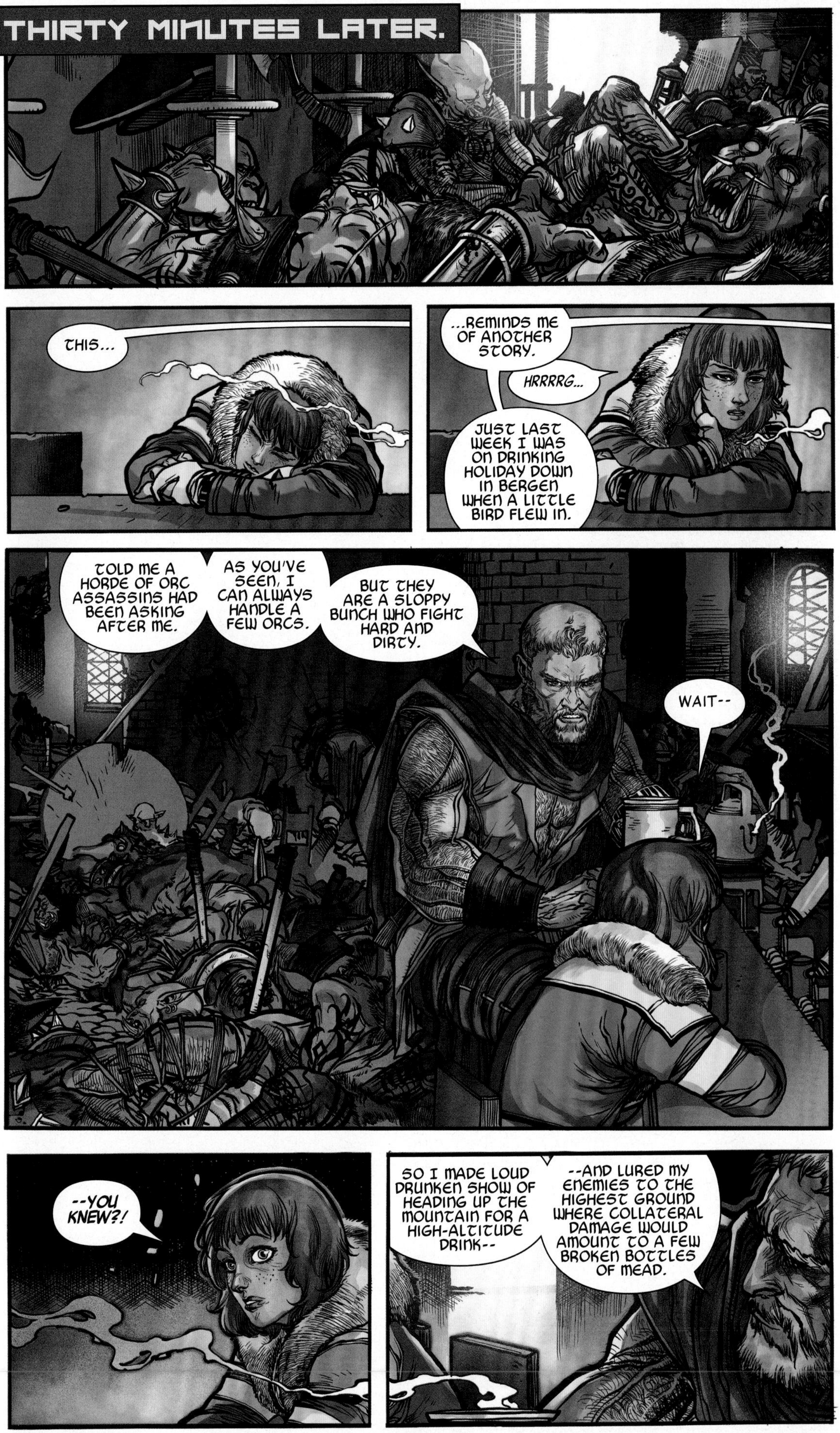
THIRTY MINUTES LATER.
THIS...
...REMINDS ME OF ANOTHER STORY.
HRRRRG...
JUST LAST WEEK I WAS ON DRINKING HOLIDAY DOWN IN BERGEN WHEN A LITTLE BIRD FLEW IN.
TOLD ME A HORDE OF ORC ASSASSINS HAD BEEN ASKING AFTER ME.
AS YOU'VE SEEN, I CAN ALWAYS HANDLE A FEW ORCS.
BUT THEY ARE A SLOPPY BUNCH WHO FIGHT HARD AND DIRTY.
WAIT--
--YOU KNEW?!
SO I MADE LOUD DRUNKEN SHOW OF HEADING UP THE MOUNTAIN FOR A HIGH-ALTITUDE DRINK--
--AND LURED MY ENEMIES TO THE HIGHEST GROUND WHERE COLLATERAL DAMAGE WOULD AMOUNT TO A FEW BROKEN BOTTLES OF MEAD.

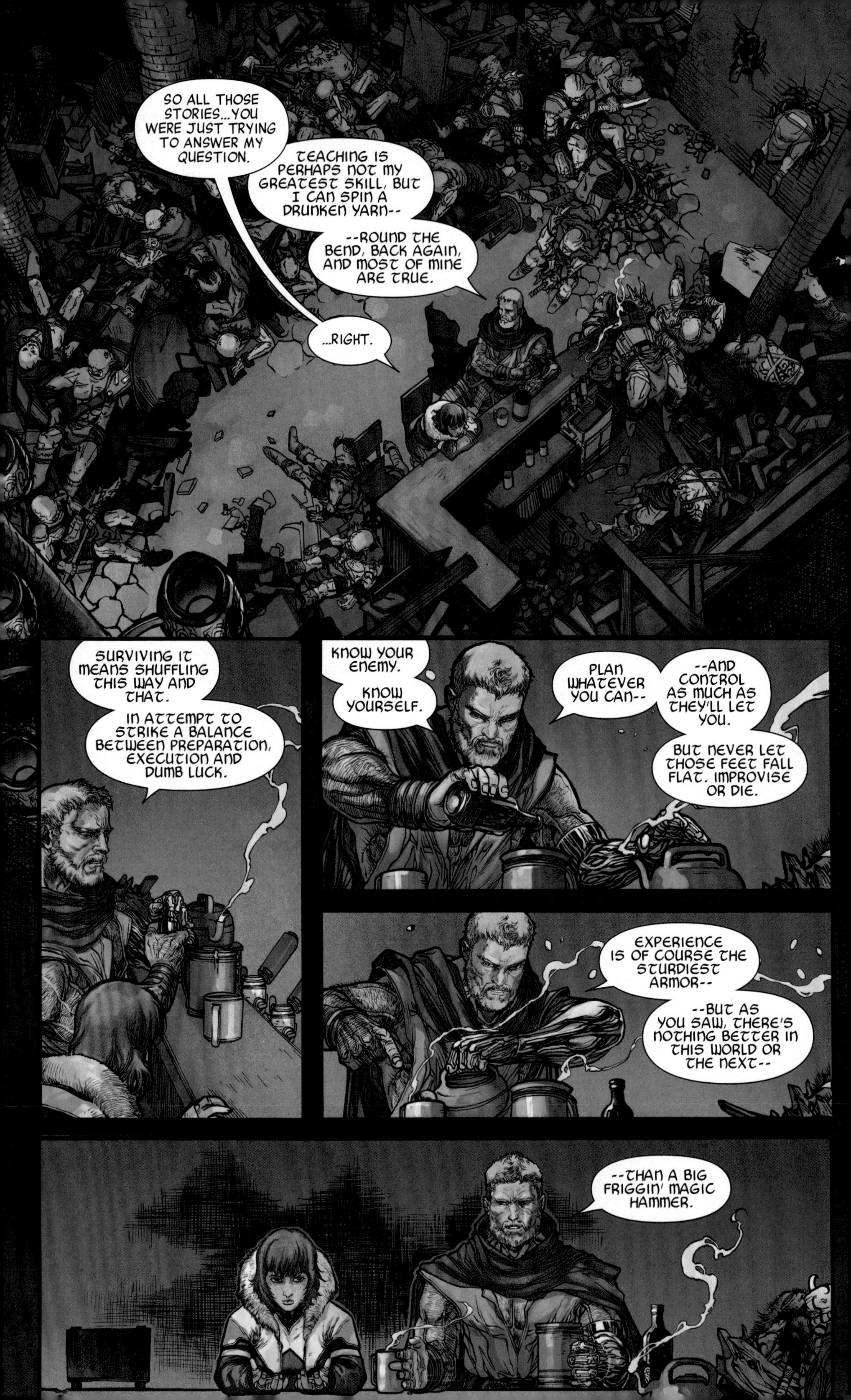
SO ALL THOSE STORIES...YOU WERE JUST TRYING TO ANSWER MY QUESTION.
TEACHING IS PERHAPS NOT MY GREATEST SKILL, BUT I CAN SPIN A DRUNKEN YARN--
--ROUND THE BEND, BACK AGAIN, AND MOST OF MINE ARE TRUE.
...RIGHT.
SURVIVING IT MEANS SHUFFLING THIS WAY AND THAT.
IN ATTEMPT TO STRIKE A BALANCE BETWEEN PREPARATION, EXECUTION AND DUMB LUCK.
KNOW YOUR ENEMY.
KNOW YOURSELF.
PLAN WHATEVER YOU CAN--
--AND CONTROL AS MUCH AS THEY'LL LET YOU.
BUT NEVER LET THOSE FEET FALL FLAT. IMPROVISE OR DIE.
EXPERIENCE IS OF COURSE THE STURDIEST ARMOR--
--BUT AS YOU SAW, THERE'S NOTHING BETTER IN THIS WORLD OR THE NEXT--
--THAN A BIG FRIGGIN' MAGIC HAMMER.

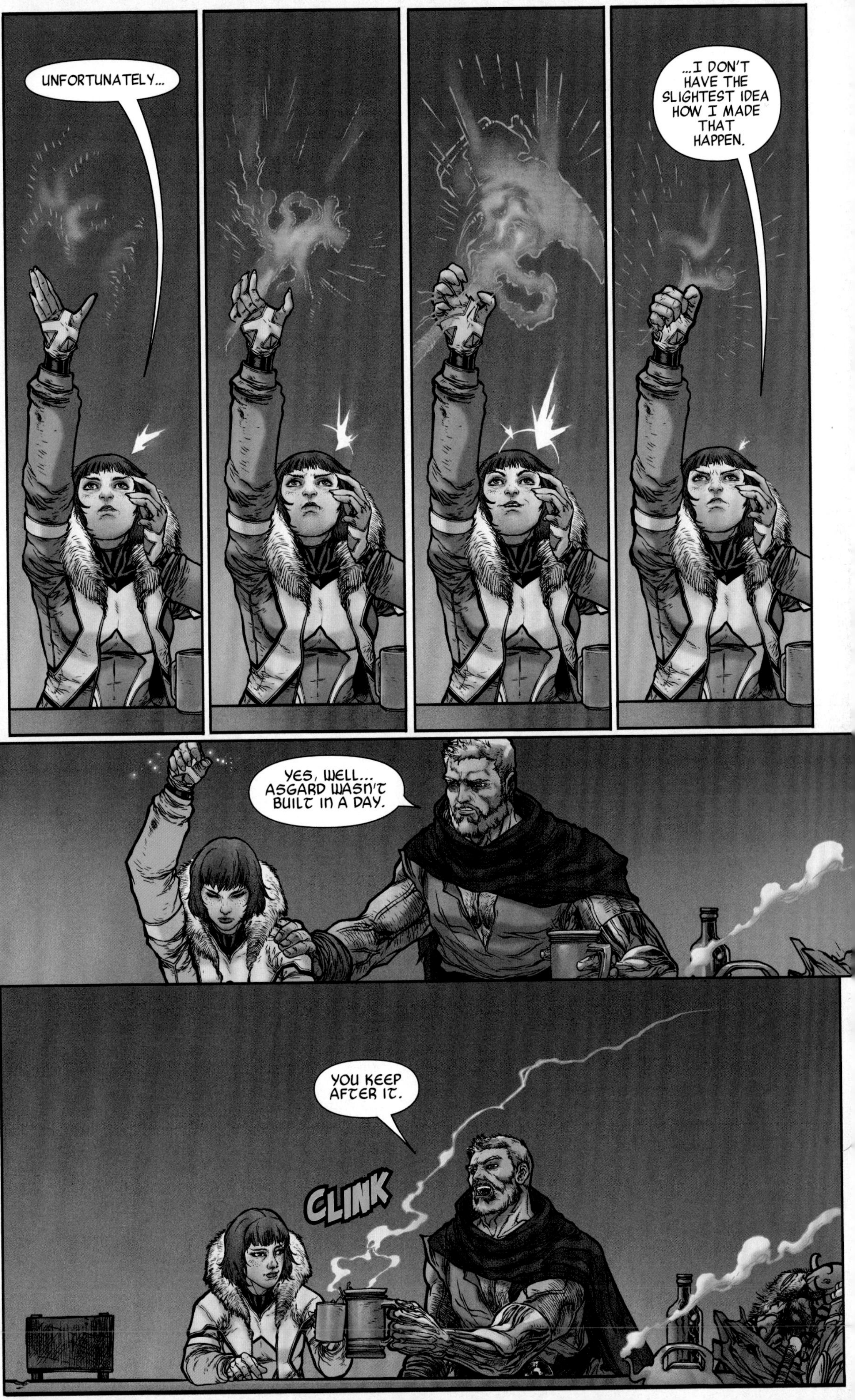
UNFORTUNATELY...
...I DON'T HAVE THE SLIGHTEST IDEA HOW I MADE THAT HAPPEN.
YES, WELL... ASGARD WASN'T BUILT IN A DAY.
YOU KEEP AFTER IT.
CLINK

5

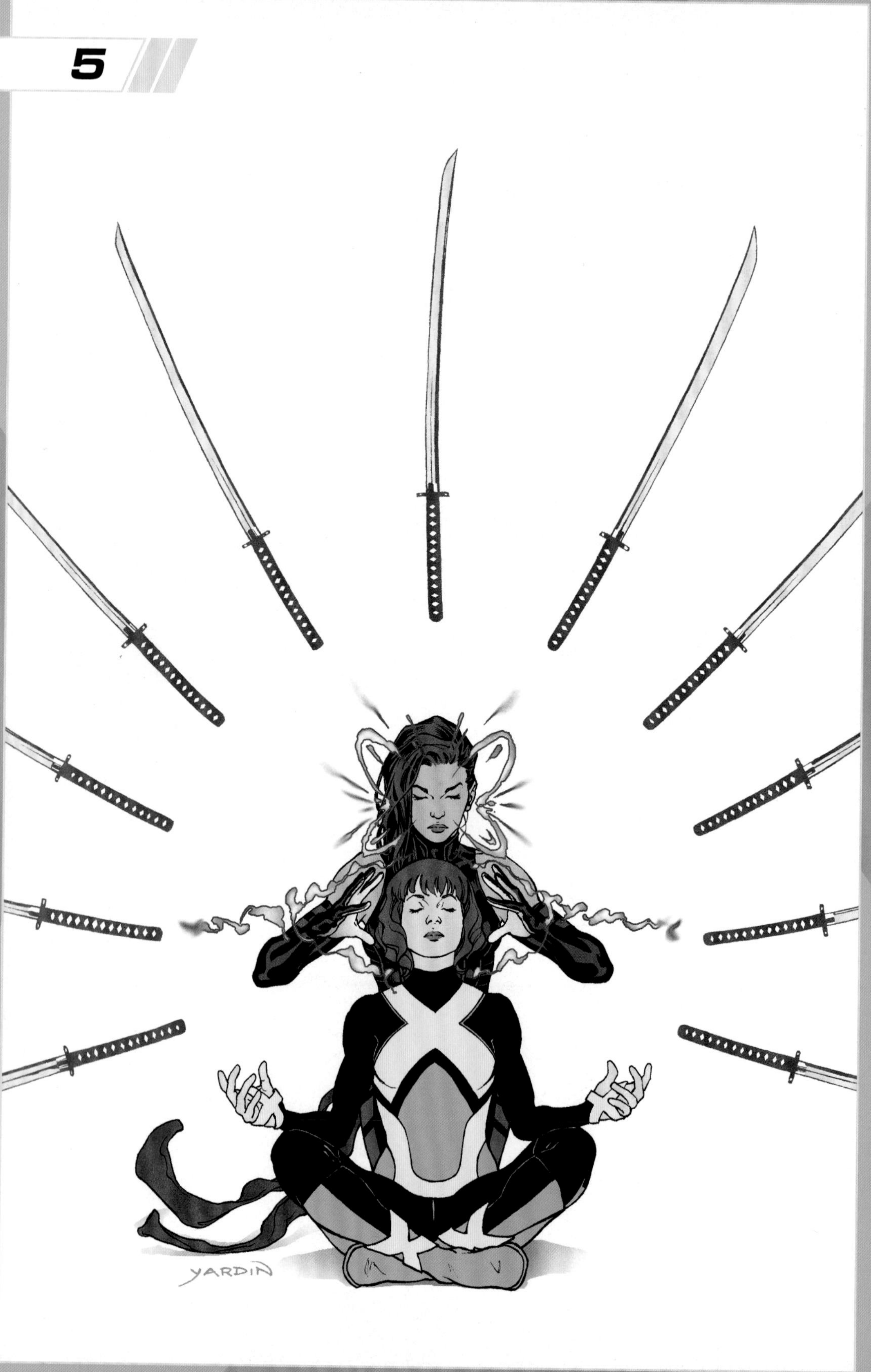
YARDIN

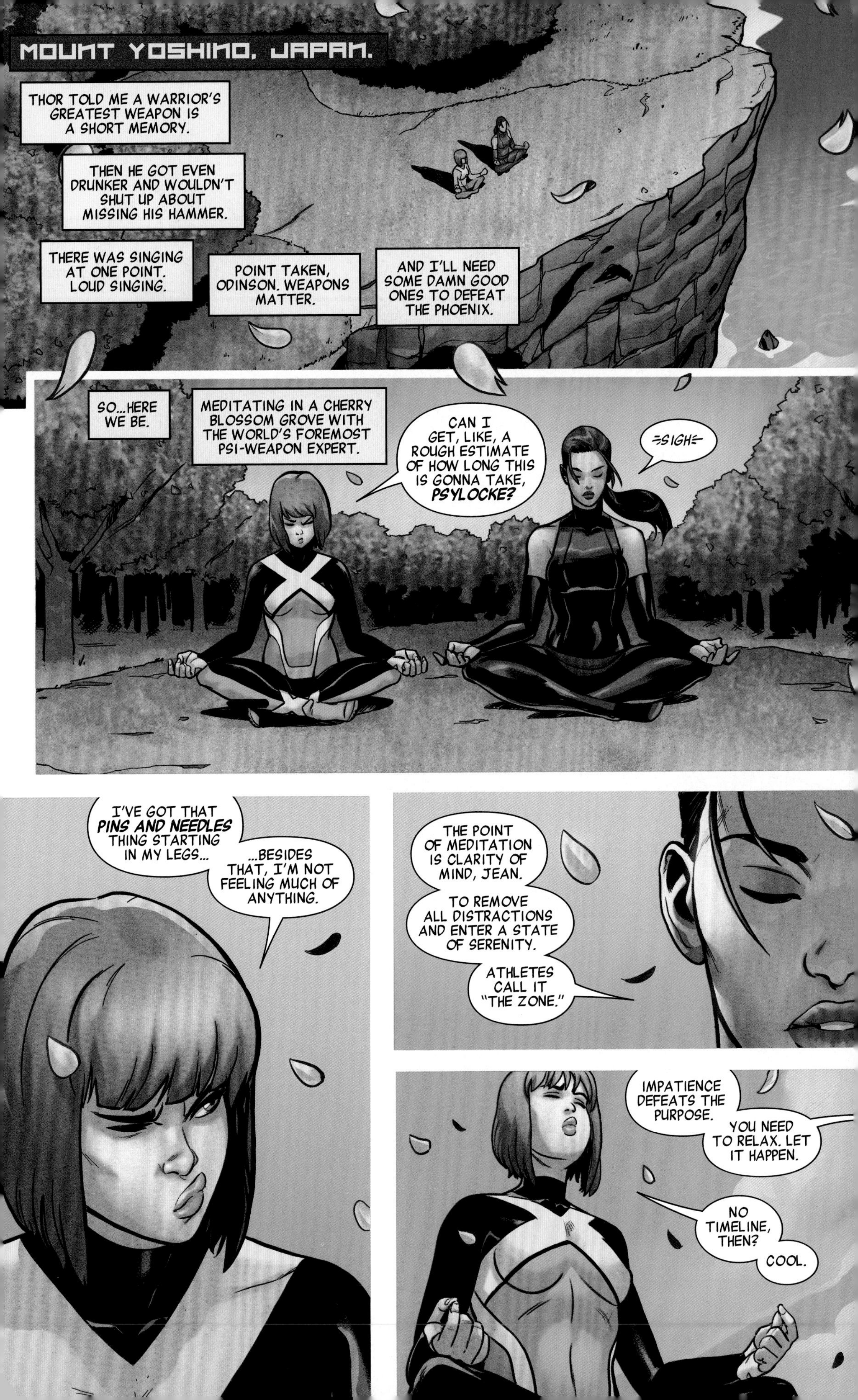
MOUNT YOSHINO, JAPAN.
THOR TOLD ME A WARRIOR'S GREATEST WEAPON IS A SHORT MEMORY.
THEN HE GOT EVEN DRUNKER AND WOULDN'T SHUT UP ABOUT MISSING HIS HAMMER.
THERE WAS SINGING AT ONE POINT. LOUD SINGING.
POINT TAKEN, ODINSON. WEAPONS MATTER.
AND I'LL NEED SOME DAMN GOOD ONES TO DEFEAT THE PHOENIX.
SO...HERE WE BE.
MEDITATING IN A CHERRY BLOSSOM GROVE WITH THE WORLD'S FOREMOST PSI-WEAPON EXPERT.
CAN I GET, LIKE, A ROUGH ESTIMATE OF HOW LONG THIS IS GONNA TAKE, PSYLOCKE?
=SIGH=
I'VE GOT THAT PINS AND NEEDLES THING STARTING IN MY LEGS...
...BESIDES THAT, I'M NOT FEELING MUCH OF ANYTHING.
THE POINT OF MEDITATION IS CLARITY OF MIND, JEAN.
TO REMOVE ALL DISTRACTIONS AND ENTER A STATE OF SERENITY.
ATHLETES CALL IT "THE ZONE."
IMPATIENCE DEFEATS THE PURPOSE.
YOU NEED TO RELAX. LET IT HAPPEN.
NO TIMELINE, THEN?
COOL.

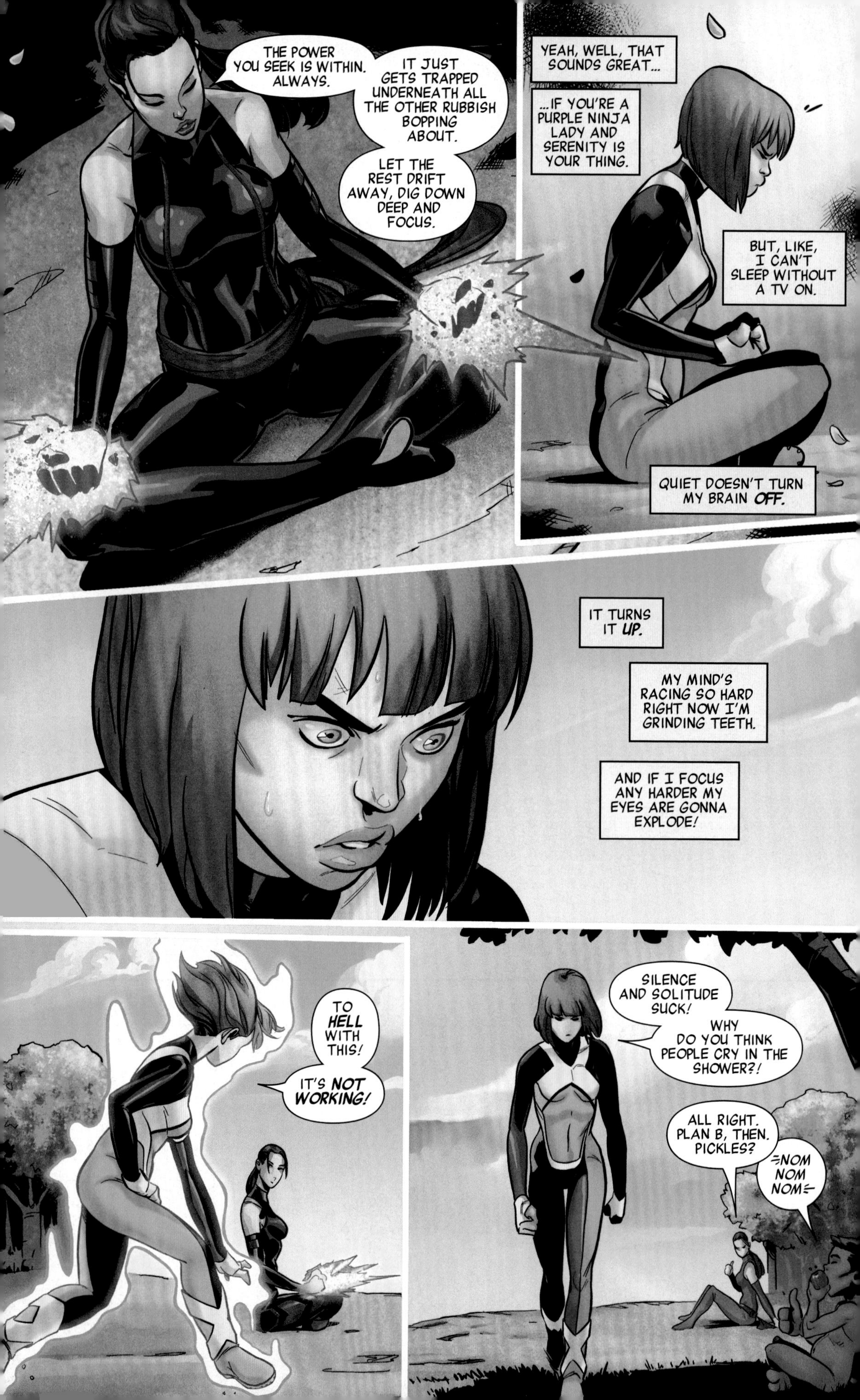
THE POWER YOU SEEK IS WITHIN. ALWAYS.
IT JUST GETS TRAPPED UNDERNEATH ALL THE OTHER RUBBISH BOPPING ABOUT.
LET THE REST DRIFT AWAY, DIG DOWN DEEP AND FOCUS.
YEAH, WELL, THAT SOUNDS GREAT...
...IF YOU'RE A PURPLE NINJA LADY AND SERENITY IS YOUR THING.
BUT, LIKE, I CAN'T SLEEP WITHOUT A TV ON.
QUIET DOESN'T TURN MY BRAIN OFF.
IT TURNS IT UP.
MY MIND'S RACING SO HARD RIGHT NOW I'M GRINDING TEETH.
AND IF I FOCUS ANY HARDER MY EYES ARE GONNA EXPLODE!
TO HELL WITH THIS!
IT'S NOT WORKING!
SILENCE AND SOLITUDE SUCK!
WHY DO YOU THINK PEOPLE CRY IN THE SHOWER?!
ALL RIGHT. PLAN B, THEN. PICKLES?
NOM NOM NOM

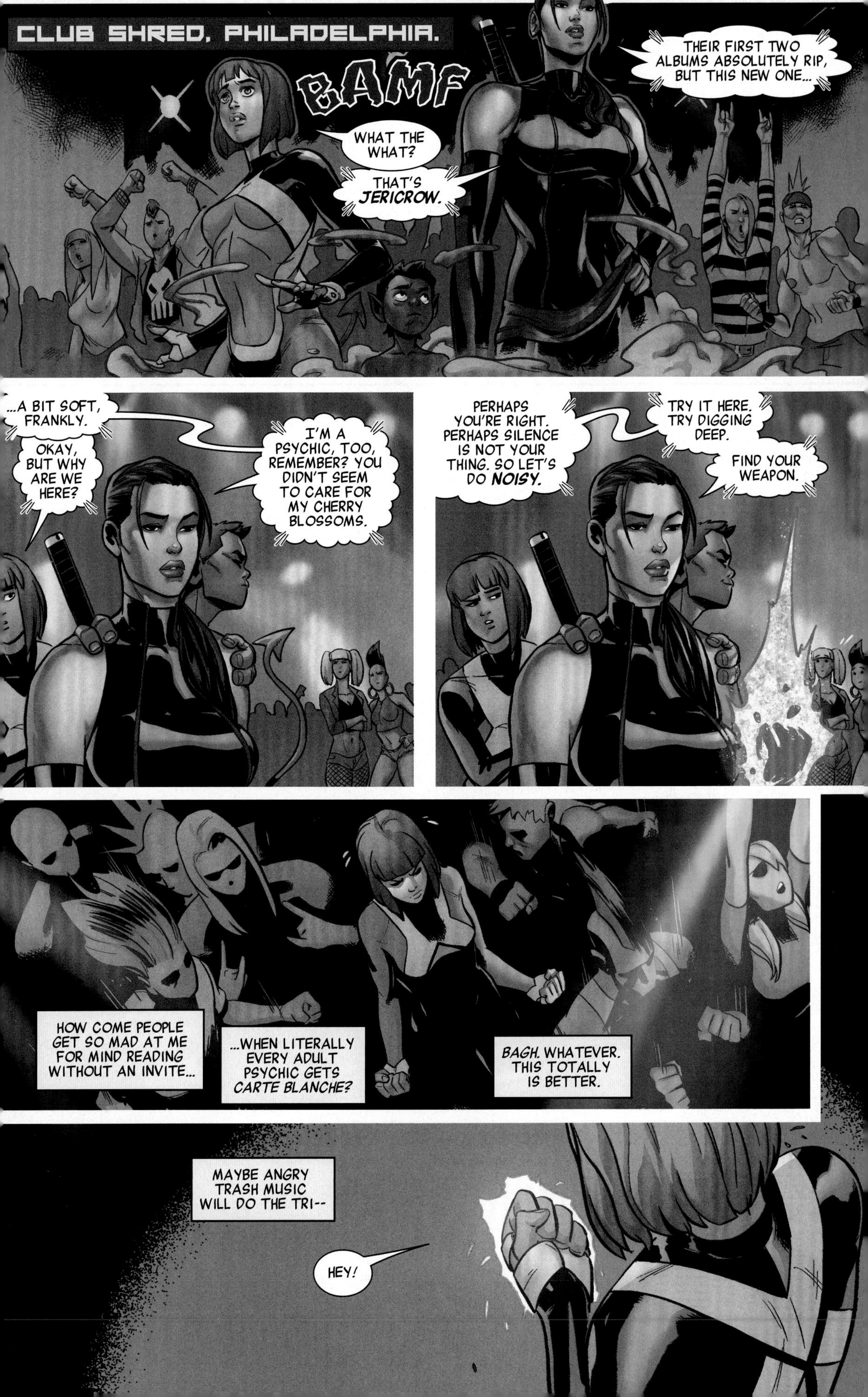
CLUB SHRED, PHILADELPHIA.
BAMF
WHAT THE WHAT?
THAT'S JERICROW.
THEIR FIRST TWO ALBUMS ABSOLUTELY RIP, BUT THIS NEW ONE...
...A BIT SOFT, FRANKLY.
OKAY, BUT WHY ARE WE HERE?
I'M A PSYCHIC, TOO, REMEMBER? YOU DIDN'T SEEM TO CARE FOR MY CHERRY BLOSSOMS.
PERHAPS YOU'RE RIGHT. PERHAPS SILENCE IS NOT YOUR THING. SO LET'S DO NOISY.
TRY IT HERE. TRY DIGGING DEEP.
FIND YOUR WEAPON.
HOW COME PEOPLE GET SO MAD AT ME FOR MIND READING WITHOUT AN INVITE...
...WHEN LITERALLY EVERY ADULT PSYCHIC GETS CARTE BLANCHE?
BAGH. WHATEVER. THIS TOTALLY IS BETTER.
MAYBE ANGRY TRASH MUSIC WILL DO THE TRI--
HEY!

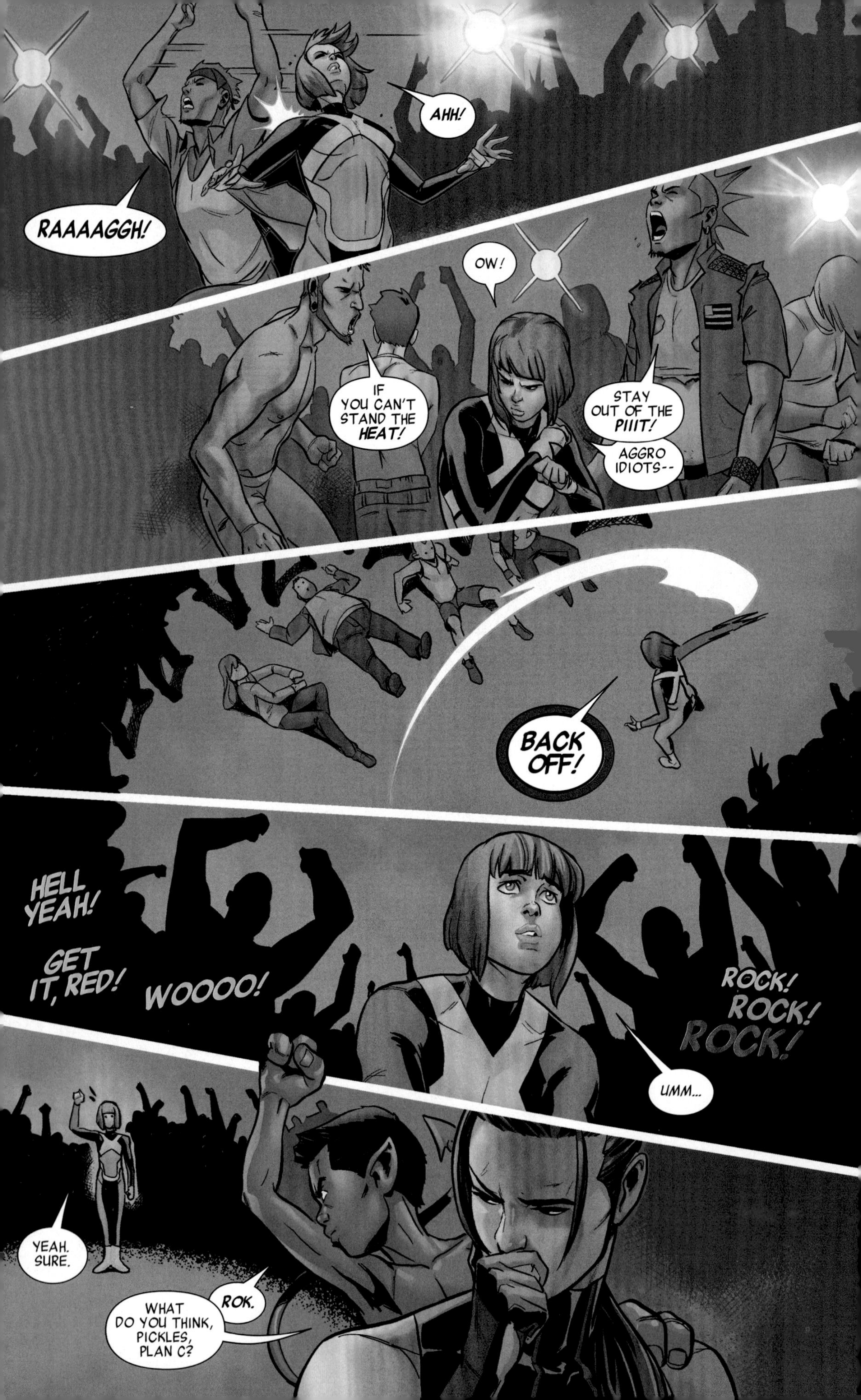
AHH!
RAAAAGGH!
OW!
IF YOU CAN'T STAND THE HEAT!
STAY OUT OF THE PIIIT!
AGGRO IDIOTS--
BACK OFF!
HELL YEAH!
GET IT, RED!
WOOOO!
ROCK! ROCK! ROCK!
UMM...
YEAH. SURE.
ROK.
WHAT DO YOU THINK, PICKLES, PLAN C?

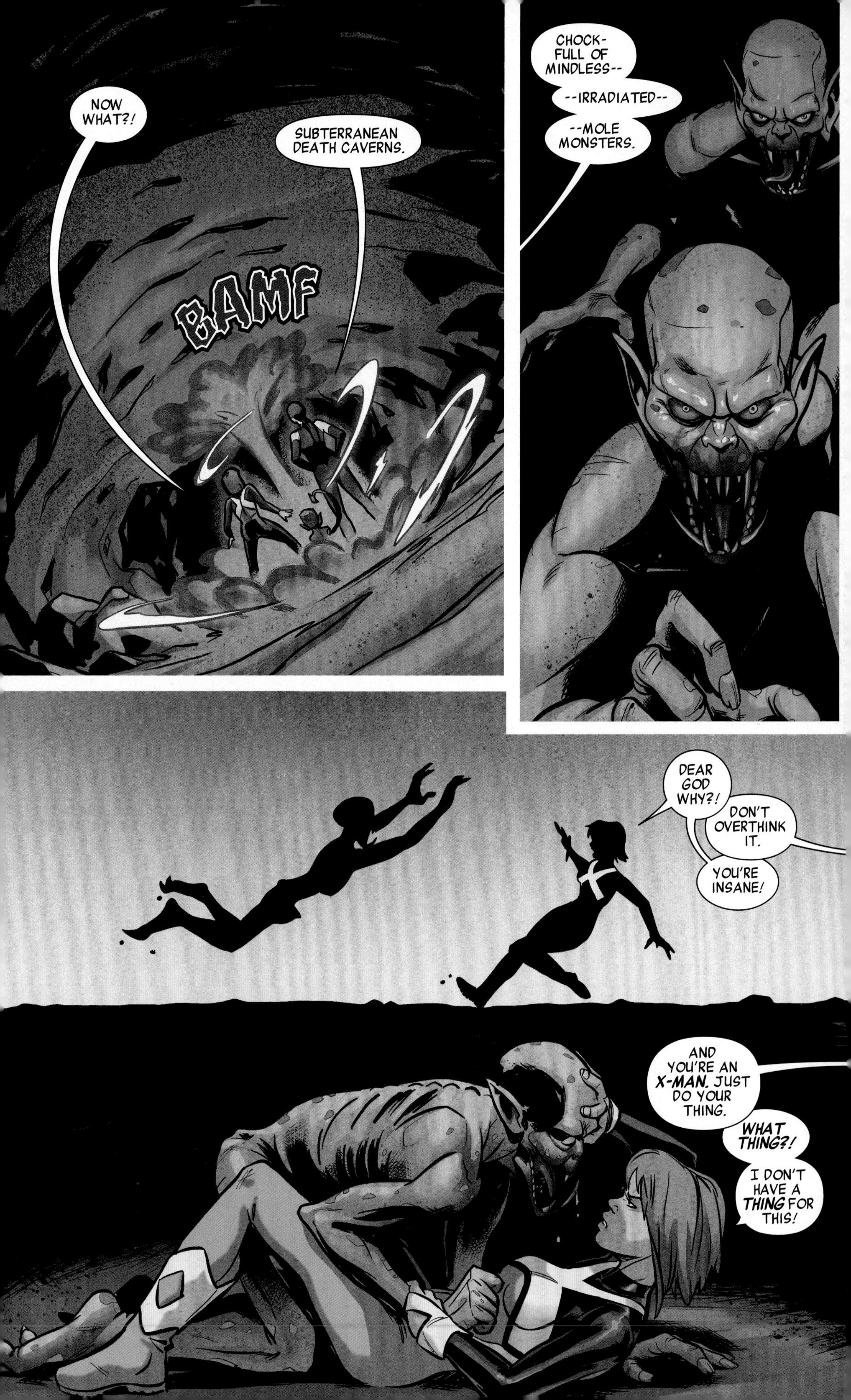
NOW WHAT?!
SUBTERRANEAN DEATH CAVERNS.
BAMF
CHOCK-FULL OF MINDLESS--
--IRRADIATED--
--MOLE MONSTERS.
DEAR GOD WHY?!
DON'T OVERTHINK IT.
YOU'RE INSANE!
AND YOU'RE AN X-MAN. JUST DO YOUR THING.
WHAT THING?!
I DON'T HAVE A THING FOR THIS!

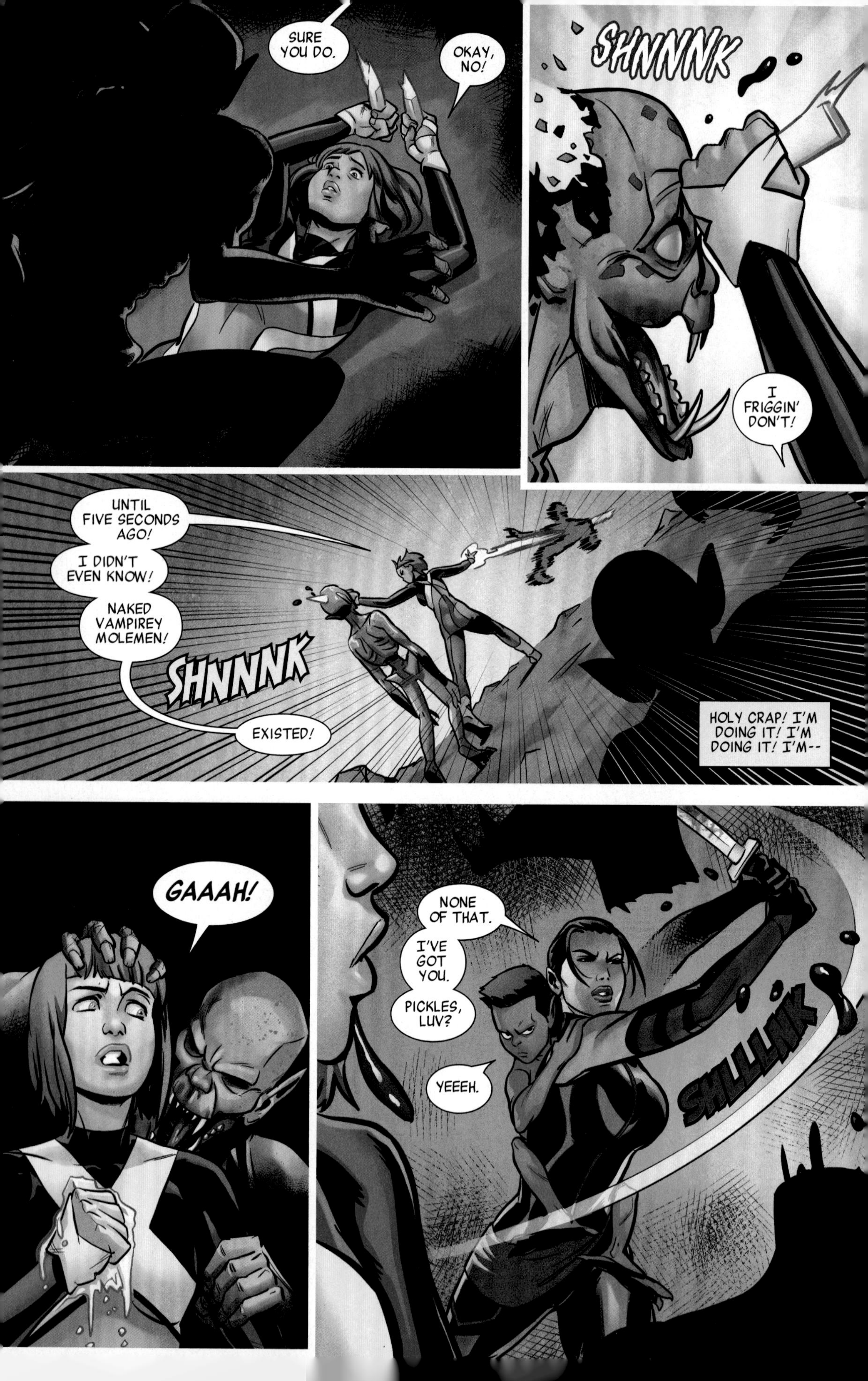
SURE YOU DO.
OKAY, NO!
SHNNNK
I FRIGGIN' DON'T!
UNTIL FIVE SECONDS AGO!
I DIDN'T EVEN KNOW!
NAKED VAMPIREY MOLEMEN!
SHNNNK
EXISTED!
HOLY CRAP! I'M DOING IT! I'M DOING IT! I'M--
GAAAH!
NONE OF THAT.
I'VE GOT YOU.
PICKLES, LUV?
YEEEH.
SHLLLNK

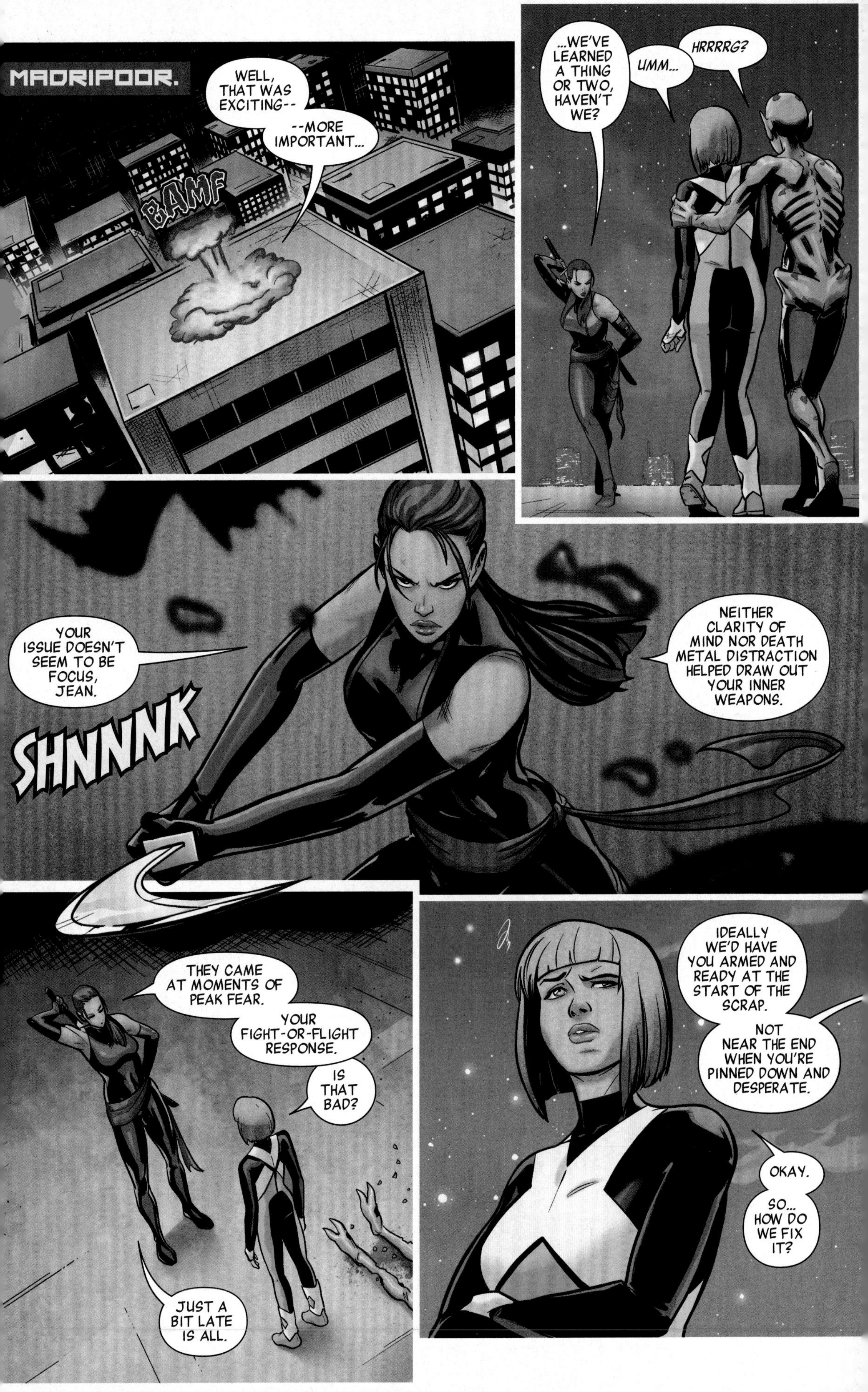

MADRIPOOR.
WELL, THAT WAS EXCITING--
--MORE IMPORTANT...
BAMF
...WE'VE LEARNED A THING OR TWO, HAVEN'T WE?
UMM...
HRRRRG?
YOUR ISSUE DOESN'T SEEM TO BE FOCUS, JEAN.
NEITHER CLARITY OF MIND NOR DEATH METAL DISTRACTION HELPED DRAW OUT YOUR INNER WEAPONS.
SHNNNK
THEY CAME AT MOMENTS OF PEAK FEAR.
YOUR FIGHT-OR-FLIGHT RESPONSE.
IS THAT BAD?
JUST A BIT LATE IS ALL.
IDEALLY WE'D HAVE YOU ARMED AND READY AT THE START OF THE SCRAP.
NOT NEAR THE END WHEN YOU'RE PINNED DOWN AND DESPERATE.
OKAY.
SO... HOW DO WE FIX IT?

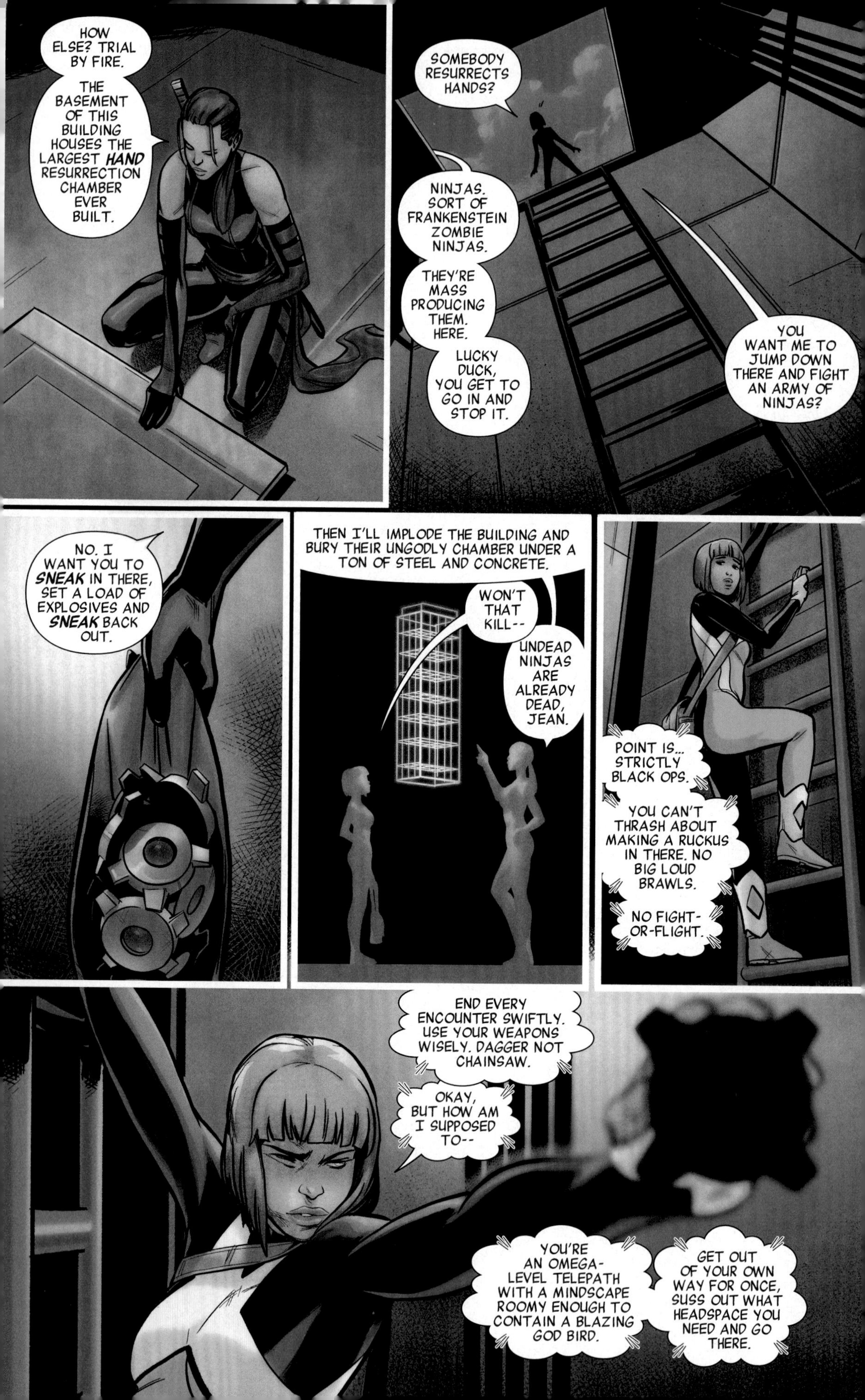

HOW ELSE? TRIAL BY FIRE.
THE BASEMENT OF THIS BUILDING HOUSES THE LARGEST HAND RESURRECTION CHAMBER EVER BUILT.
SOMEBODY RESURRECTS HANDS?
NINJAS. SORT OF FRANKENSTEIN ZOMBIE NINJAS.
THEY'RE MASS PRODUCING THEM. HERE.
LUCKY DUCK, YOU GET TO GO IN AND STOP IT.
YOU WANT ME TO JUMP DOWN THERE AND FIGHT AN ARMY OF NINJAS?
NO. I WANT YOU TO SNEAK IN THERE, SET A LOAD OF EXPLOSIVES AND SNEAK BACK OUT.
THEN I'LL IMPLODE THE BUILDING AND BURY THEIR UNGODLY CHAMBER UNDER A TON OF STEEL AND CONCRETE.
WON'T THAT KILL--
UNDEAD NINJAS ARE ALREADY DEAD, JEAN.
POINT IS... STRICTLY BLACK OPS.
YOU CAN'T THRASH ABOUT MAKING A RUCKUS IN THERE. NO BIG LOUD BRAWLS.
NO FIGHT-OR-FLIGHT.
END EVERY ENCOUNTER SWIFTLY. USE YOUR WEAPONS WISELY. DAGGER NOT CHAINSAW.
OKAY, BUT HOW AM I SUPPOSED TO--
YOU'RE AN OMEGA-LEVEL TELEPATH WITH A MINDSCAPE ROOMY ENOUGH TO CONTAIN A BLAZING GOD BIRD.
GET OUT OF YOUR OWN WAY FOR ONCE, SUSS OUT WHAT HEADSPACE YOU NEED AND GO THERE.

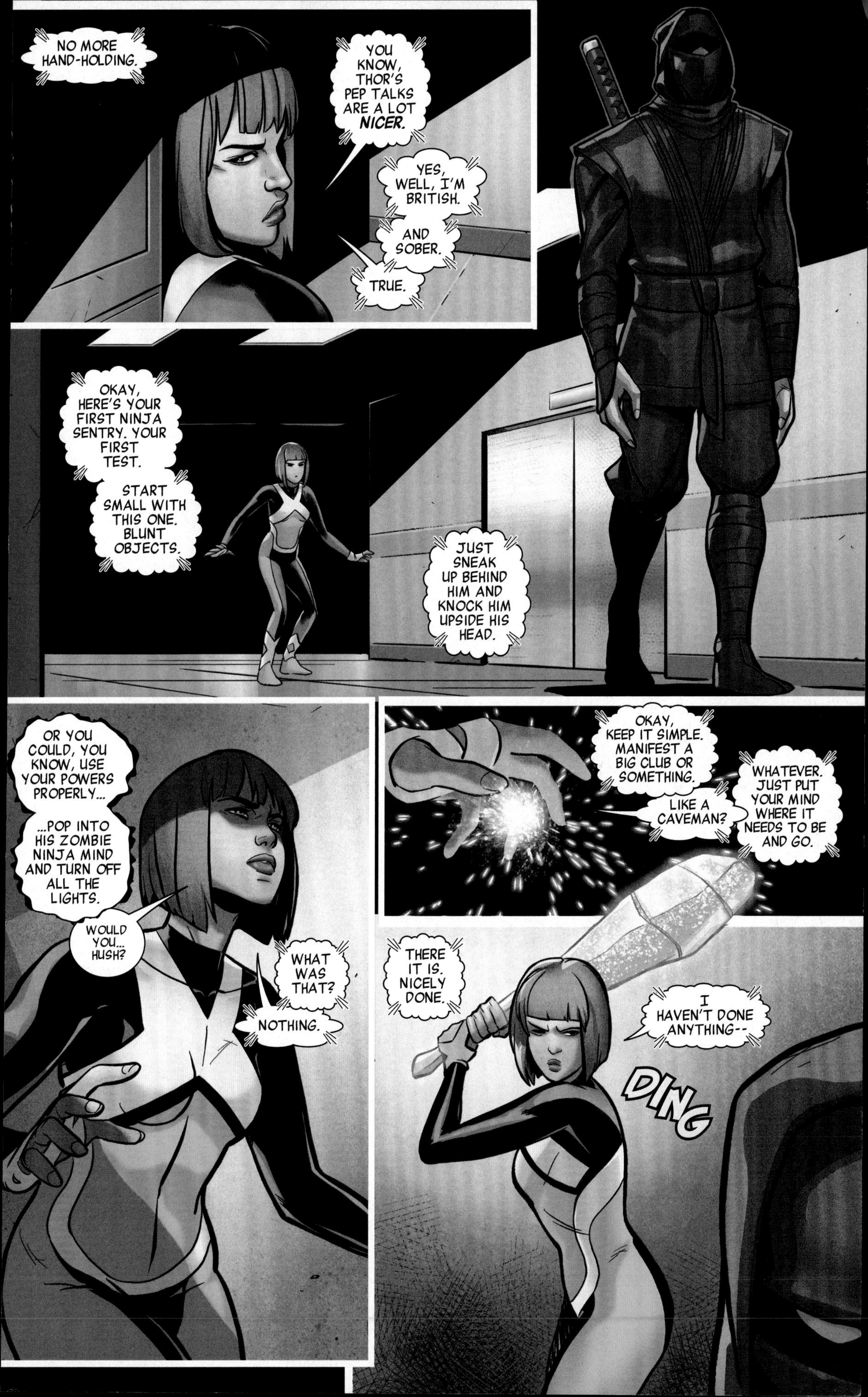
NO MORE HAND-HOLDING.
YOU KNOW, THOR'S PEP TALKS ARE A LOT NICER.
YES, WELL, I'M BRITISH.
AND SOBER.
TRUE.
OKAY, HERE'S YOUR FIRST NINJA SENTRY. YOUR FIRST TEST.
START SMALL WITH THIS ONE. BLUNT OBJECTS.
JUST SNEAK UP BEHIND HIM AND KNOCK HIM UPSIDE HIS HEAD.
OR YOU COULD, YOU KNOW, USE YOUR POWERS PROPERLY...
...POP INTO HIS ZOMBIE NINJA MIND AND TURN OFF ALL THE LIGHTS.
WOULD YOU... HUSH?
WHAT WAS THAT?
NOTHING.
OKAY, KEEP IT SIMPLE. MANIFEST A BIG CLUB OR SOMETHING.
LIKE A CAVEMAN?
WHATEVER. JUST PUT YOUR MIND WHERE IT NEEDS TO BE AND GO.
THERE IT IS. NICELY DONE.
I HAVEN'T DONE ANYTHING--
DING

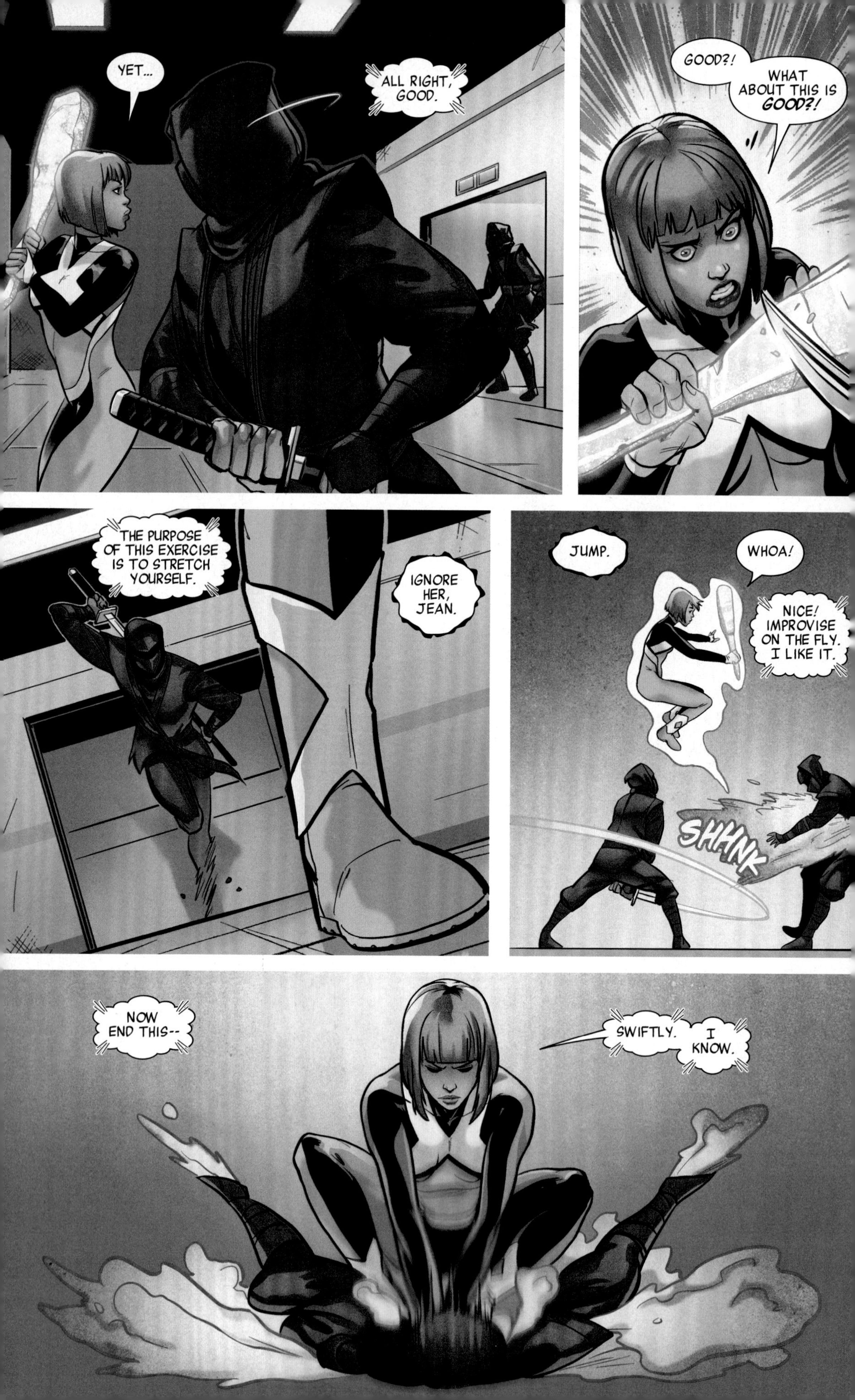
YET...
ALL RIGHT, GOOD.
GOOD?!
WHAT ABOUT THIS IS GOOD?!
THE PURPOSE OF THIS EXERCISE IS TO STRETCH YOURSELF.
IGNORE HER, JEAN.
JUMP.
WHOA!
NICE! IMPROVISE ON THE FLY. I LIKE IT.
SHHNK
NOW END THIS--
SWIFTLY.
I KNOW.

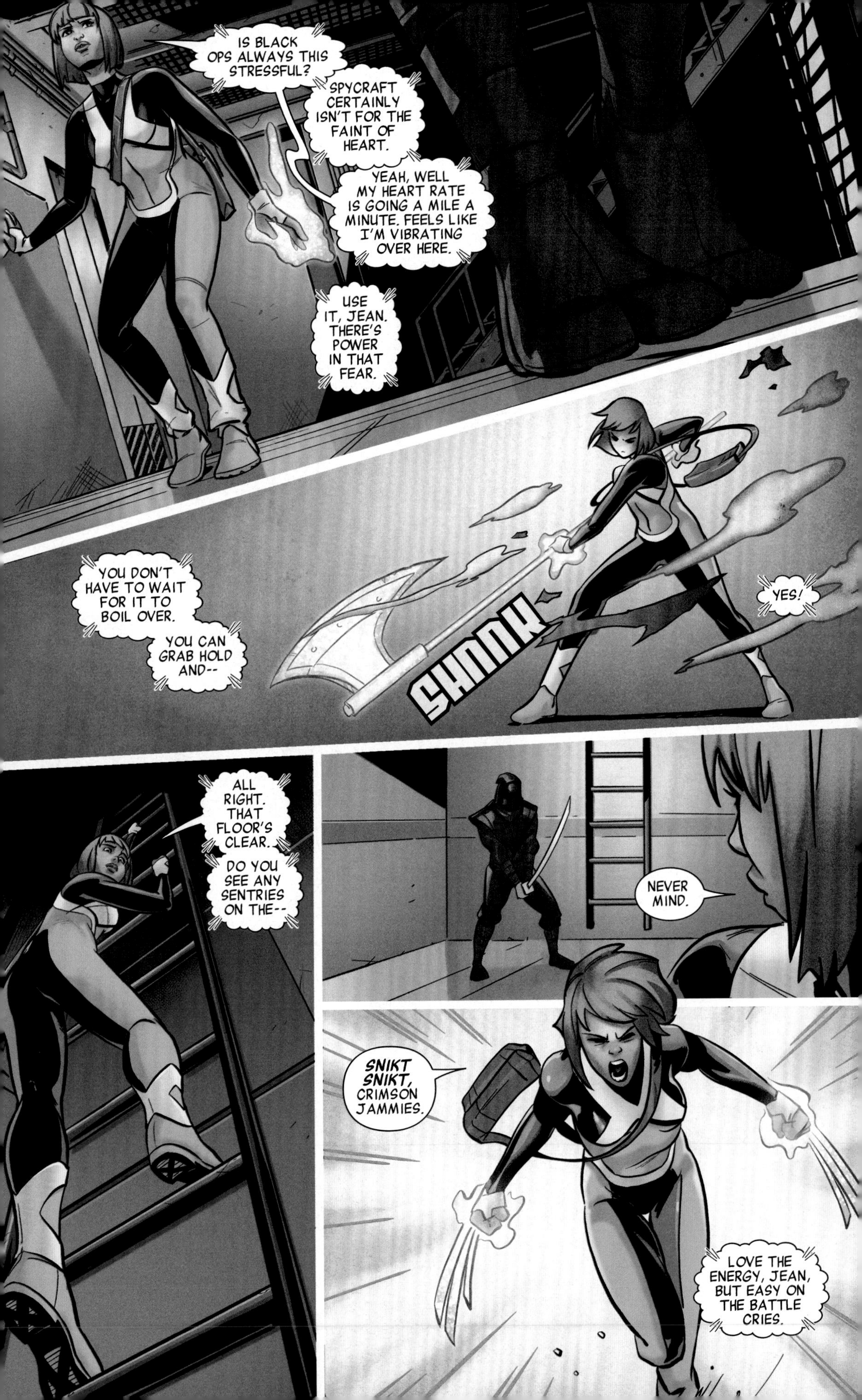
IS BLACK OPS ALWAYS THIS STRESSFUL?
SPYCRAFT CERTAINLY ISN'T FOR THE FAINT OF HEART.
YEAH, WELL MY HEART RATE IS GOING A MILE A MINUTE. FEELS LIKE I'M VIBRATING OVER HERE.
USE IT, JEAN. THERE'S POWER IN THAT FEAR.
YOU DON'T HAVE TO WAIT FOR IT TO BOIL OVER.
YOU CAN GRAB HOLD AND--
SHNNK
YES!
ALL RIGHT. THAT FLOOR'S CLEAR.
DO YOU SEE ANY SENTRIES ON THE--
NEVER MIND.
SNIKT SNIKT, CRIMSON JAMMIES.
LOVE THE ENERGY, JEAN, BUT EASY ON THE BATTLE CRIES.

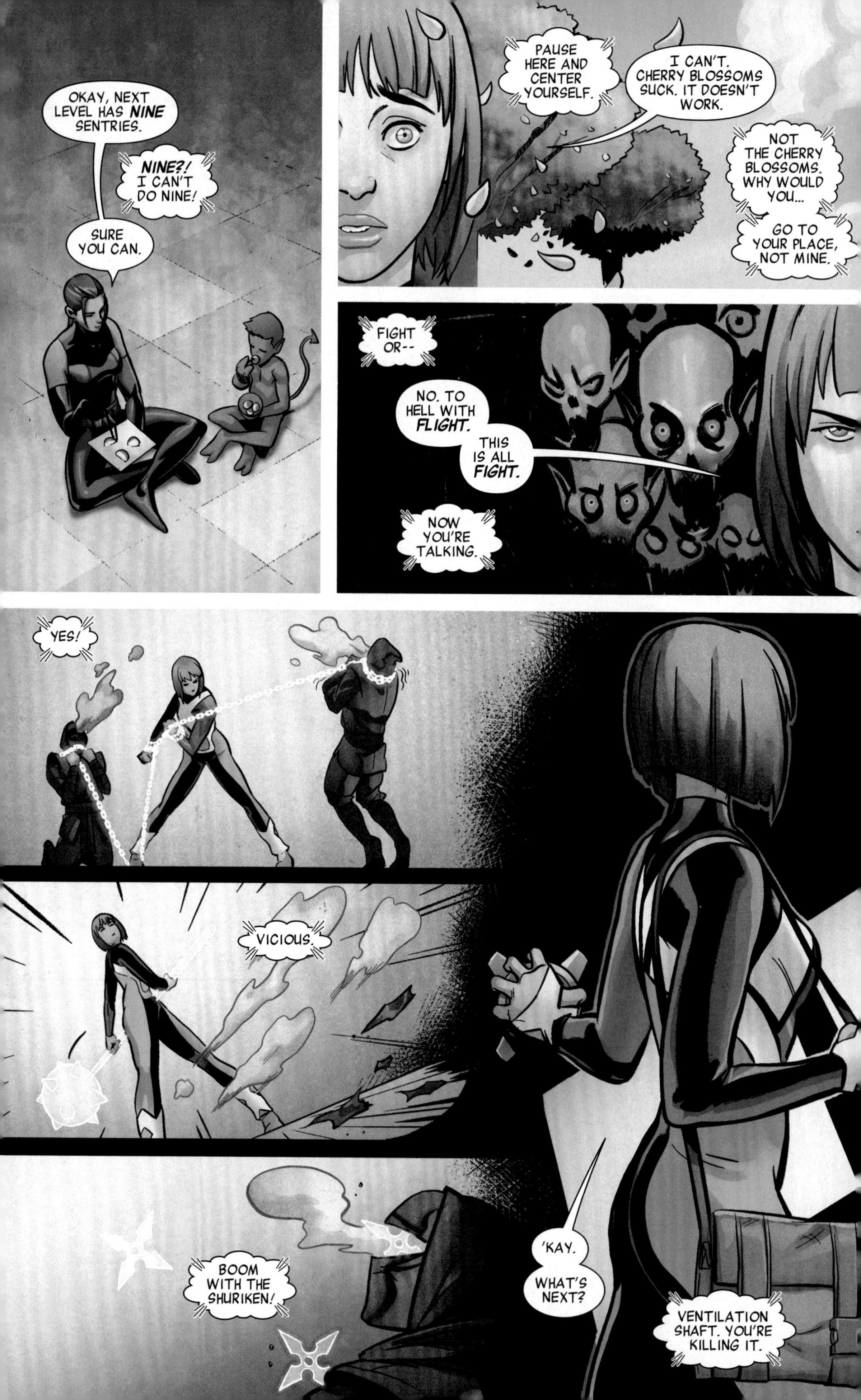
OKAY, NEXT LEVEL HAS NINE SENTRIES.
NINE?! I CAN'T DO NINE!
SURE YOU CAN.
PAUSE HERE AND CENTER YOURSELF.
I CAN'T. CHERRY BLOSSOMS SUCK. IT DOESN'T WORK.
NOT THE CHERRY BLOSSOMS. WHY WOULD YOU...
GO TO YOUR PLACE, NOT MINE.
FIGHT OR--
NO. TO HELL WITH FLIGHT.
THIS IS ALL FIGHT.
NOW YOU'RE TALKING.
YES!
VICIOUS.
BOOM WITH THE SHURIKEN!
'KAY.
WHAT'S NEXT?
VENTILATION SHAFT. YOU'RE KILLING IT.

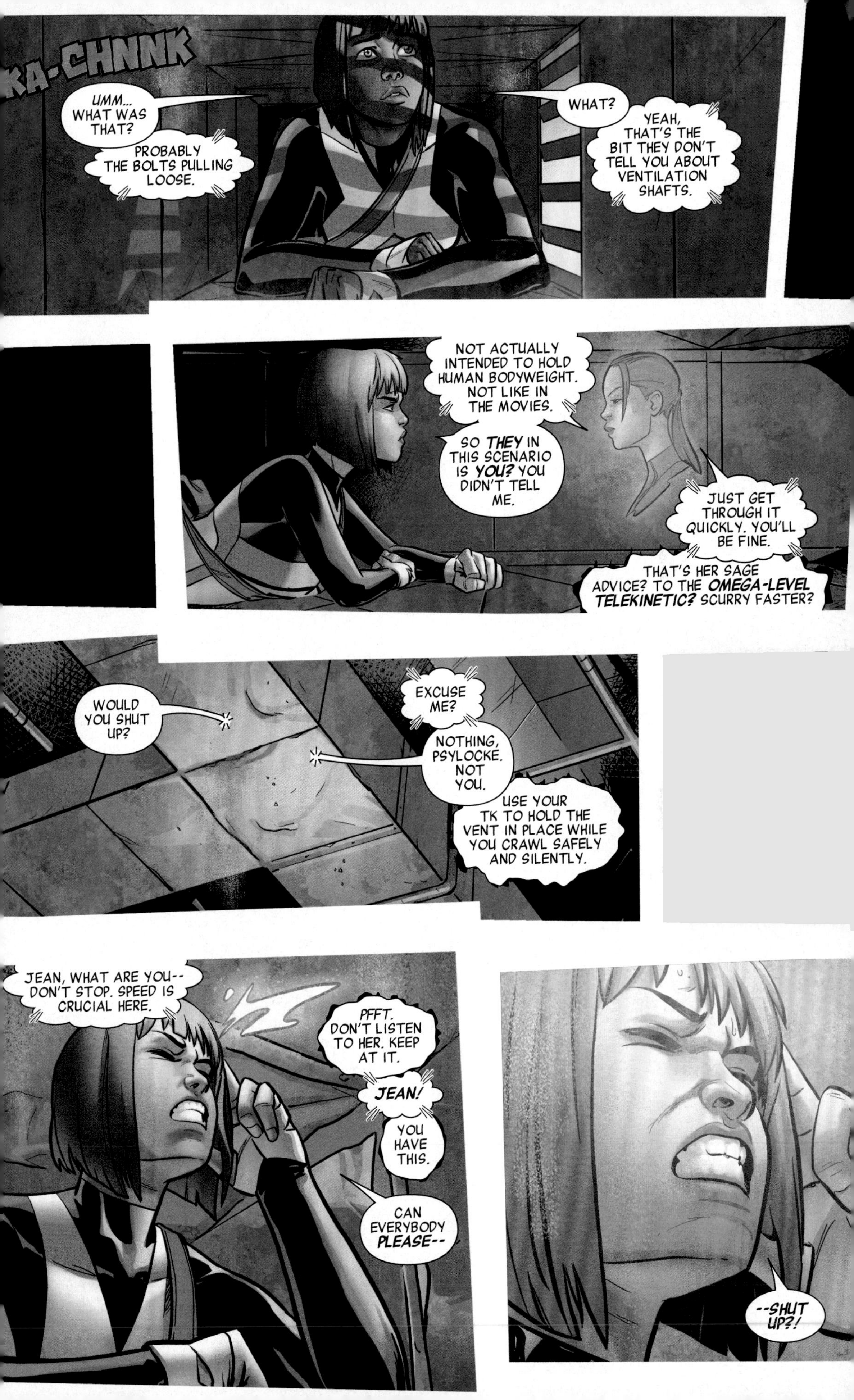
KA-CHNNK
UMM... WHAT WAS THAT?
PROBABLY THE BOLTS PULLING LOOSE.
WHAT?
YEAH, THAT'S THE BIT THEY DON'T TELL YOU ABOUT VENTILATION SHAFTS.
NOT ACTUALLY INTENDED TO HOLD HUMAN BODYWEIGHT. NOT LIKE IN THE MOVIES.
SO THEY IN THIS SCENARIO IS YOU? YOU DIDN'T TELL ME.
JUST GET THROUGH IT QUICKLY. YOU'LL BE FINE.
THAT'S HER SAGE ADVICE? TO THE OMEGA-LEVEL TELEKINETIC? SCURRY FASTER?
WOULD YOU SHUT UP?
EXCUSE ME?
NOTHING, PSYLOCKE. NOT YOU.
USE YOUR TK TO HOLD THE VENT IN PLACE WHILE YOU CRAWL SAFELY AND SILENTLY.
JEAN, WHAT ARE YOU-- DON'T STOP. SPEED IS CRUCIAL HERE.
PFFT. DON'T LISTEN TO HER. KEEP AT IT.
JEAN!
YOU HAVE THIS.
CAN EVERYBODY PLEASE--
--SHUT UP?!

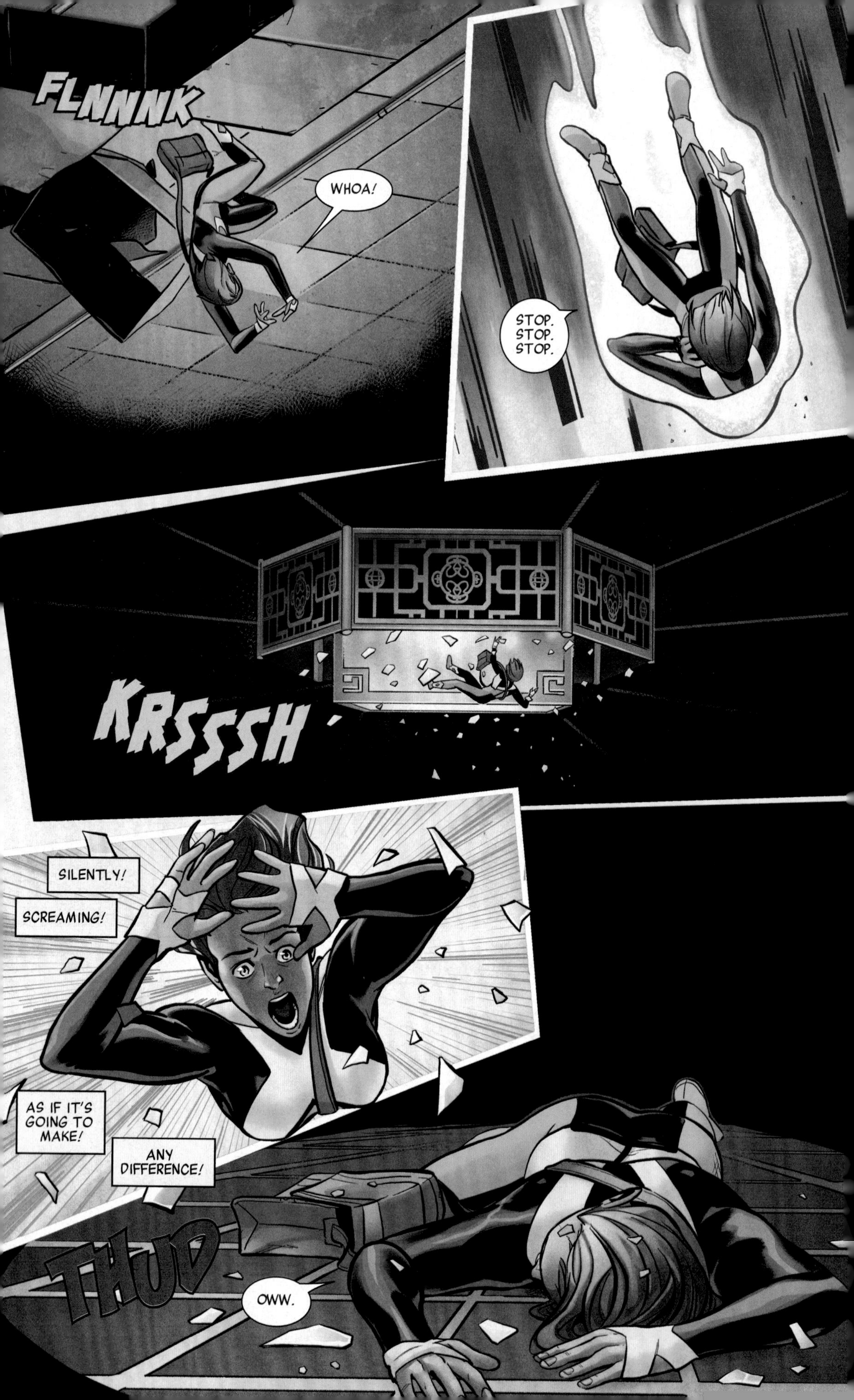
FLNNNK
WHOA!
STOP. STOP. STOP.
KRSSSH
SILENTLY!
SCREAMING!
AS IF IT'S GOING TO MAKE!
ANY DIFFERENCE!
THUD
OWW.

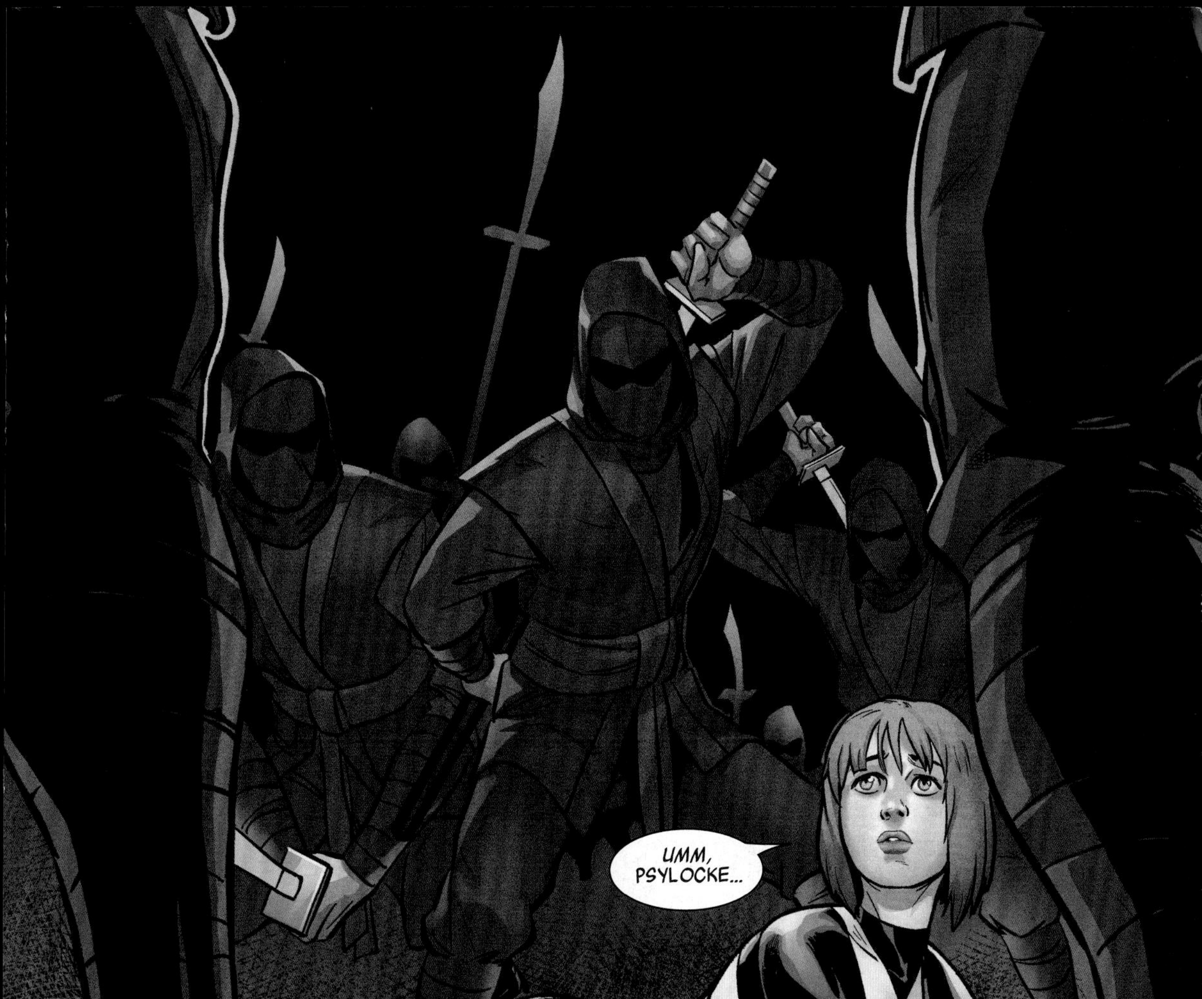
UMM, PSYLOCKE...

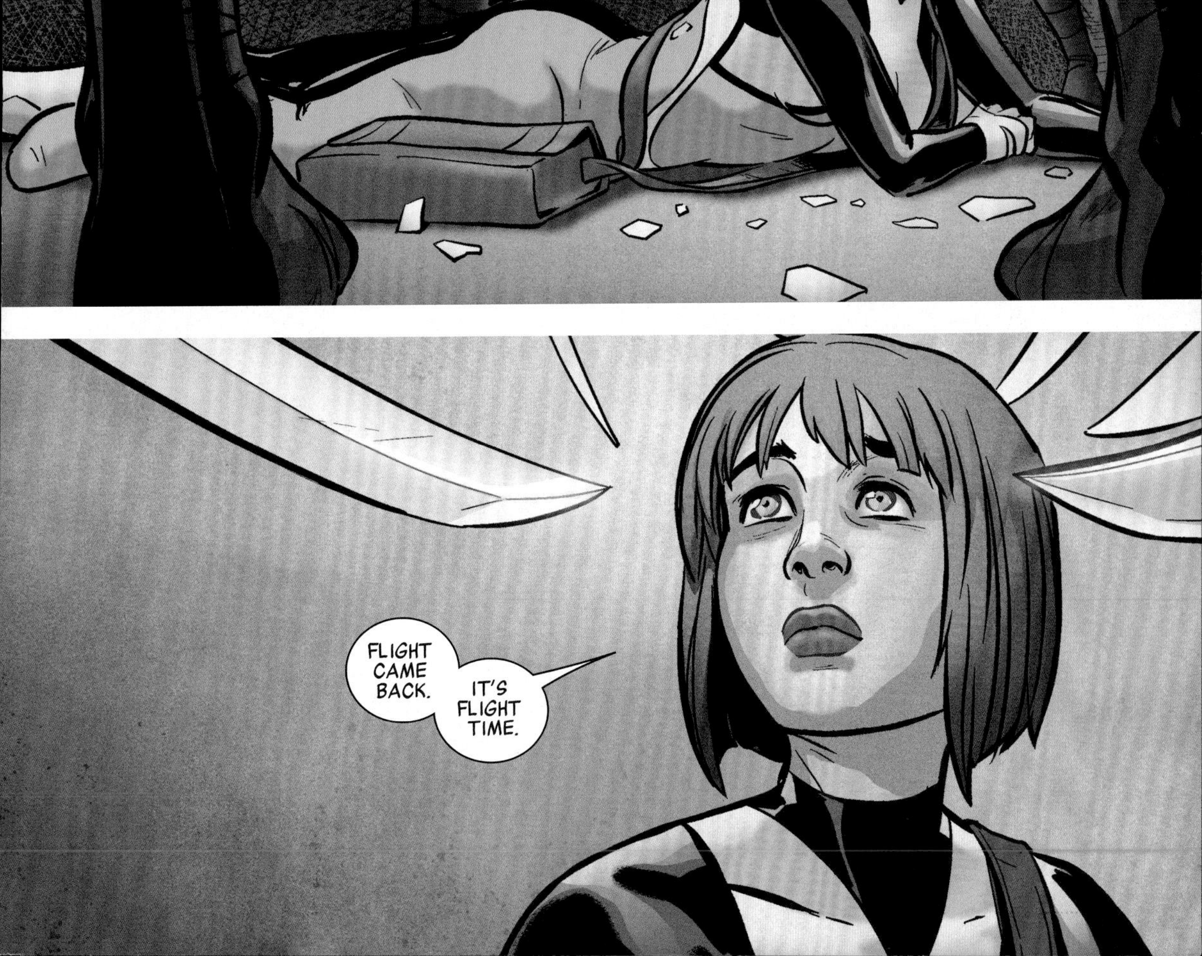
FLIGHT CAME BACK.
IT'S FLIGHT TIME.

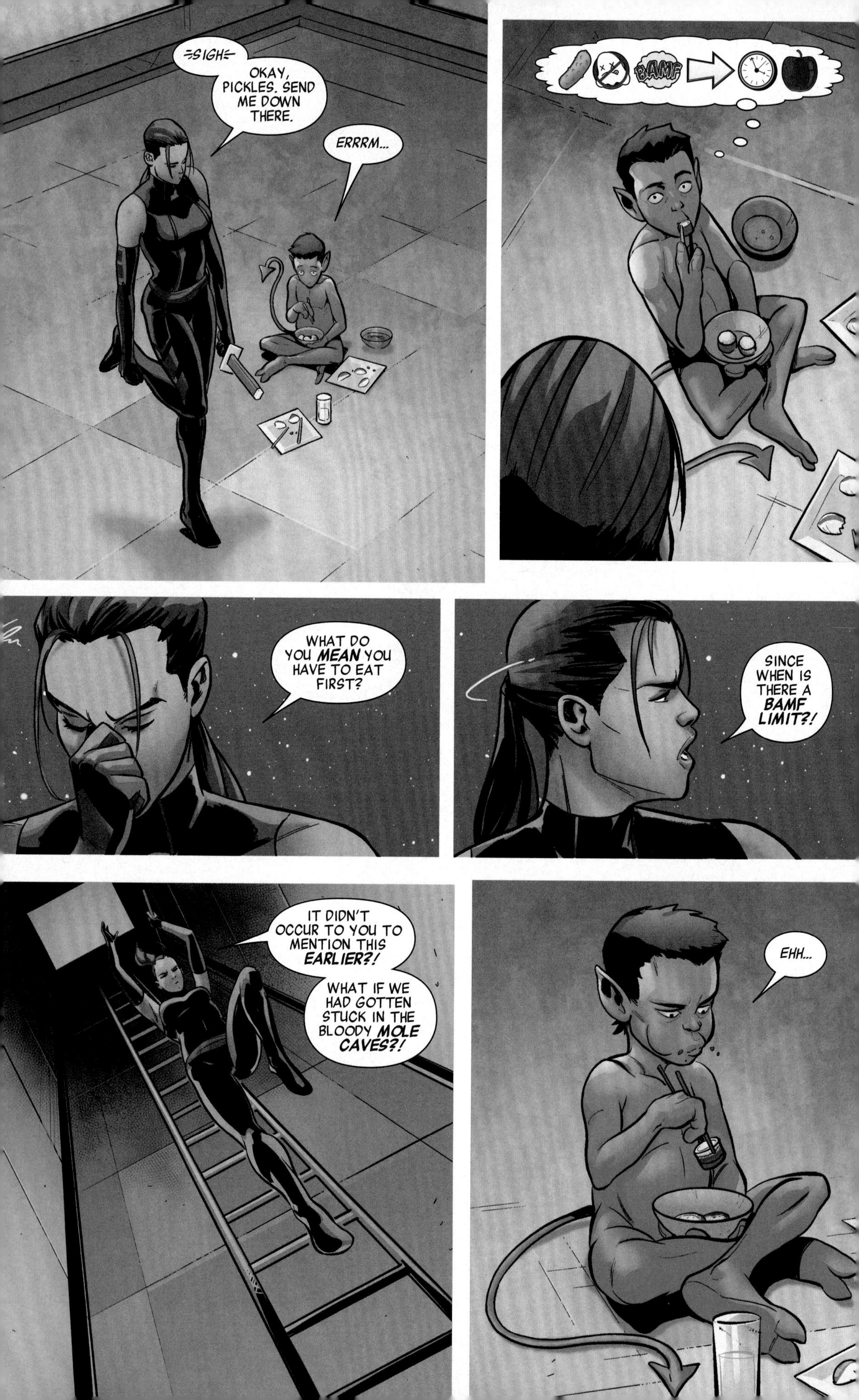

=SIGH=
OKAY, PICKLES. SEND ME DOWN THERE.
ERRRM...
BAMF
WHAT DO YOU **MEAN** YOU HAVE TO EAT FIRST?
SINCE WHEN IS THERE A **BAMF LIMIT?!**
IT DIDN'T OCCUR TO YOU TO MENTION THIS **EARLIER?!**
WHAT IF WE HAD GOTTEN STUCK IN THE BLOODY **MOLE CAVES?!**
EHH...

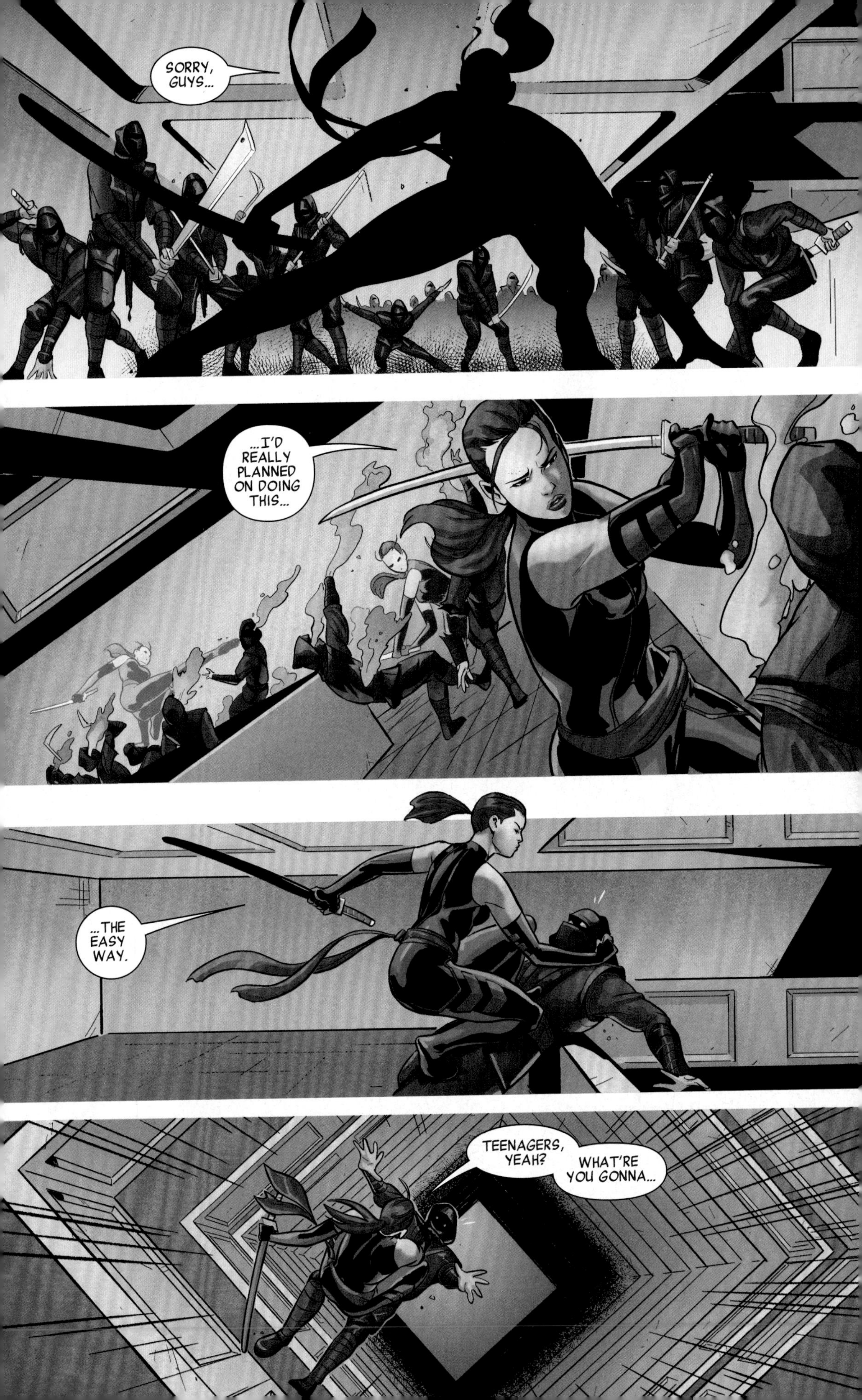
SORRY, GUYS...
...I'D REALLY PLANNED ON DOING THIS...
...THE EASY WAY.
TEENAGERS, YEAH?
WHAT'RE YOU GONNA...

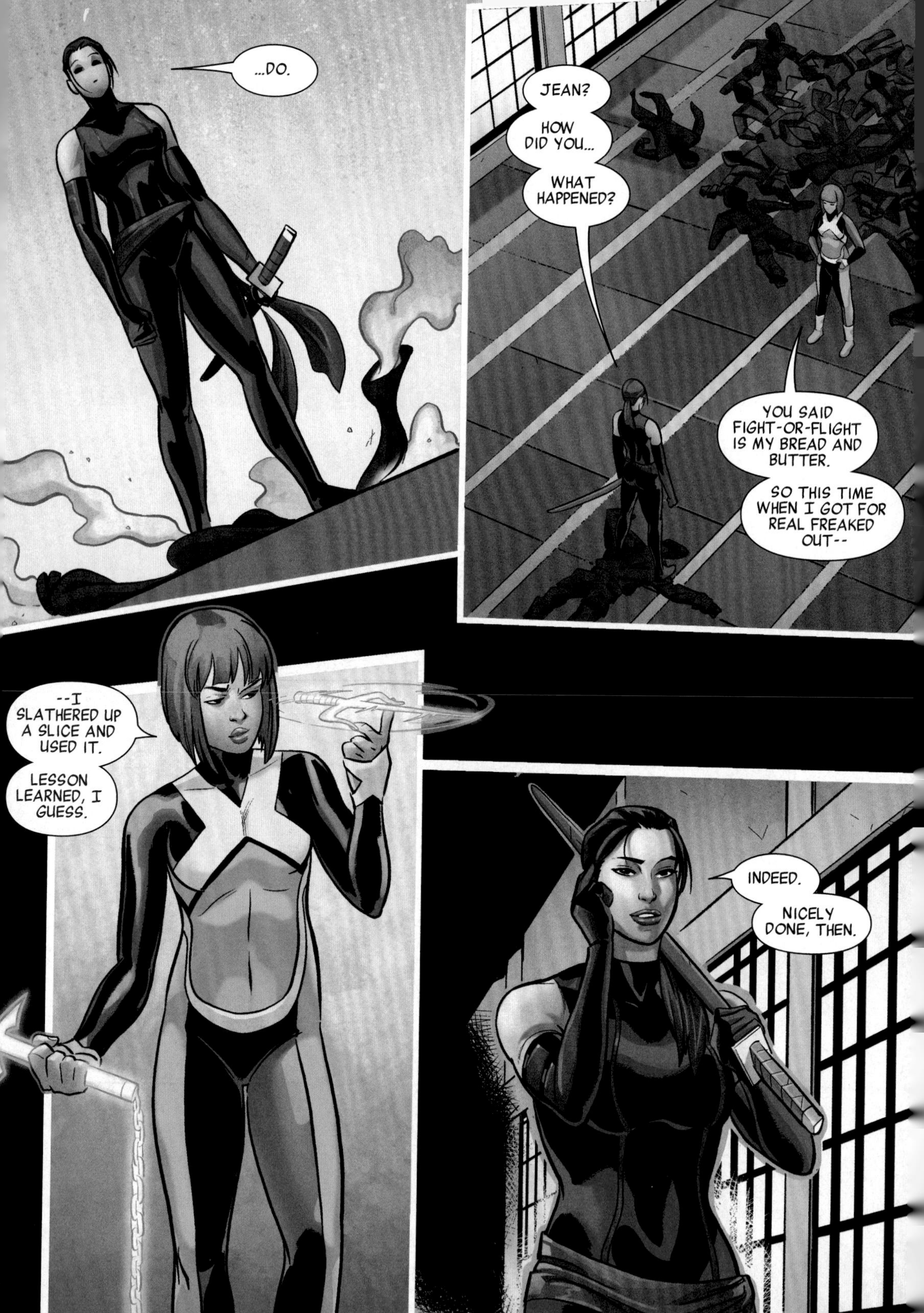
...DO.
JEAN?
HOW DID YOU...
WHAT HAPPENED?
YOU SAID FIGHT-OR-FLIGHT IS MY BREAD AND BUTTER.
SO THIS TIME WHEN I GOT FOR REAL FREAKED OUT--
--I SLATHERED UP A SLICE AND USED IT.
LESSON LEARNED, I GUESS.
INDEED.
NICELY DONE, THEN.

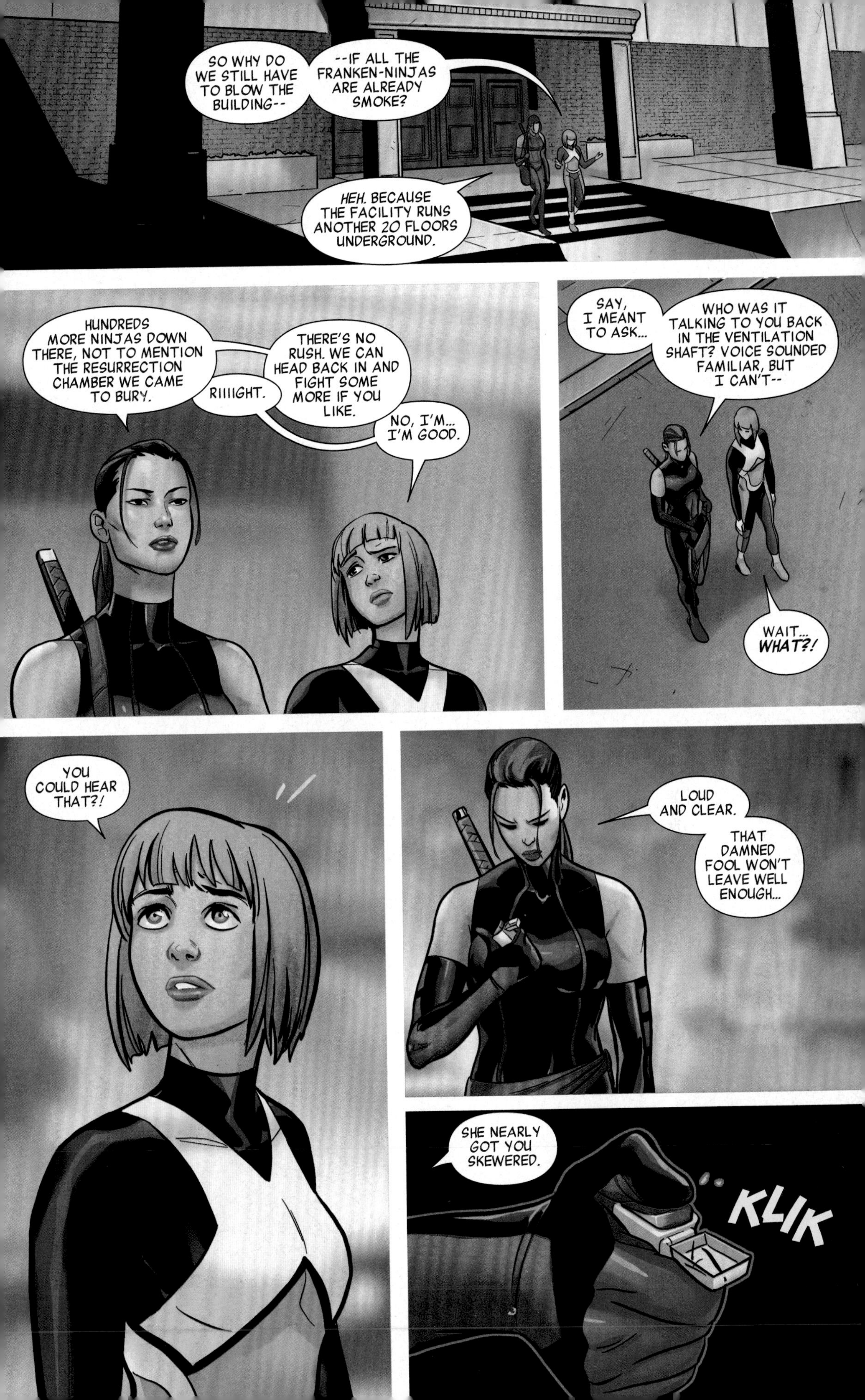
SO WHY DO WE STILL HAVE TO BLOW THE BUILDING--
--IF ALL THE FRANKEN-NINJAS ARE ALREADY SMOKE?
HEH. BECAUSE THE FACILITY RUNS ANOTHER 20 FLOORS UNDERGROUND.
HUNDREDS MORE NINJAS DOWN THERE, NOT TO MENTION THE RESURRECTION CHAMBER WE CAME TO BURY.
RIIIIGHT.
THERE'S NO RUSH. WE CAN HEAD BACK IN AND FIGHT SOME MORE IF YOU LIKE.
NO, I'M... I'M GOOD.
SAY, I MEANT TO ASK...
WHO WAS IT TALKING TO YOU BACK IN THE VENTILATION SHAFT? VOICE SOUNDED FAMILIAR, BUT I CAN'T--
WAIT... WHAT?!
YOU COULD HEAR THAT?!
LOUD AND CLEAR.
THAT DAMNED FOOL WON'T LEAVE WELL ENOUGH...
SHE NEARLY GOT YOU SKEWERED.
KLIK

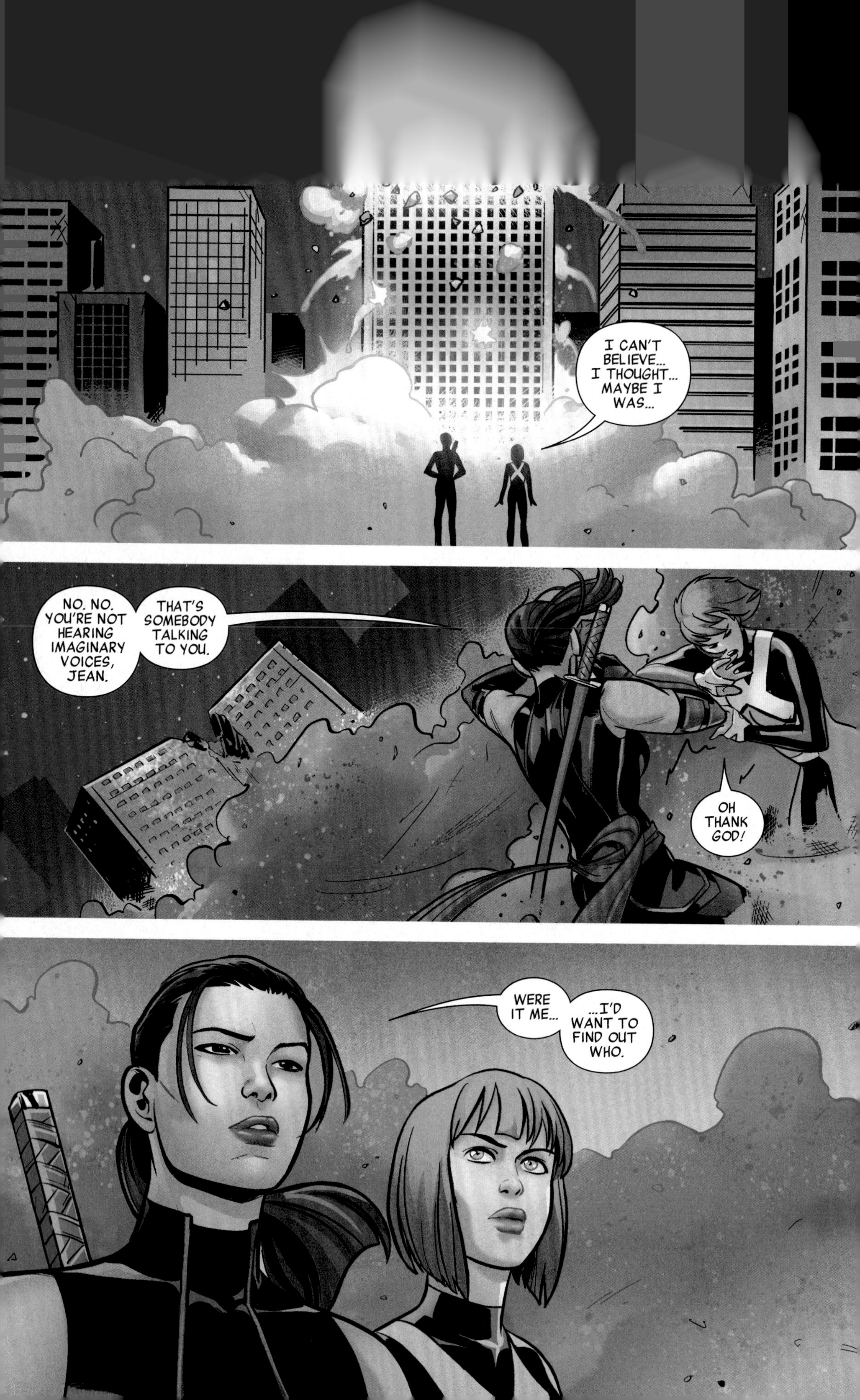
I CAN'T BELIEVE... I THOUGHT... MAYBE I WAS...
NO. NO. YOU'RE NOT HEARING IMAGINARY VOICES, JEAN.
THAT'S SOMEBODY TALKING TO YOU.
OH THANK GOD!
WERE IT ME...
...I'D WANT TO FIND OUT WHO.

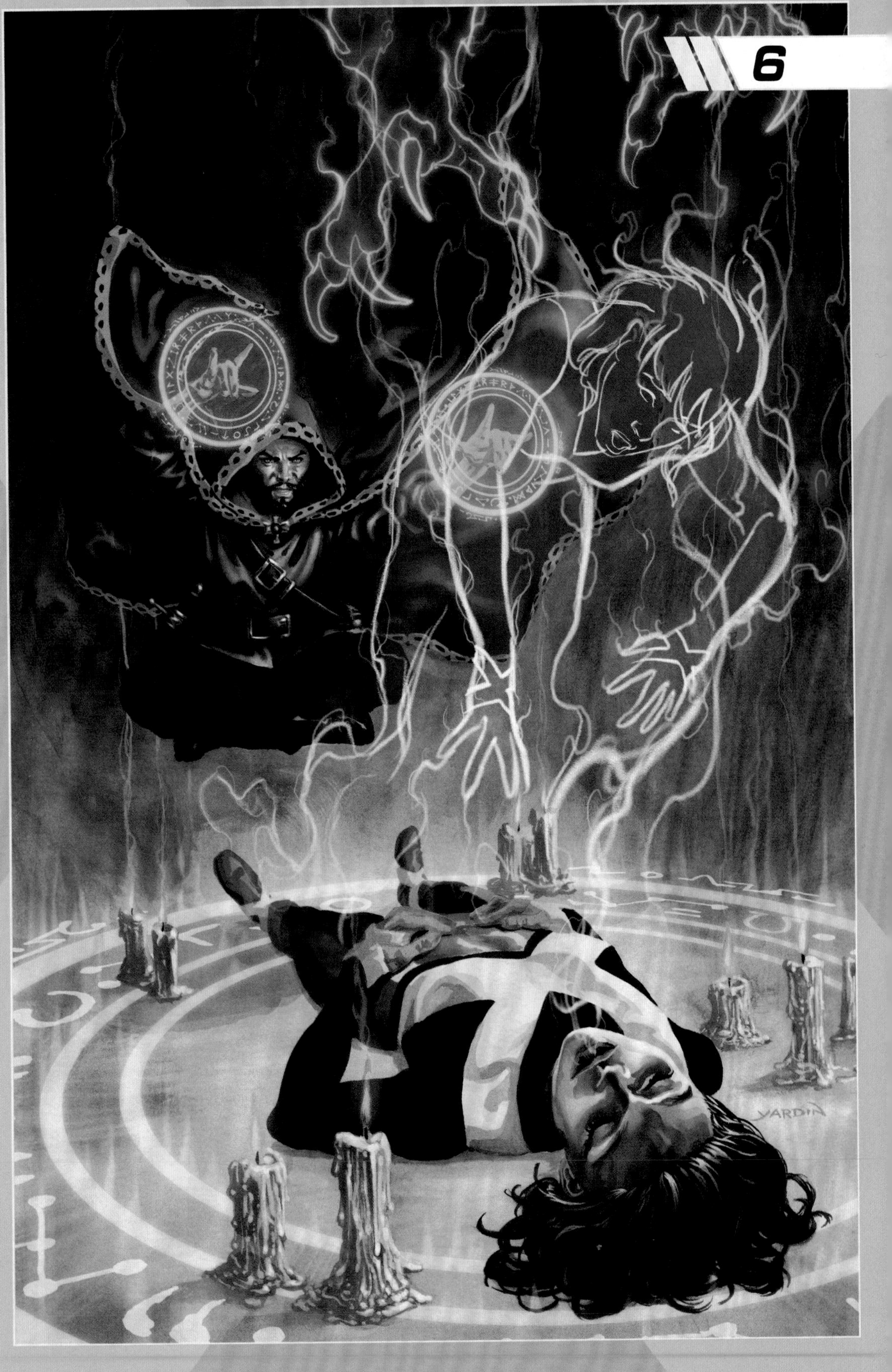
6
YARDIN

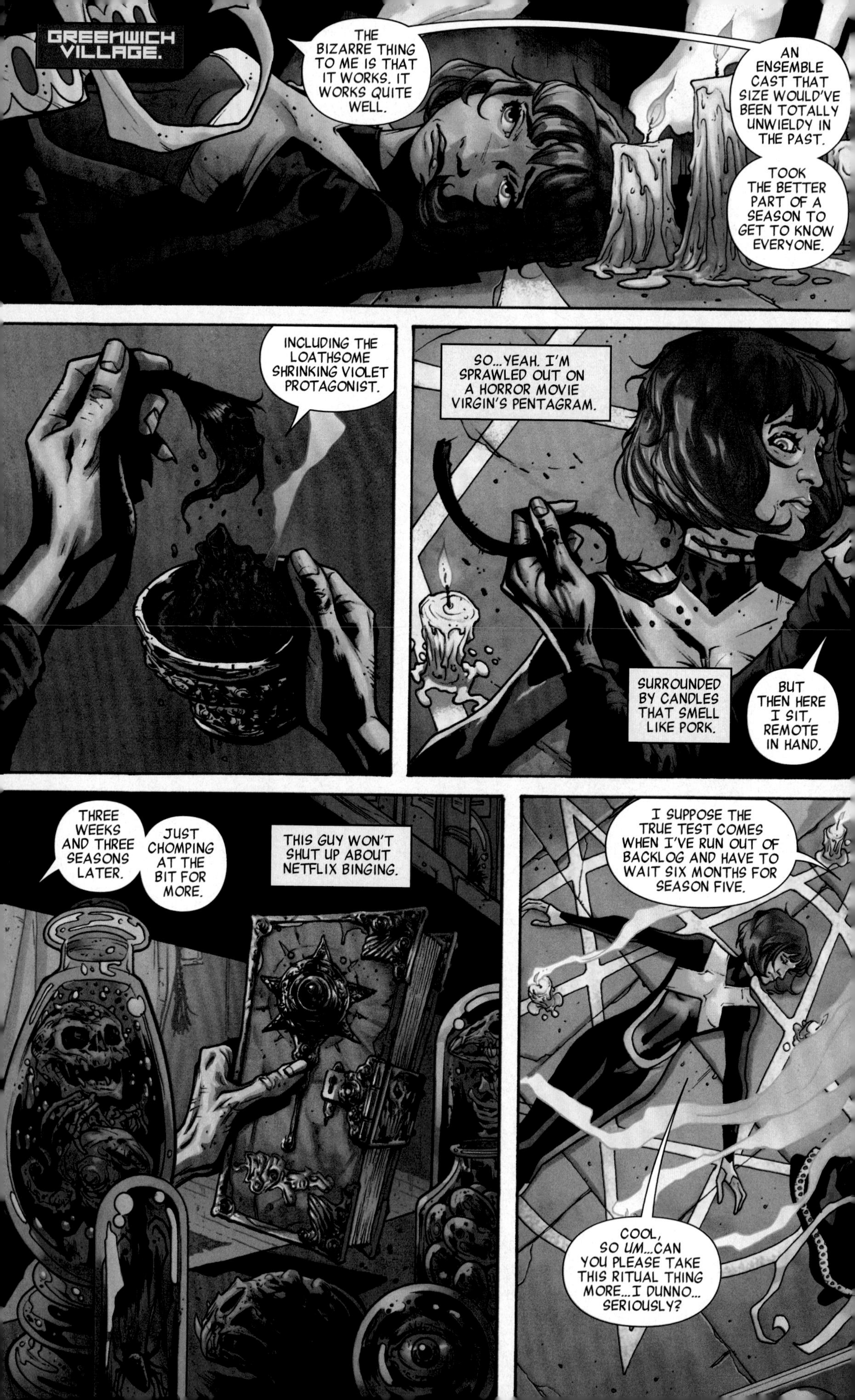
GREENWICH VILLAGE.
THE BIZARRE THING TO ME IS THAT IT WORKS. IT WORKS QUITE WELL.
AN ENSEMBLE CAST THAT SIZE WOULD'VE BEEN TOTALLY UNWIELDY IN THE PAST.
TOOK THE BETTER PART OF A SEASON TO GET TO KNOW EVERYONE.
INCLUDING THE LOATHSOME SHRINKING VIOLET PROTAGONIST.
SO...YEAH. I'M SPRAWLED OUT ON A HORROR MOVIE VIRGIN'S PENTAGRAM.
SURROUNDED BY CANDLES THAT SMELL LIKE PORK.
BUT THEN HERE I SIT, REMOTE IN HAND.
THREE WEEKS AND THREE SEASONS LATER.
JUST CHOMPING AT THE BIT FOR MORE.
THIS GUY WON'T SHUT UP ABOUT NETFLIX BINGING.
I SUPPOSE THE TRUE TEST COMES WHEN I'VE RUN OUT OF BACKLOG AND HAVE TO WAIT SIX MONTHS FOR SEASON FIVE.
COOL, SO UM...CAN YOU PLEASE TAKE THIS RITUAL THING MORE...I DUNNO... SERIOUSLY?

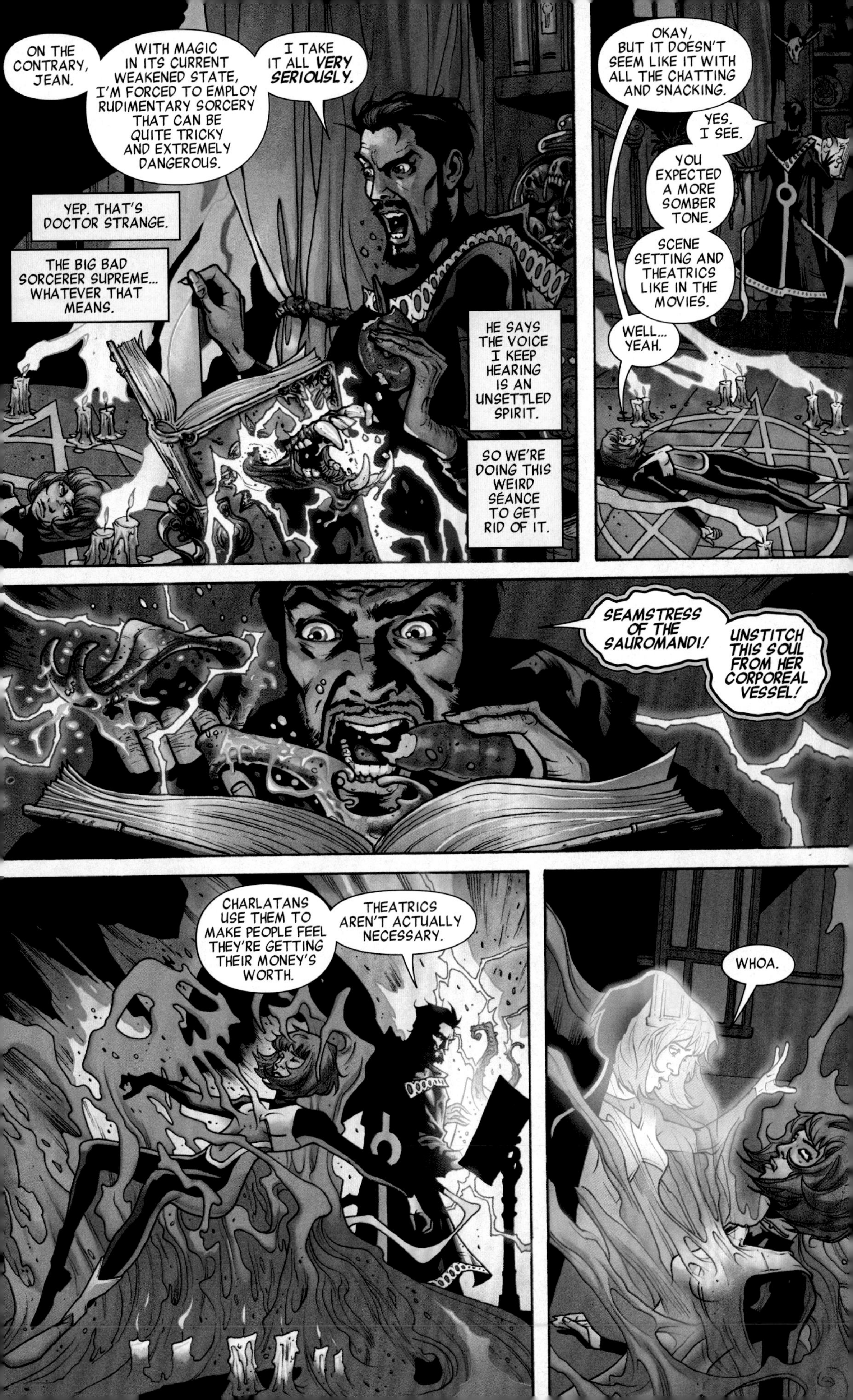
ON THE CONTRARY, JEAN.
WITH MAGIC IN ITS CURRENT WEAKENED STATE, I'M FORCED TO EMPLOY RUDIMENTARY SORCERY THAT CAN BE QUITE TRICKY AND EXTREMELY DANGEROUS.
I TAKE IT ALL VERY SERIOUSLY.
YEP. THAT'S DOCTOR STRANGE.
THE BIG BAD SORCERER SUPREME... WHATEVER THAT MEANS.
HE SAYS THE VOICE I KEEP HEARING IS AN UNSETTLED SPIRIT.
SO WE'RE DOING THIS WEIRD SÉANCE TO GET RID OF IT.
OKAY, BUT IT DOESN'T SEEM LIKE IT WITH ALL THE CHATTING AND SNACKING.
YES. I SEE.
YOU EXPECTED A MORE SOMBER TONE.
SCENE SETTING AND THEATRICS LIKE IN THE MOVIES.
WELL... YEAH.
SEAMSTRESS OF THE SAUROMANDI!
UNSTITCH THIS SOUL FROM HER CORPOREAL VESSEL!
THEATRICS AREN'T ACTUALLY NECESSARY.
CHARLATANS USE THEM TO MAKE PEOPLE FEEL THEY'RE GETTING THEIR MONEY'S WORTH.
WHOA.

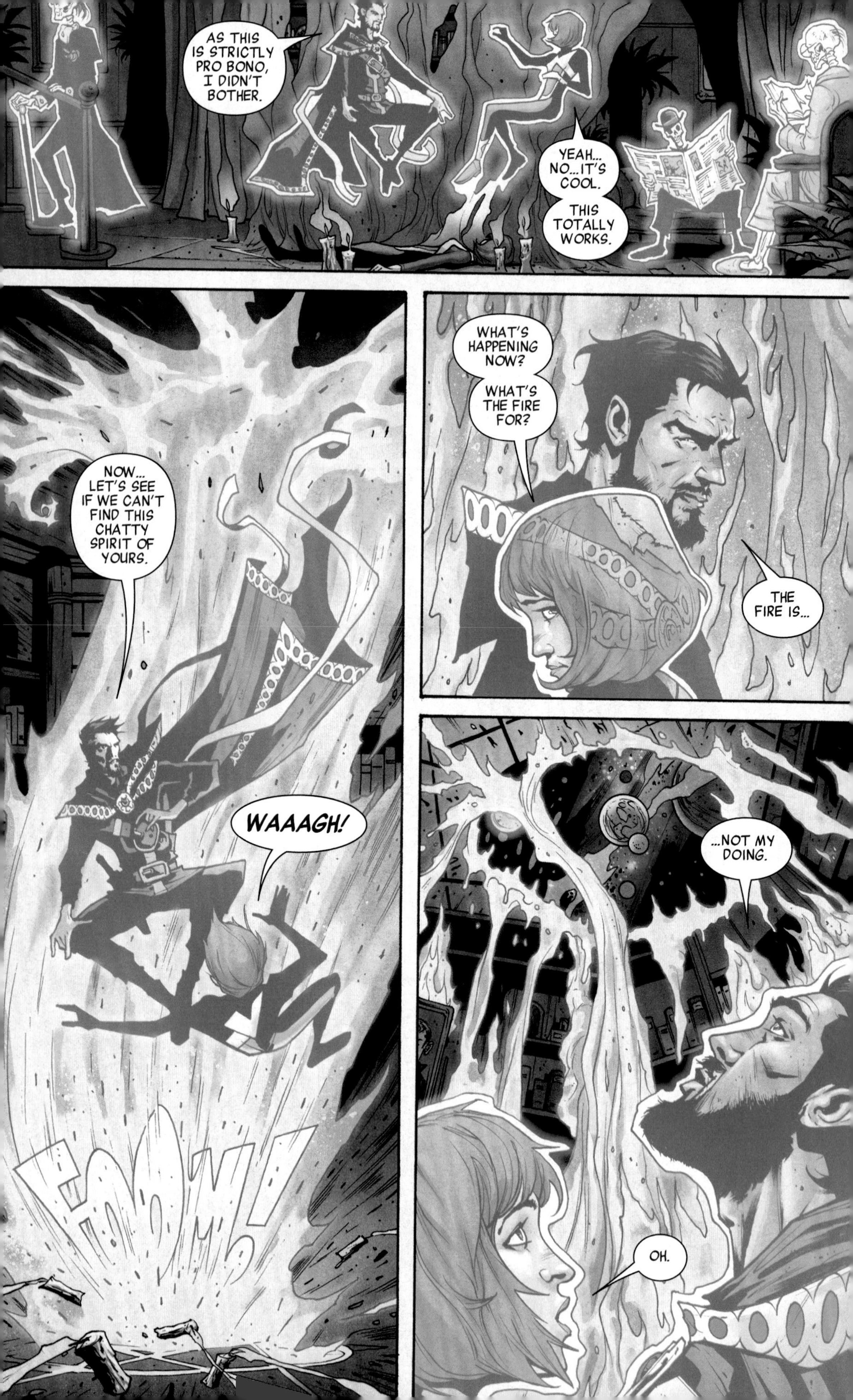
AS THIS IS STRICTLY PRO BONO, I DIDN'T BOTHER.
YEAH... NO...IT'S COOL.
THIS TOTALLY WORKS.
NOW... LET'S SEE IF WE CAN'T FIND THIS CHATTY SPIRIT OF YOURS.
WAAAGH!
WHAT'S HAPPENING NOW?
WHAT'S THE FIRE FOR?
THE FIRE IS...
...NOT MY DOING.
OH.

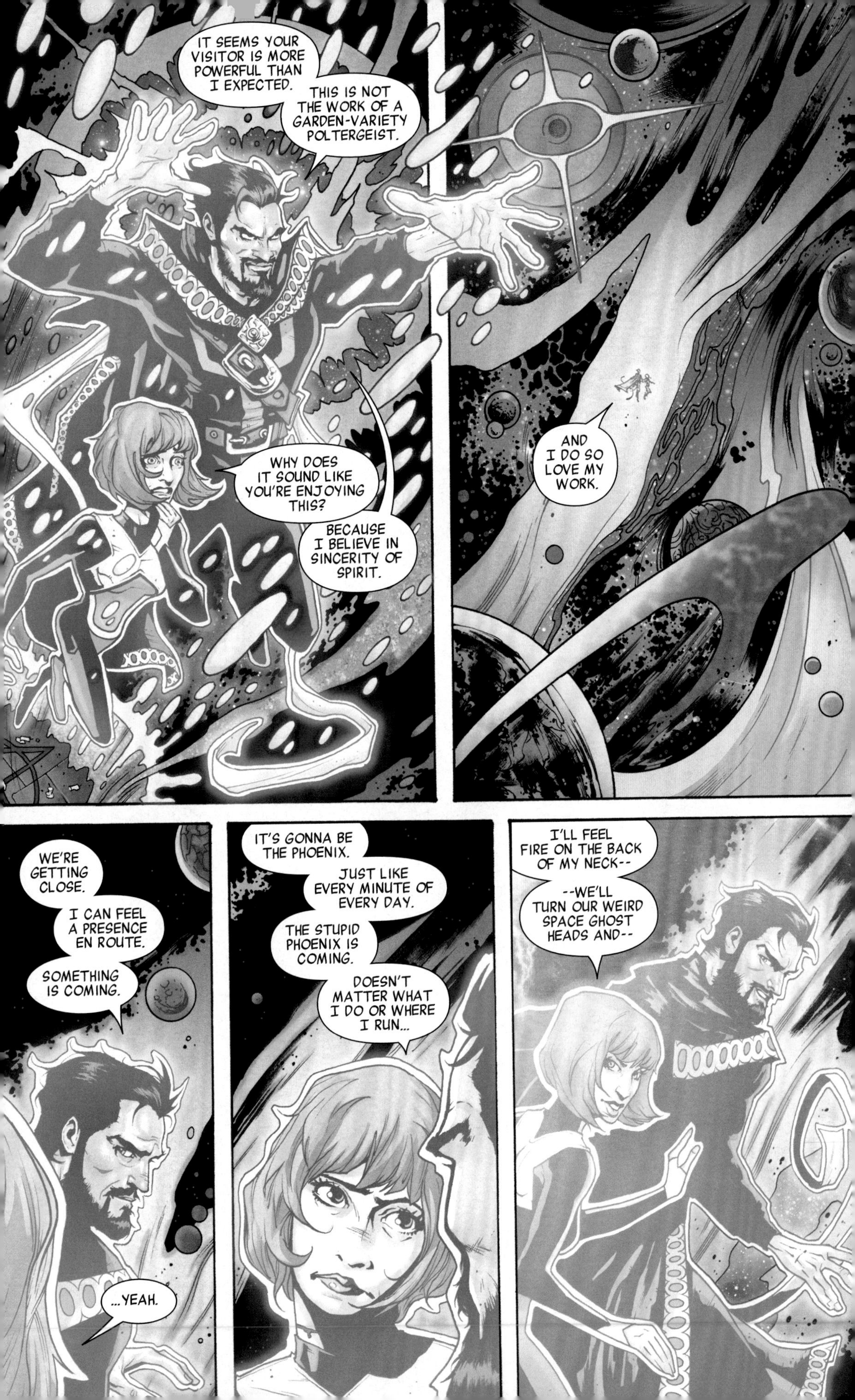
IT SEEMS YOUR VISITOR IS MORE POWERFUL THAN I EXPECTED.
THIS IS NOT THE WORK OF A GARDEN-VARIETY POLTERGEIST.
WHY DOES IT SOUND LIKE YOU'RE ENJOYING THIS?
BECAUSE I BELIEVE IN SINCERITY OF SPIRIT.
AND I DO SO LOVE MY WORK.
WE'RE GETTING CLOSE.
I CAN FEEL A PRESENCE EN ROUTE.
SOMETHING IS COMING.
...YEAH.
IT'S GONNA BE THE PHOENIX.
JUST LIKE EVERY MINUTE OF EVERY DAY.
THE STUPID PHOENIX IS COMING.
DOESN'T MATTER WHAT I DO OR WHERE I RUN...
I'LL FEEL FIRE ON THE BACK OF MY NECK--
--WE'LL TURN OUR WEIRD SPACE GHOST HEADS AND--

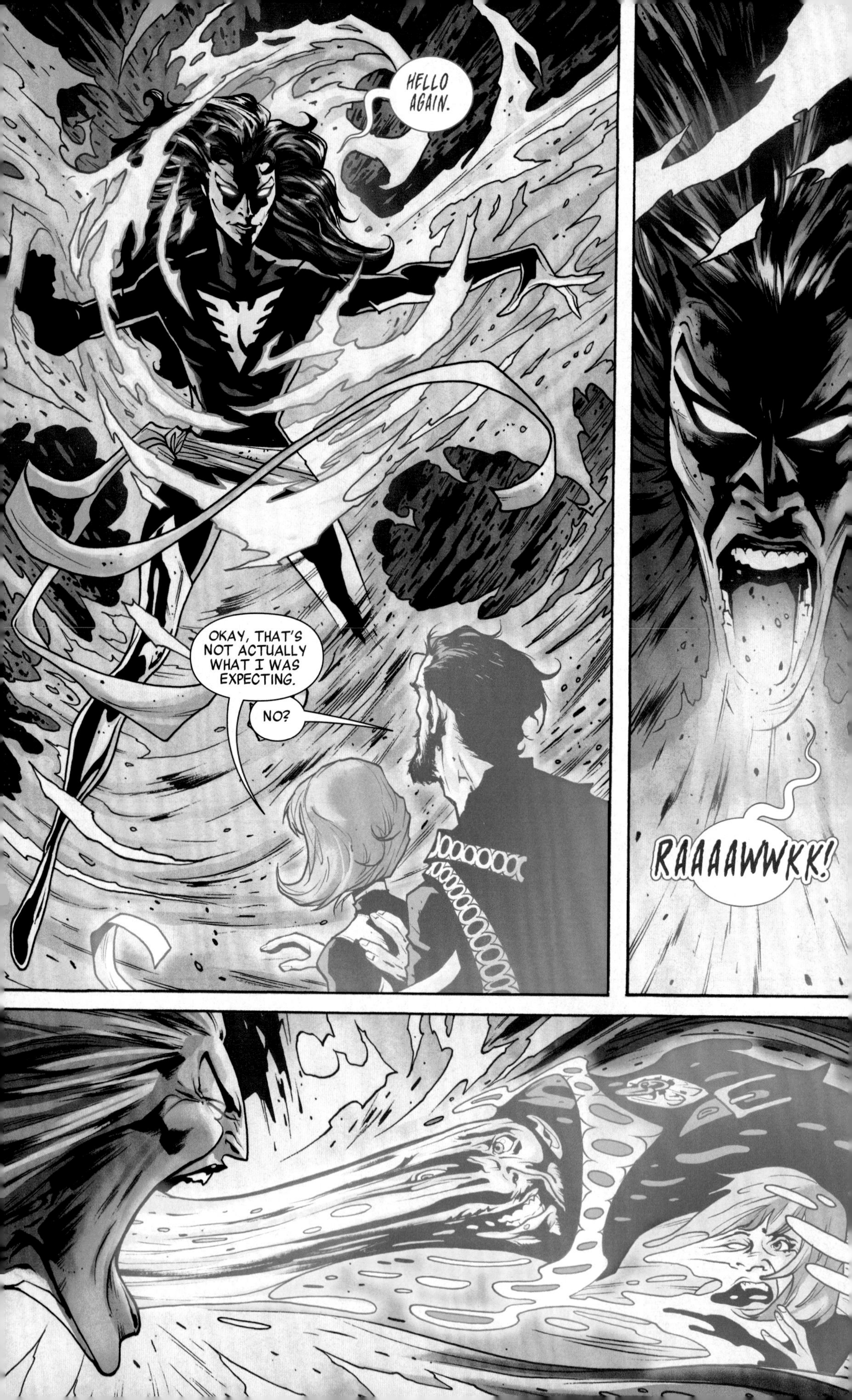
HELLO AGAIN.
OKAY, THAT'S NOT ACTUALLY WHAT I WAS EXPECTING.
NO?
RAAAAWWKK!

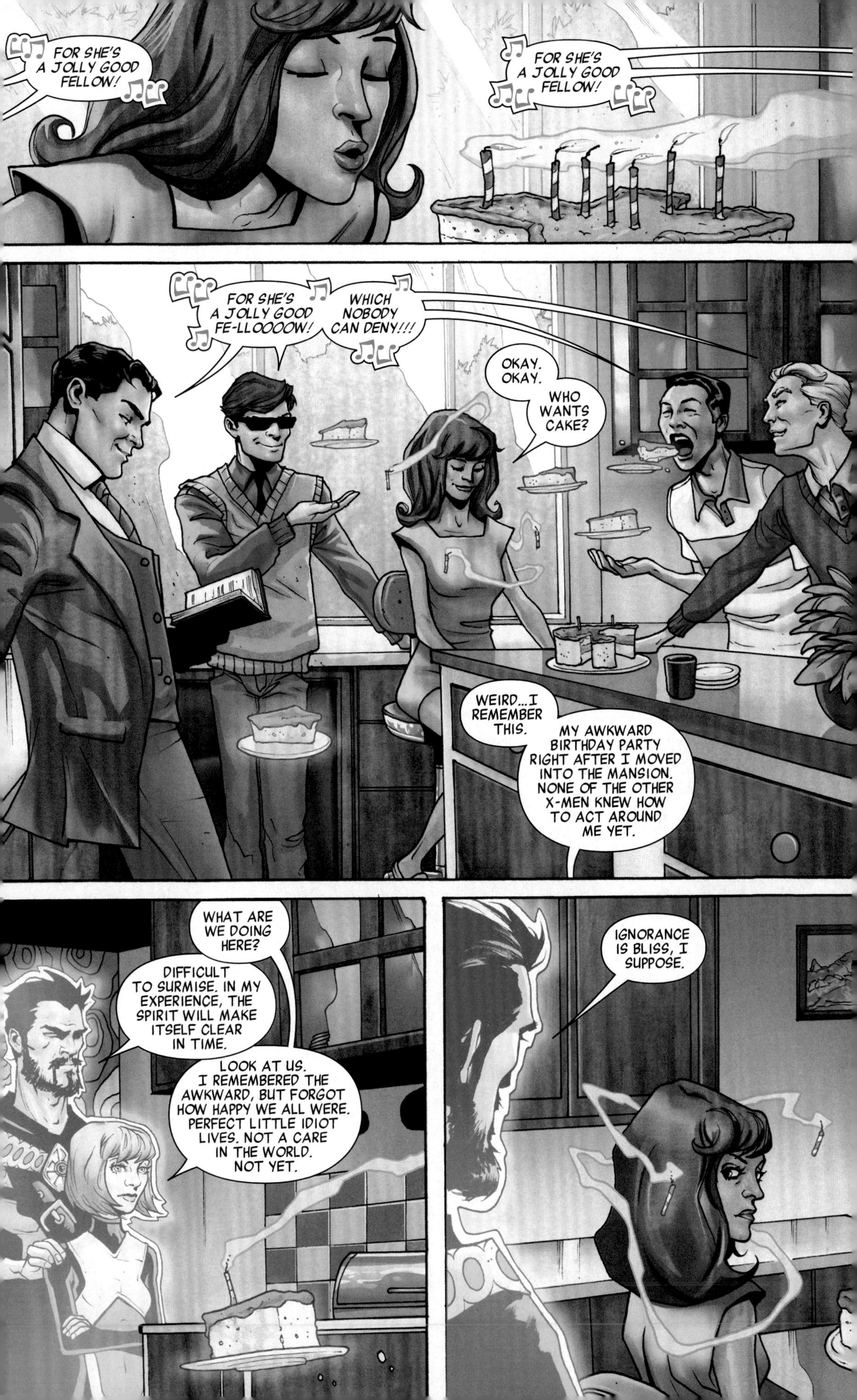
FOR SHE'S A JOLLY GOOD FELLOW!
FOR SHE'S A JOLLY GOOD FELLOW!
FOR SHE'S A JOLLY GOOD FE-LLOOOOW!
WHICH NOBODY CAN DENY!!!
OKAY. OKAY.
WHO WANTS CAKE?
WEIRD...I REMEMBER THIS.
MY AWKWARD BIRTHDAY PARTY RIGHT AFTER I MOVED INTO THE MANSION. NONE OF THE OTHER X-MEN KNEW HOW TO ACT AROUND ME YET.
WHAT ARE WE DOING HERE?
DIFFICULT TO SURMISE. IN MY EXPERIENCE, THE SPIRIT WILL MAKE ITSELF CLEAR IN TIME.
LOOK AT US. I REMEMBERED THE AWKWARD, BUT FORGOT HOW HAPPY WE ALL WERE. PERFECT LITTLE IDIOT LIVES. NOT A CARE IN THE WORLD. NOT YET.
IGNORANCE IS BLISS, I SUPPOSE.

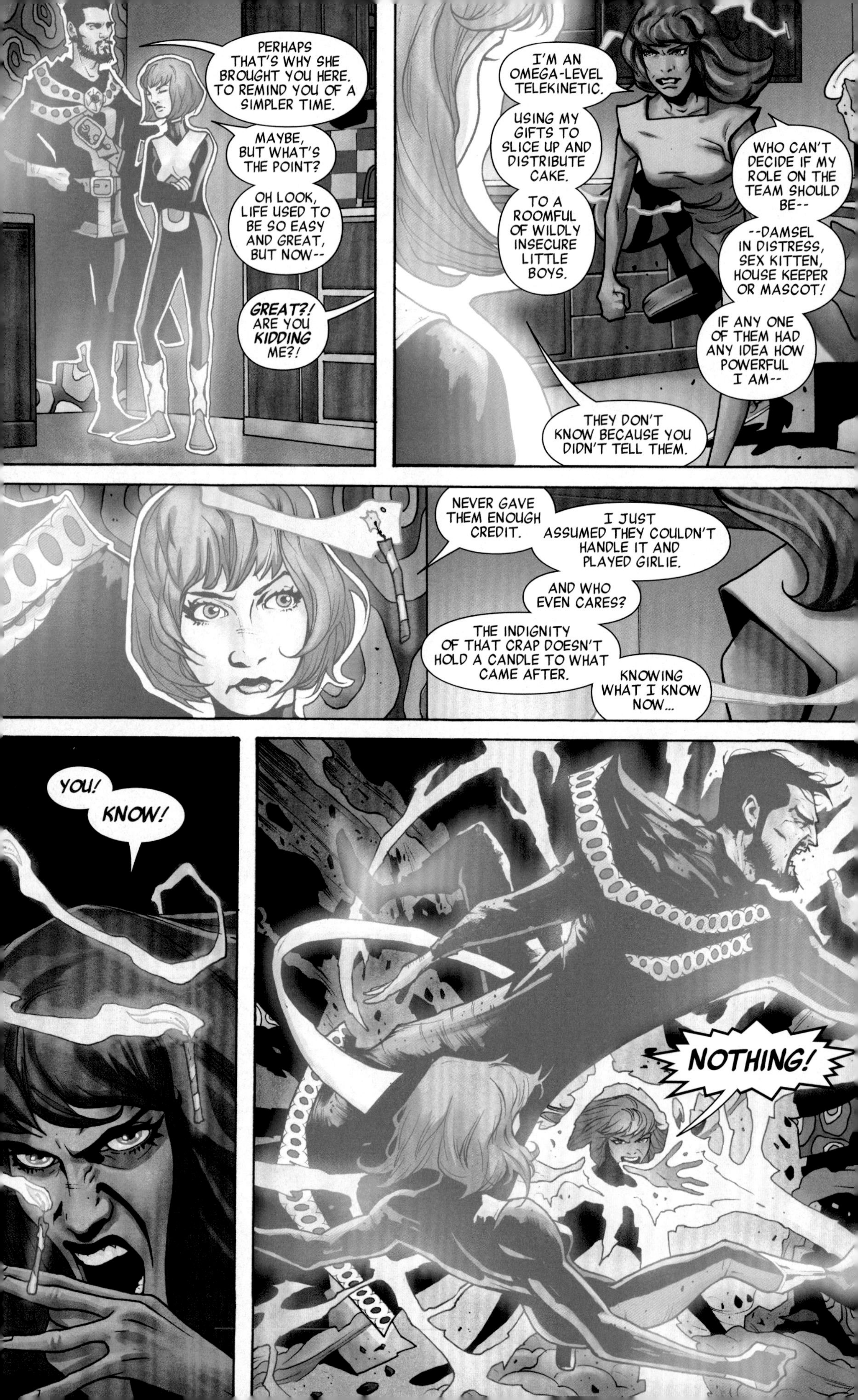

PERHAPS THAT'S WHY SHE BROUGHT YOU HERE. TO REMIND YOU OF A SIMPLER TIME.
MAYBE, BUT WHAT'S THE POINT?
OH LOOK, LIFE USED TO BE SO EASY AND GREAT, BUT NOW--
GREAT?! ARE YOU KIDDING ME?!
I'M AN OMEGA-LEVEL TELEKINETIC.
USING MY GIFTS TO SLICE UP AND DISTRIBUTE CAKE.
TO A ROOMFUL OF WILDLY INSECURE LITTLE BOYS.
WHO CAN'T DECIDE IF MY ROLE ON THE TEAM SHOULD BE--
--DAMSEL IN DISTRESS, SEX KITTEN, HOUSE KEEPER OR MASCOT!
IF ANY ONE OF THEM HAD ANY IDEA HOW POWERFUL I AM--
THEY DON'T KNOW BECAUSE YOU DIDN'T TELL THEM.
NEVER GAVE THEM ENOUGH CREDIT.
I JUST ASSUMED THEY COULDN'T HANDLE IT AND PLAYED GIRLIE.
AND WHO EVEN CARES?
THE INDIGNITY OF THAT CRAP DOESN'T HOLD A CANDLE TO WHAT CAME AFTER.
KNOWING WHAT I KNOW NOW...
YOU!
KNOW!
NOTHING!

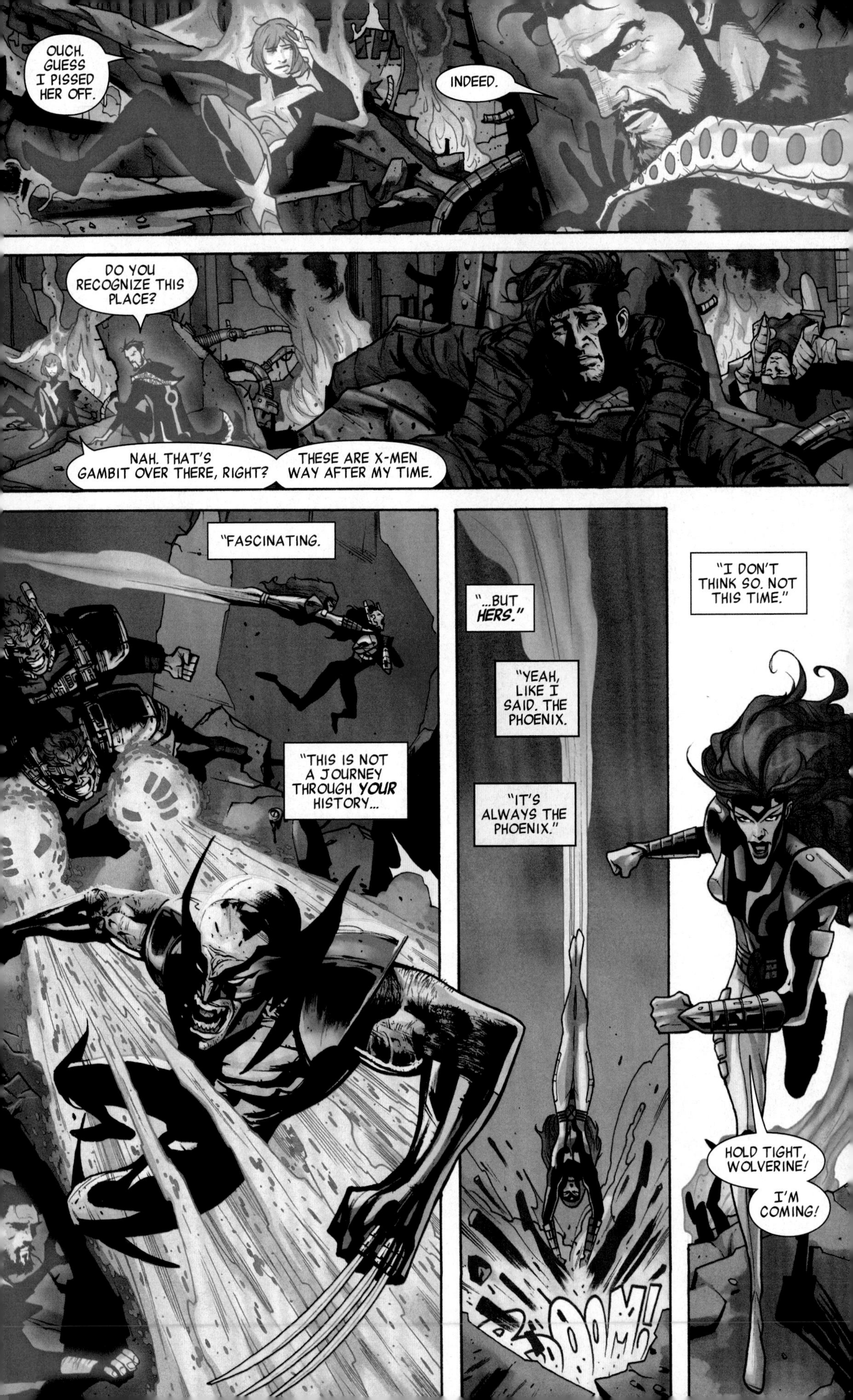
OUCH. GUESS I PISSED HER OFF.
INDEED.
DO YOU RECOGNIZE THIS PLACE?
NAH. THAT'S GAMBIT OVER THERE, RIGHT?
THESE ARE X-MEN WAY AFTER MY TIME.
"FASCINATING.
"THIS IS NOT A JOURNEY THROUGH YOUR HISTORY...
"...BUT HERS."
"YEAH, LIKE I SAID. THE PHOENIX.
"IT'S ALWAYS THE PHOENIX."
"I DON'T THINK SO. NOT THIS TIME."
HOLD TIGHT, WOLVERINE!
I'M COMING!
TOOOOM!

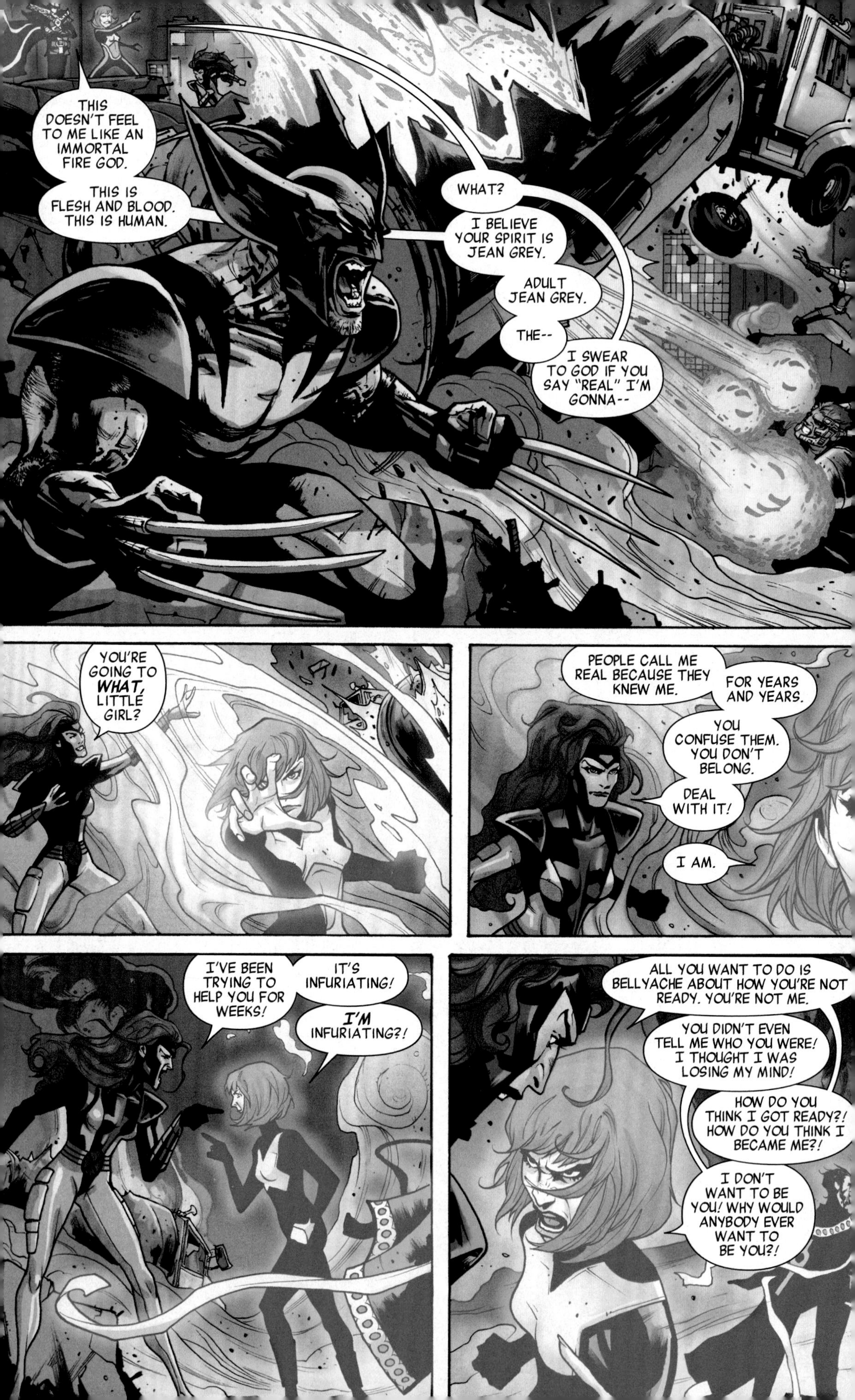
THIS DOESN'T FEEL TO ME LIKE AN IMMORTAL FIRE GOD.
THIS IS FLESH AND BLOOD. THIS IS HUMAN.
WHAT?
I BELIEVE YOUR SPIRIT IS JEAN GREY.
ADULT JEAN GREY.
THE--
I SWEAR TO GOD IF YOU SAY "REAL" I'M GONNA--
YOU'RE GOING TO WHAT, LITTLE GIRL?
PEOPLE CALL ME REAL BECAUSE THEY KNEW ME.
FOR YEARS AND YEARS.
YOU CONFUSE THEM. YOU DON'T BELONG.
DEAL WITH IT!
I AM.
I'VE BEEN TRYING TO HELP YOU FOR WEEKS!
IT'S INFURIATING!
I'M INFURIATING?!
ALL YOU WANT TO DO IS BELLYACHE ABOUT HOW YOU'RE NOT READY. YOU'RE NOT ME.
YOU DIDN'T EVEN TELL ME WHO YOU WERE! I THOUGHT I WAS LOSING MY MIND!
HOW DO YOU THINK I GOT READY?! HOW DO YOU THINK I BECAME ME?!
I DON'T WANT TO BE YOU! WHY WOULD ANYBODY EVER WANT TO BE YOU?!

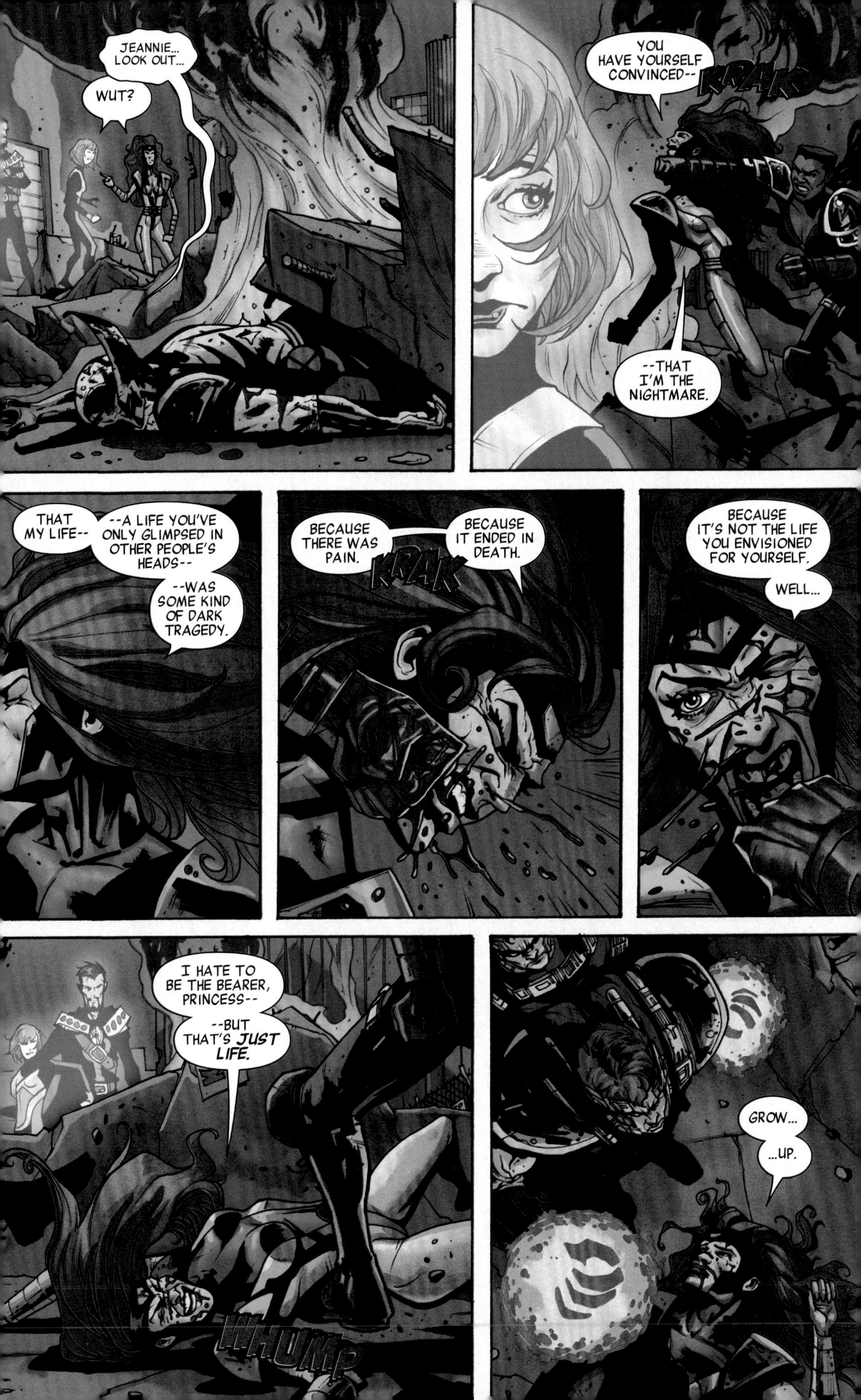
JEANNIE... LOOK OUT...
WUT?
YOU HAVE YOURSELF CONVINCED--
KRAK
--THAT I'M THE NIGHTMARE.
THAT MY LIFE--
--A LIFE YOU'VE ONLY GLIMPSED IN OTHER PEOPLE'S HEADS--
--WAS SOME KIND OF DARK TRAGEDY.
BECAUSE THERE WAS PAIN.
BECAUSE IT ENDED IN DEATH.
KRAK
BECAUSE IT'S NOT THE LIFE YOU ENVISIONED FOR YOURSELF.
WELL...
I HATE TO BE THE BEARER, PRINCESS--
--BUT THAT'S *JUST LIFE.*
WHUMP
GROW...
...UP.

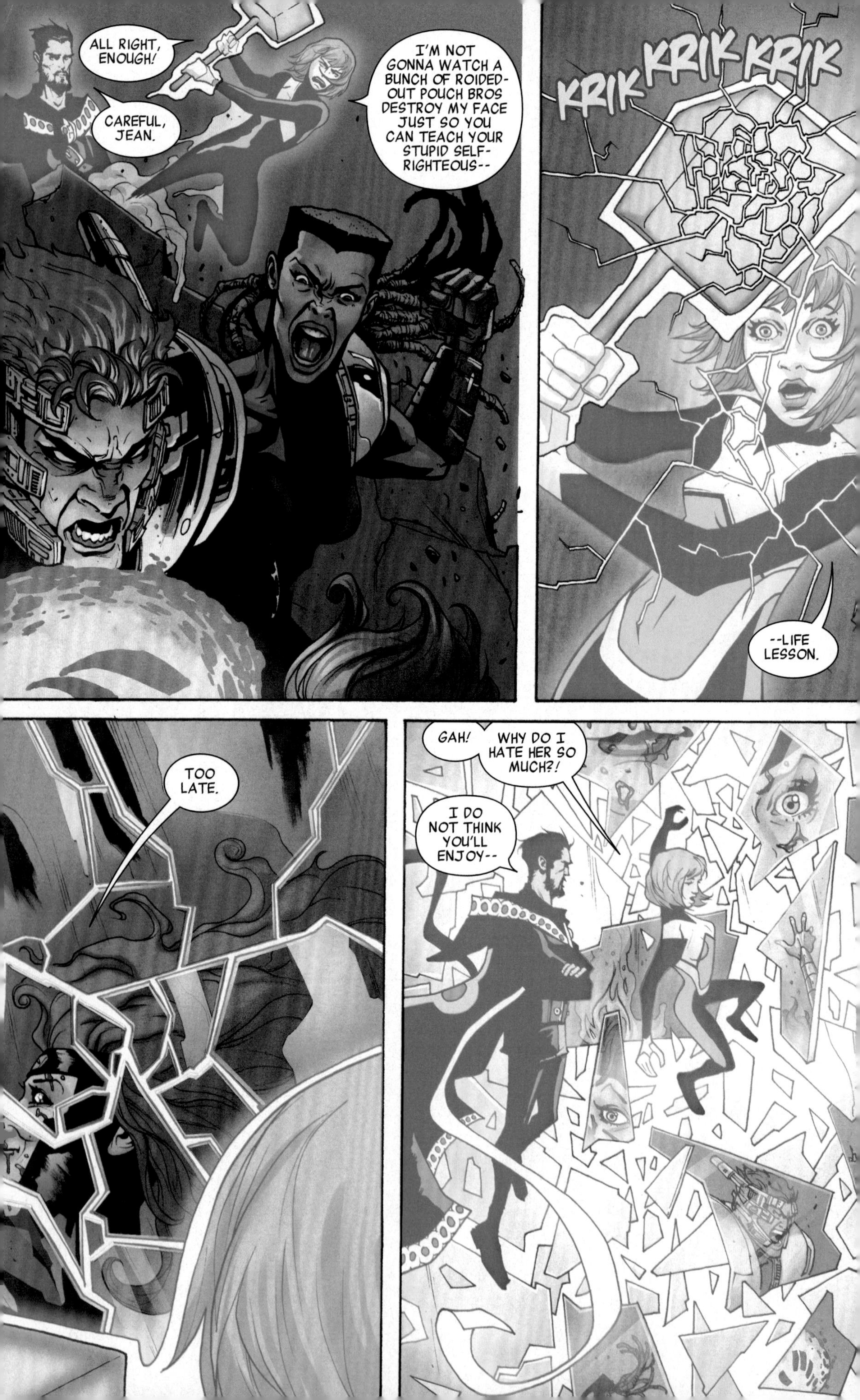
ALL RIGHT, ENOUGH!
CAREFUL, JEAN.
I'M NOT GONNA WATCH A BUNCH OF ROIDED-OUT POUCH BROS DESTROY MY FACE JUST SO YOU CAN TEACH YOUR STUPID SELF-RIGHTEOUS--
KRIK KRIK KRIK
--LIFE LESSON.
TOO LATE.
GAH!
WHY DO I HATE HER SO MUCH?!
I DO NOT THINK YOU'LL ENJOY--

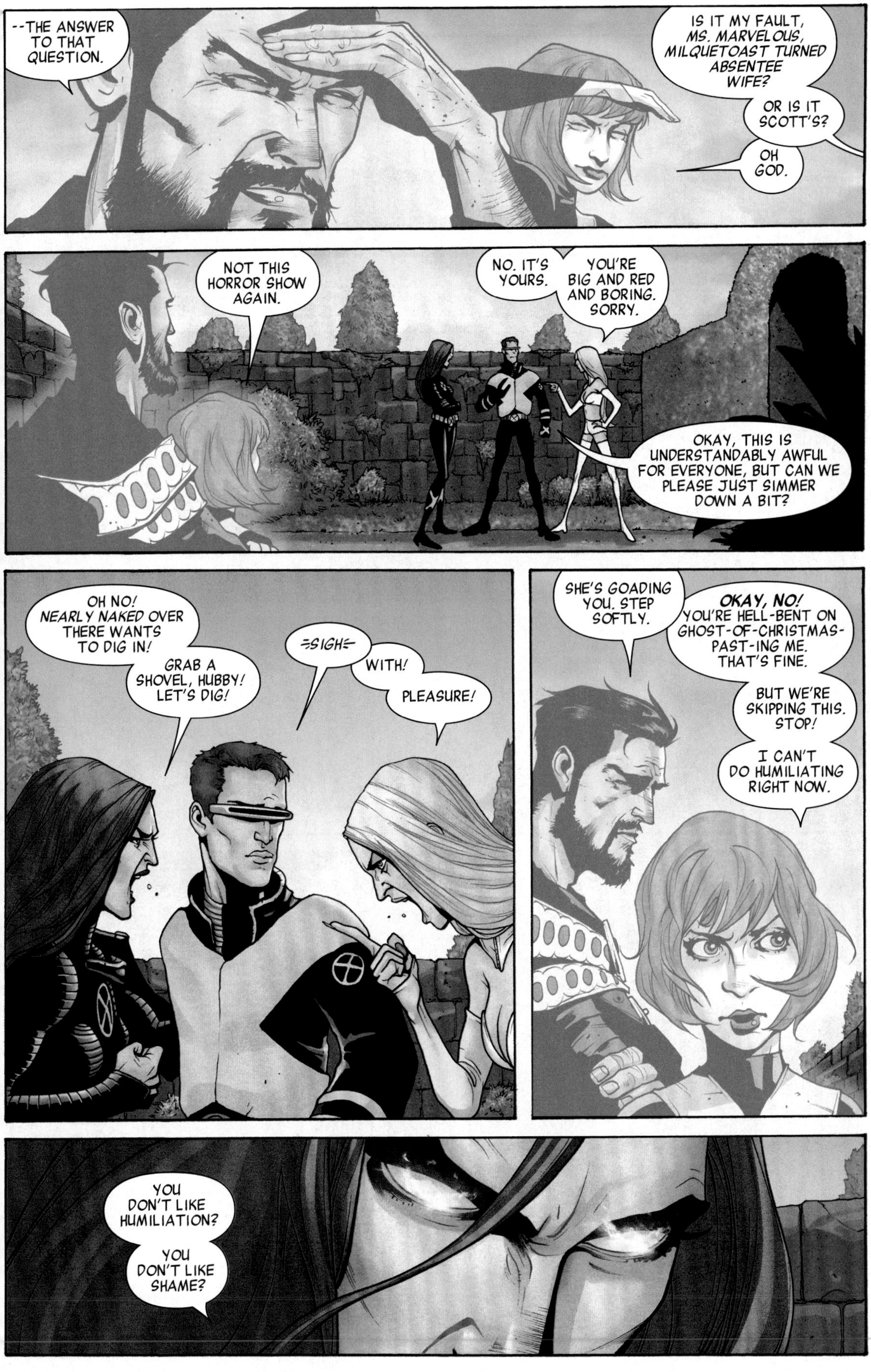
--THE ANSWER TO THAT QUESTION.
IS IT MY FAULT, MS. MARVELOUS, MILQUETOAST TURNED ABSENTEE WIFE?
OR IS IT SCOTT'S?
OH GOD.
NOT THIS HORROR SHOW AGAIN.
NO. IT'S YOURS.
YOU'RE BIG AND RED AND BORING. SORRY.
OKAY, THIS IS UNDERSTANDABLY AWFUL FOR EVERYONE, BUT CAN WE PLEASE JUST SIMMER DOWN A BIT?
OH NO! NEARLY NAKED OVER THERE WANTS TO DIG IN!
GRAB A SHOVEL, HUBBY! LET'S DIG!
=SIGH=
WITH!
PLEASURE!
SHE'S GOADING YOU. STEP SOFTLY.
OKAY, NO! YOU'RE HELL-BENT ON GHOST-OF-CHRISTMAS-PAST-ING ME. THAT'S FINE.
BUT WE'RE SKIPPING THIS. STOP!
I CAN'T DO HUMILIATING RIGHT NOW.
YOU DON'T LIKE HUMILIATION?
YOU DON'T LIKE SHAME?

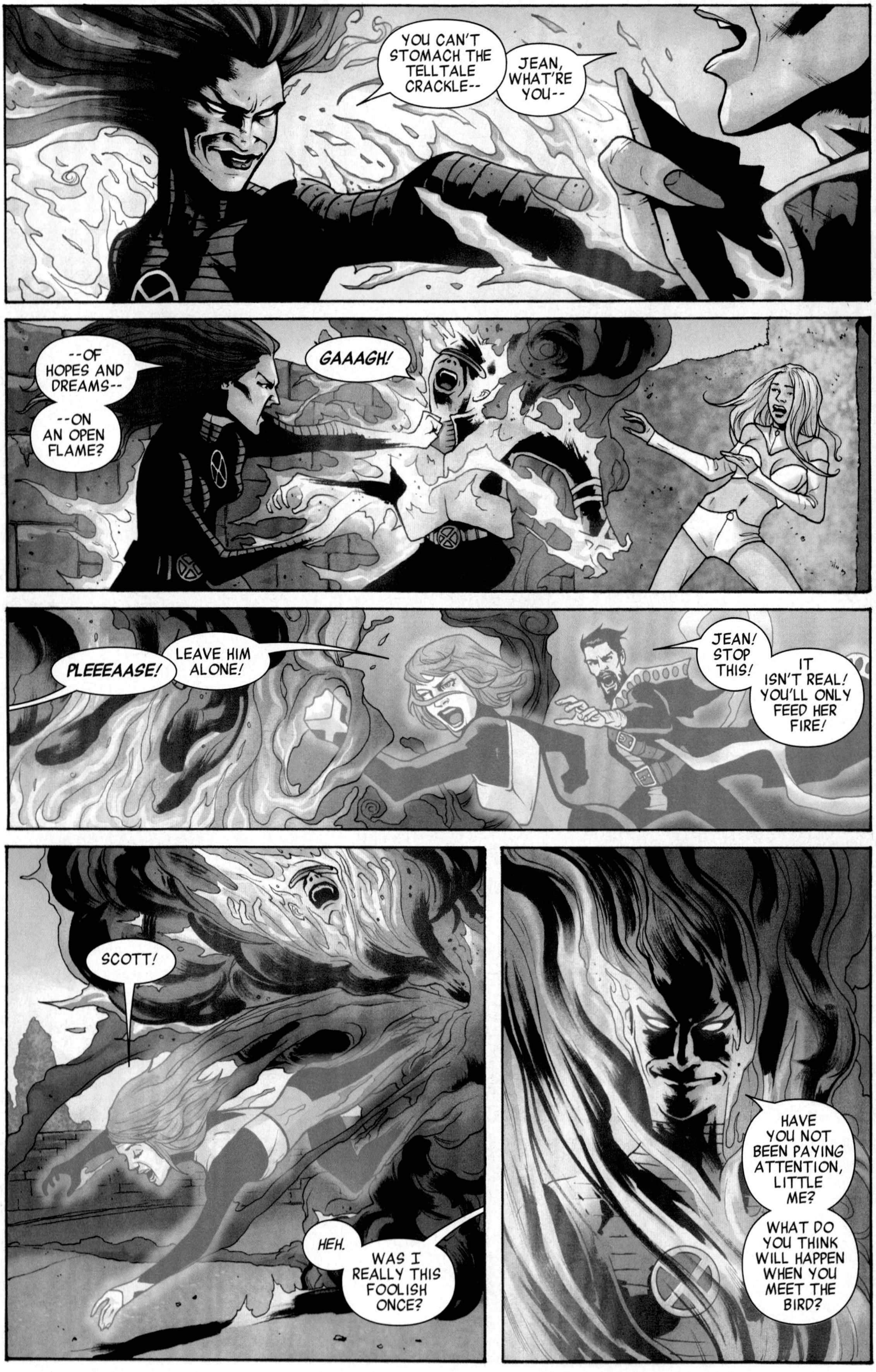

YOU CAN'T STOMACH THE TELLTALE CRACKLE--
JEAN, WHAT'RE YOU--
--OF HOPES AND DREAMS--
--ON AN OPEN FLAME?
GAAAGH!
PLEEEAASE!
LEAVE HIM ALONE!
JEAN! STOP THIS!
IT ISN'T REAL! YOU'LL ONLY FEED HER FIRE!
SCOTT!
HEH.
WAS I REALLY THIS FOOLISH ONCE?
HAVE YOU NOT BEEN PAYING ATTENTION, LITTLE ME?
WHAT DO YOU THINK WILL HAPPEN WHEN YOU MEET THE BIRD?

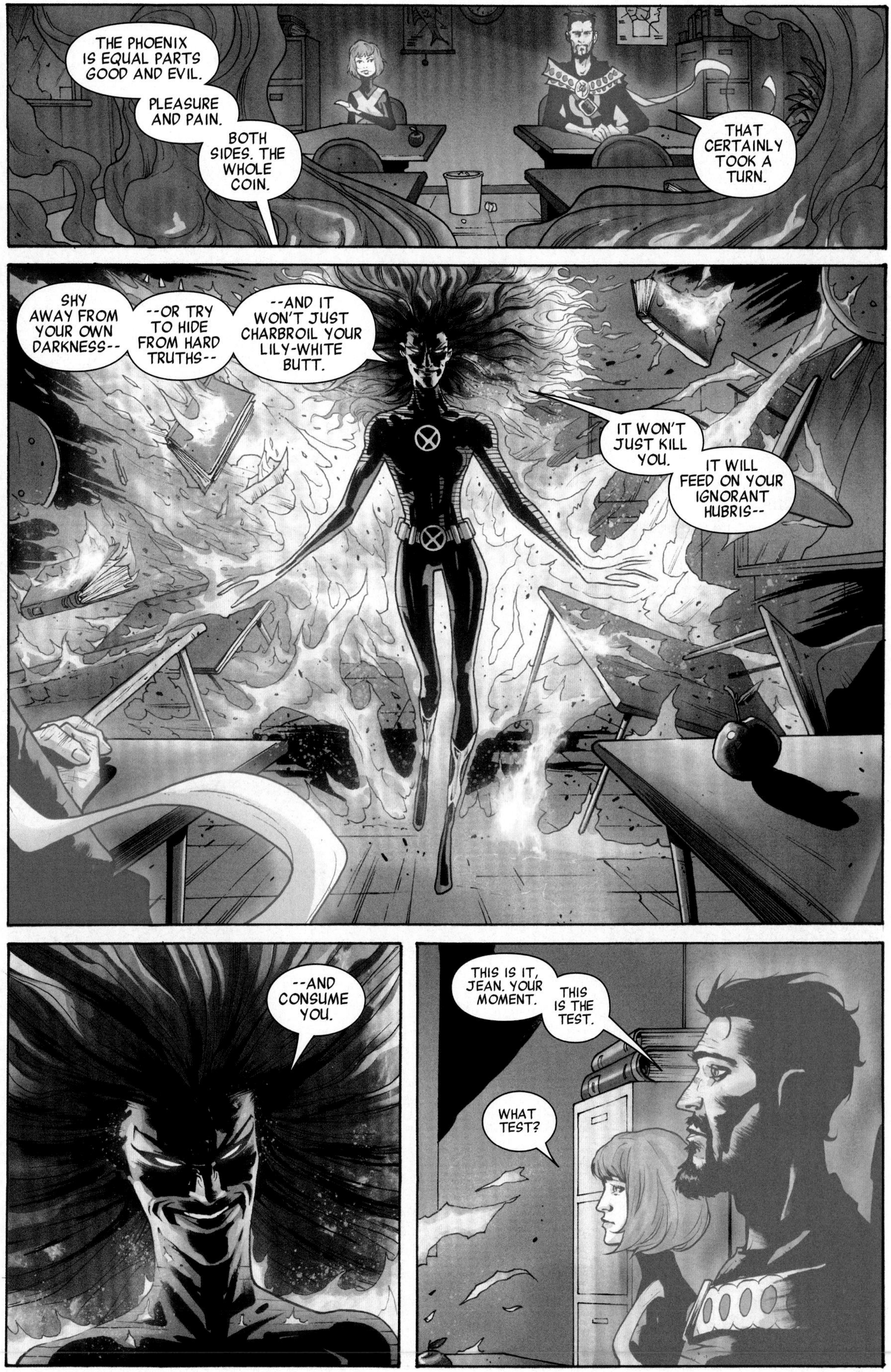
THE PHOENIX IS EQUAL PARTS GOOD AND EVIL.
PLEASURE AND PAIN.
BOTH SIDES. THE WHOLE COIN.
THAT CERTAINLY TOOK A TURN.
SHY AWAY FROM YOUR OWN DARKNESS--
--OR TRY TO HIDE FROM HARD TRUTHS--
--AND IT WON'T JUST CHARBROIL YOUR LILY-WHITE BUTT.
IT WON'T JUST KILL YOU.
IT WILL FEED ON YOUR IGNORANT HUBRIS--
--AND CONSUME YOU.
THIS IS IT, JEAN. YOUR MOMENT.
THIS IS THE TEST.
WHAT TEST?

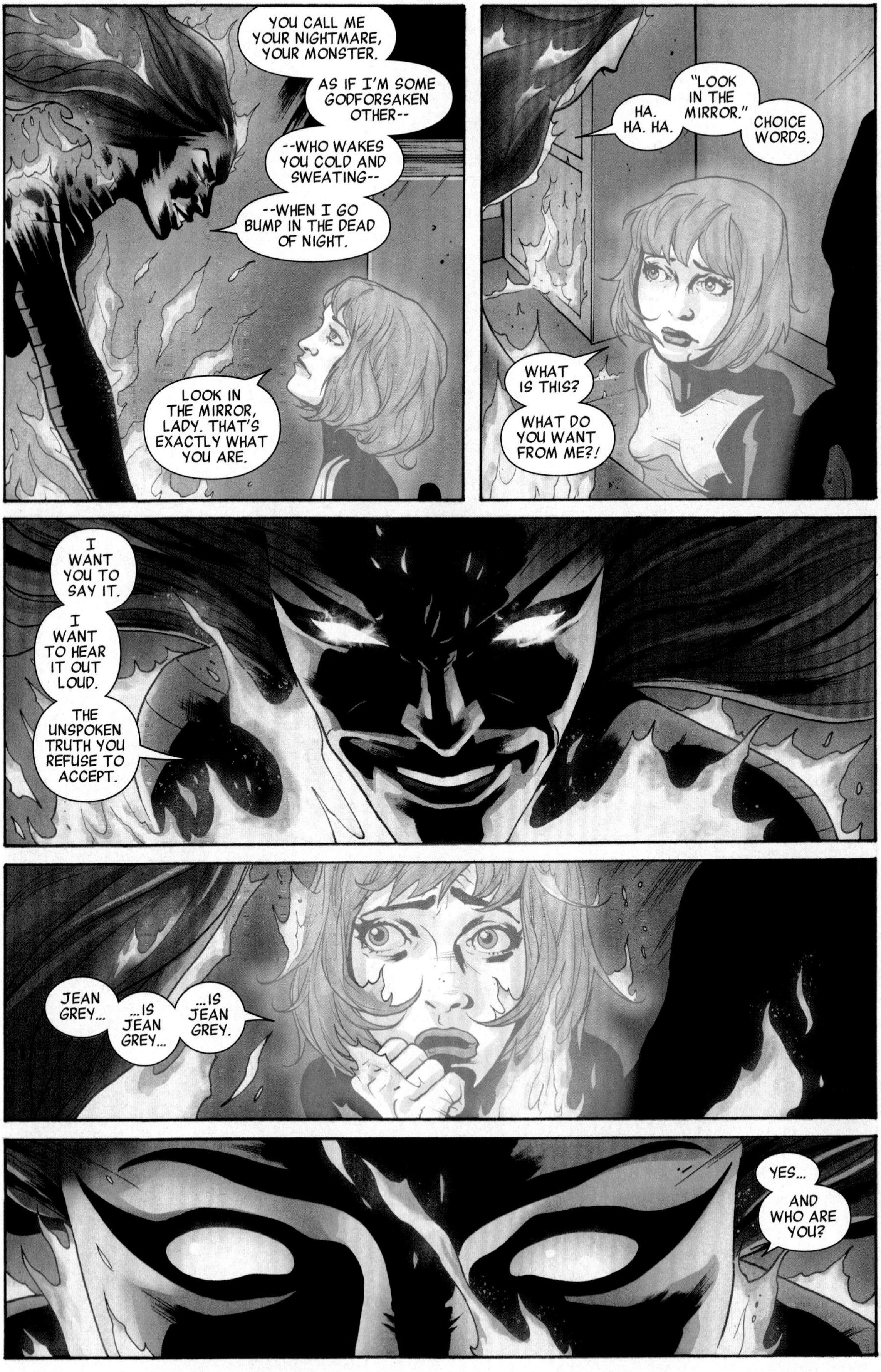
YOU CALL ME YOUR NIGHTMARE, YOUR MONSTER.
AS IF I'M SOME GODFORSAKEN OTHER--
--WHO WAKES YOU COLD AND SWEATING--
--WHEN I GO BUMP IN THE DEAD OF NIGHT.
LOOK IN THE MIRROR, LADY. THAT'S EXACTLY WHAT YOU ARE.
HA. HA. HA.
"LOOK IN THE MIRROR."
CHOICE WORDS.
WHAT IS THIS?
WHAT DO YOU WANT FROM ME?!
I WANT YOU TO SAY IT.
I WANT TO HEAR IT OUT LOUD.
THE UNSPOKEN TRUTH YOU REFUSE TO ACCEPT.
JEAN GREY...
...IS JEAN GREY...
...IS JEAN GREY.
YES...
AND WHO ARE YOU?

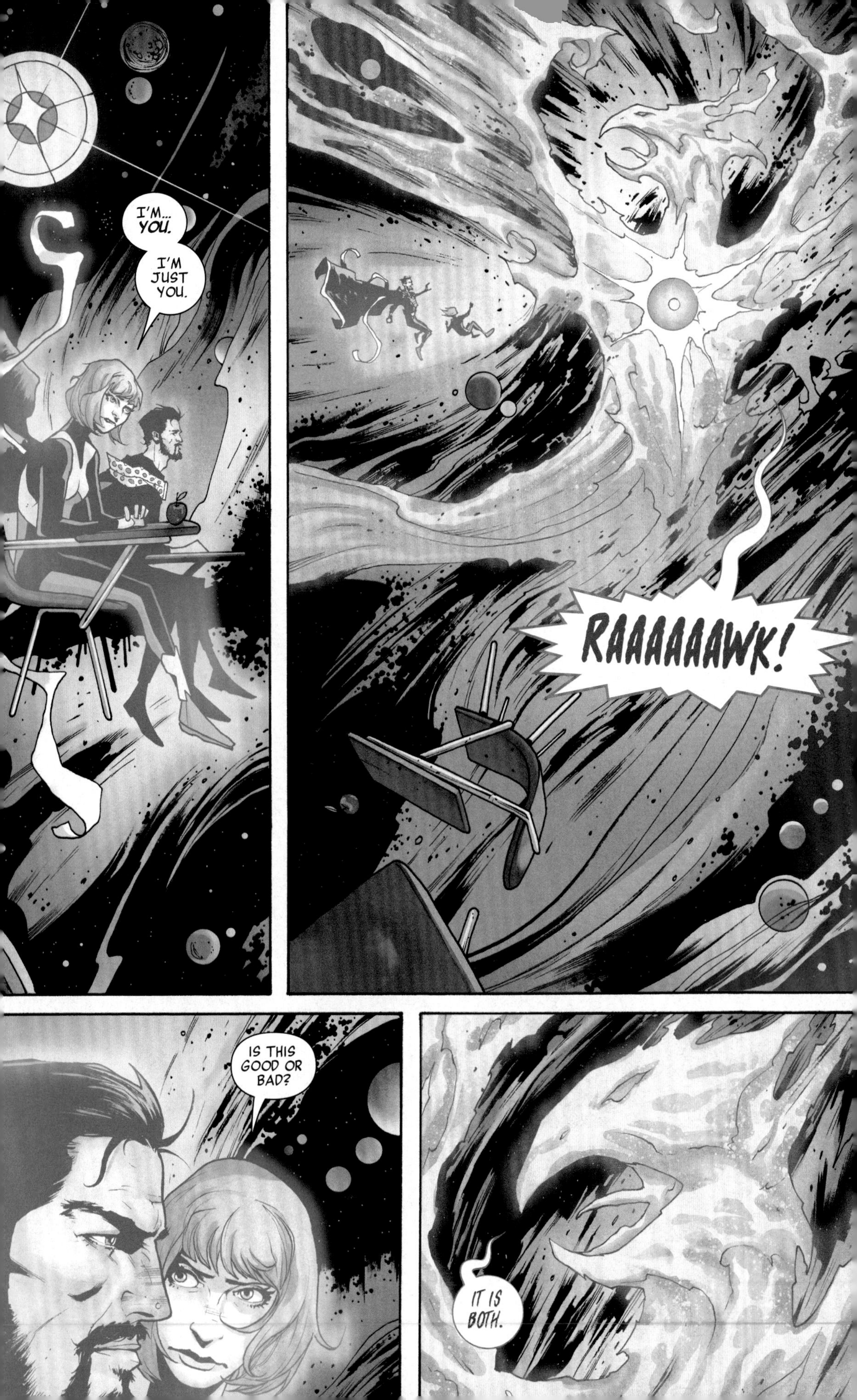
I'M... YOU.
I'M JUST YOU.
RAAAAAAAWK!
IS THIS GOOD OR BAD?
IT IS BOTH.

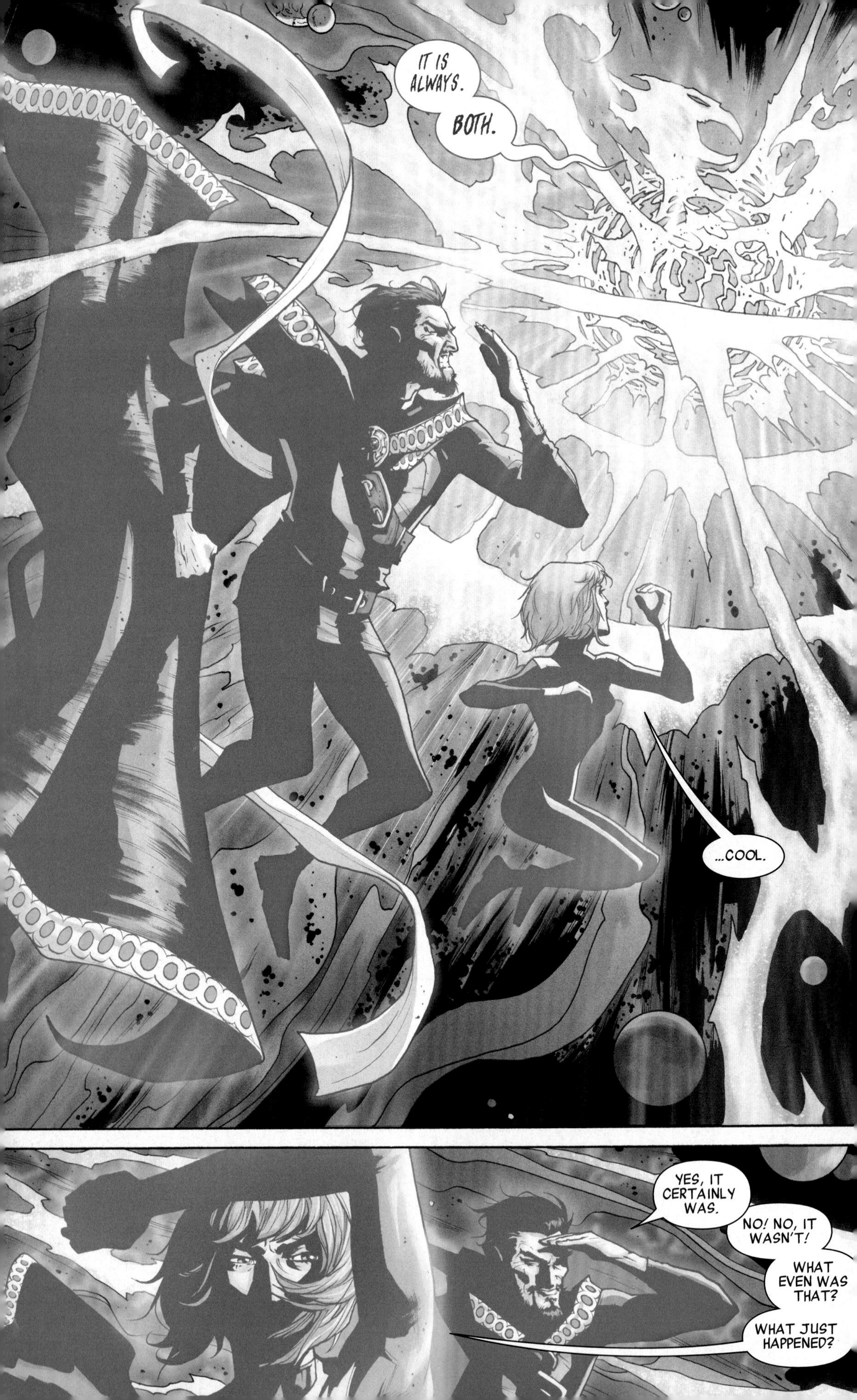
IT IS ALWAYS.
BOTH.
...COOL.
YES, IT CERTAINLY WAS.
NO! NO, IT WASN'T!
WHAT EVEN WAS THAT?
WHAT JUST HAPPENED?

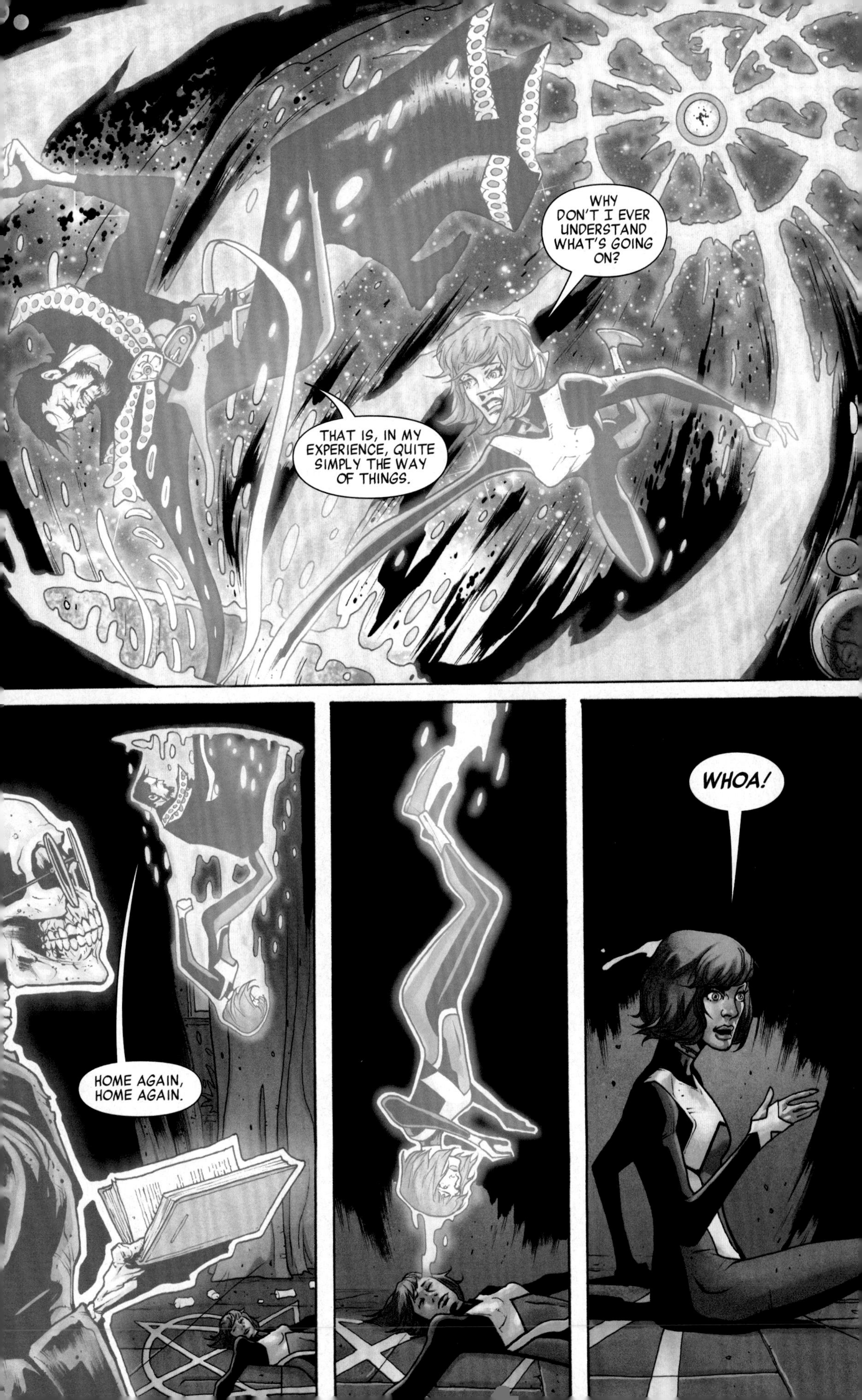
WHY DON'T I EVER UNDERSTAND WHAT'S GOING ON?
THAT IS, IN MY EXPERIENCE, QUITE SIMPLY THE WAY OF THINGS.
HOME AGAIN, HOME AGAIN.
WHOA!

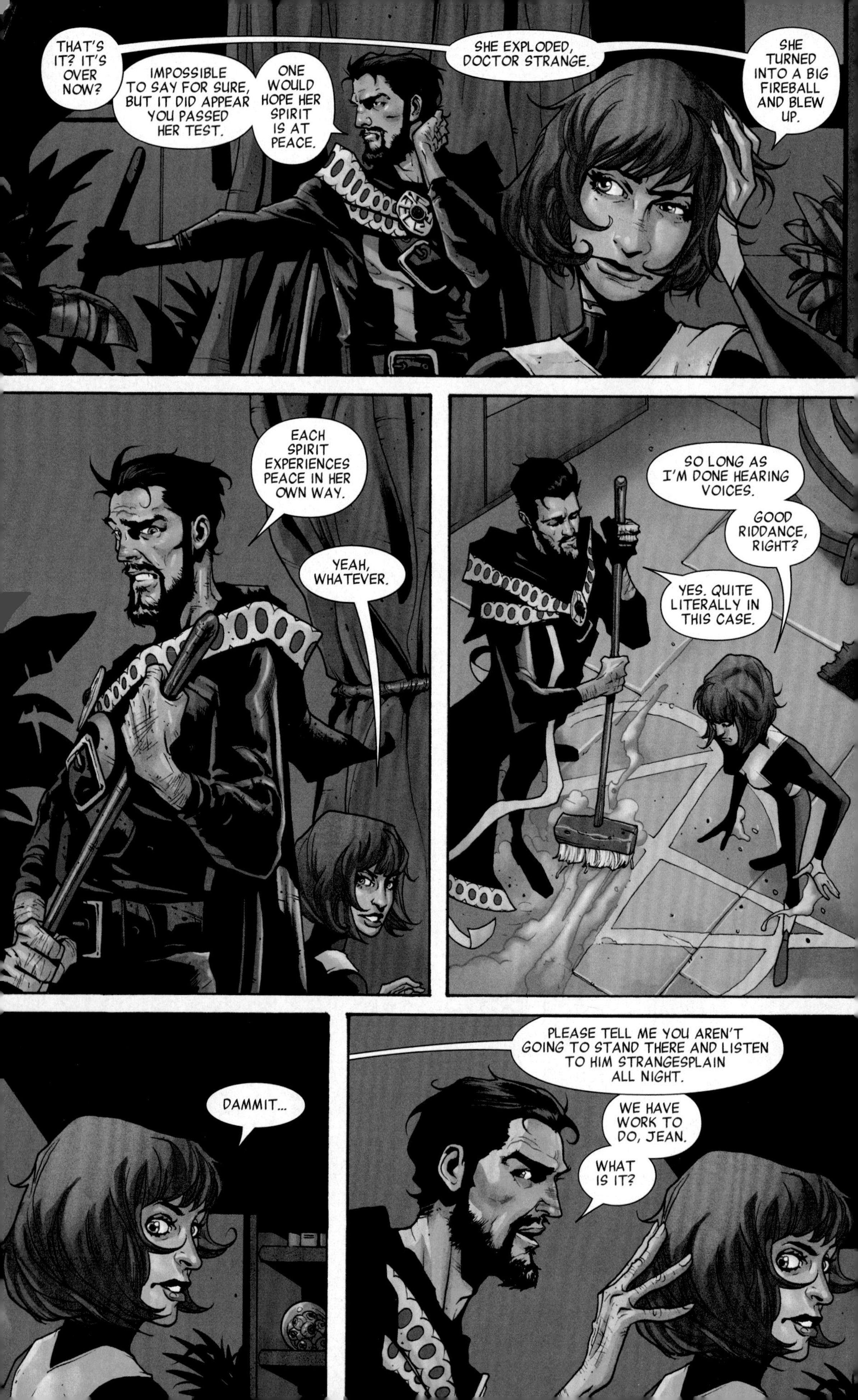
THAT'S IT? IT'S OVER NOW?
IMPOSSIBLE TO SAY FOR SURE, BUT IT DID APPEAR YOU PASSED HER TEST.
ONE WOULD HOPE HER SPIRIT IS AT PEACE.
SHE EXPLODED, DOCTOR STRANGE.
SHE TURNED INTO A BIG FIREBALL AND BLEW UP.
EACH SPIRIT EXPERIENCES PEACE IN HER OWN WAY.
YEAH, WHATEVER.
SO LONG AS I'M DONE HEARING VOICES.
GOOD RIDDANCE, RIGHT?
YES. QUITE LITERALLY IN THIS CASE.
DAMMIT...
PLEASE TELL ME YOU AREN'T GOING TO STAND THERE AND LISTEN TO HIM STRANGESPLAIN ALL NIGHT.
WE HAVE WORK TO DO, JEAN.
WHAT IS IT?

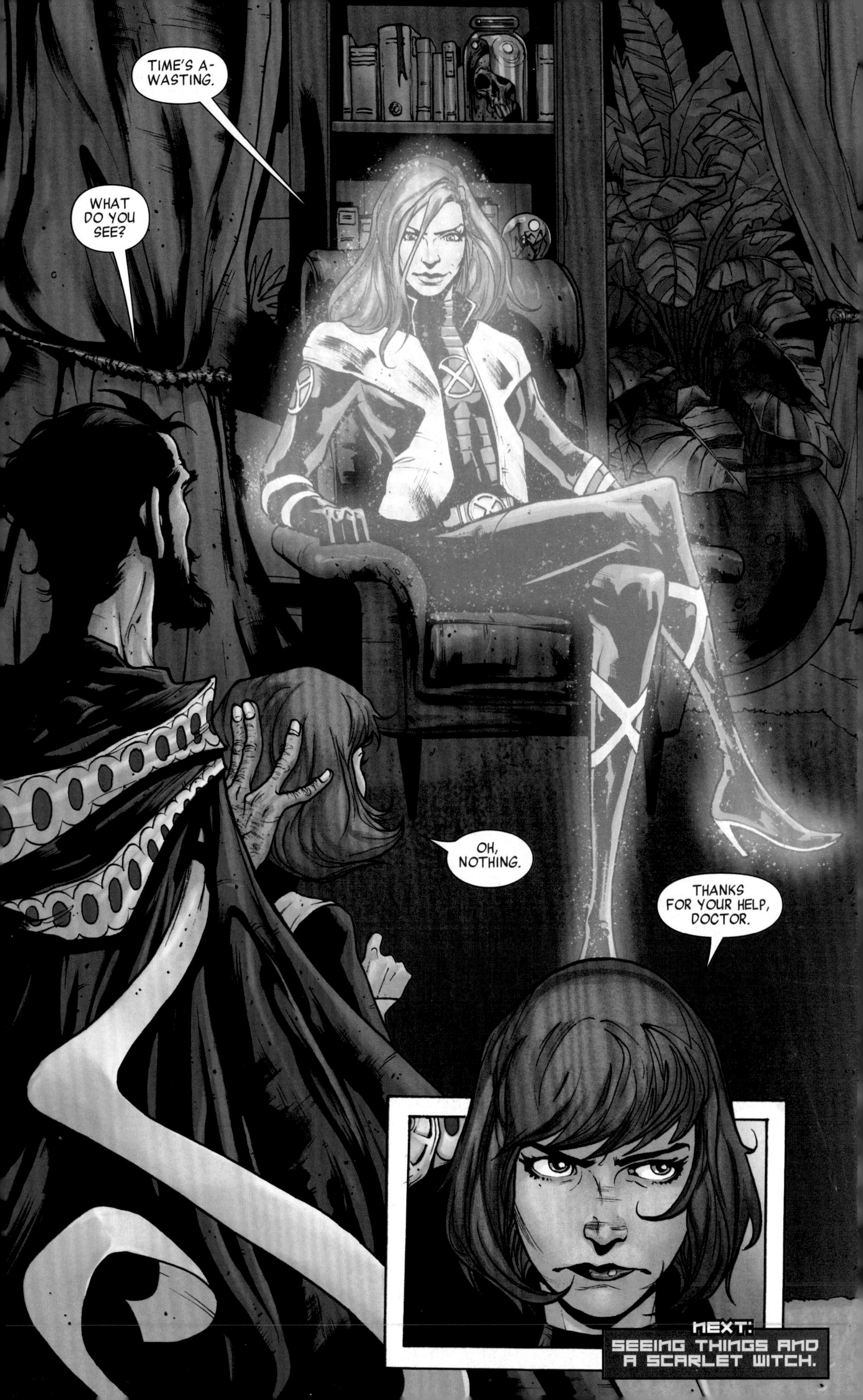
TIME'S A-WASTING.
WHAT DO YOU SEE?
OH, NOTHING.
THANKS FOR YOUR HELP, DOCTOR.
NEXT:
SEEING THINGS AND A SCARLET WITCH.

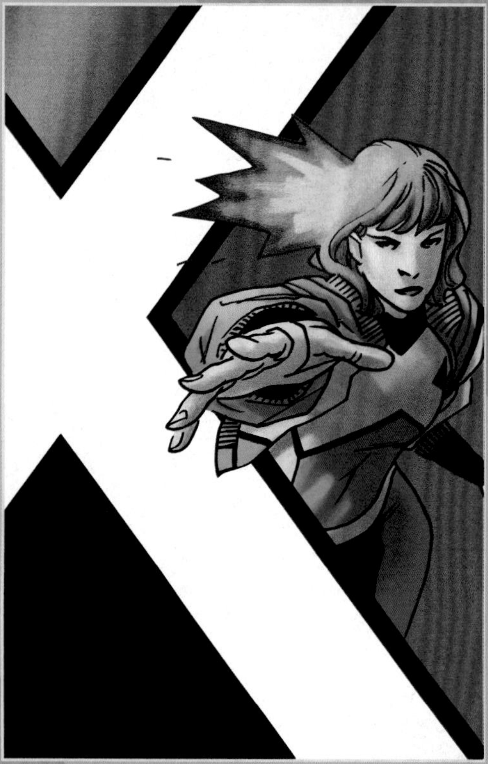

#1 CORNER BOX VARIANT
BY **LEONARD KIRK**
& **MICHAEL GARLAND**

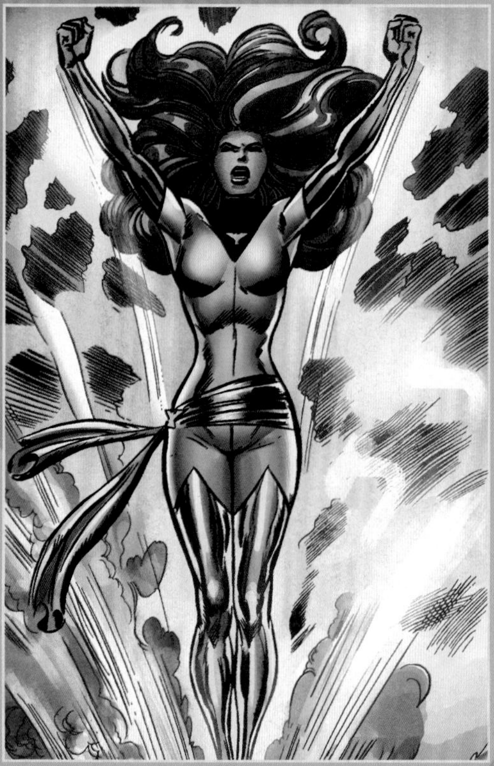

#1 REMASTERED VARIANT
BY **DAVE COCKRUM**
& **PAUL MOUNTS**

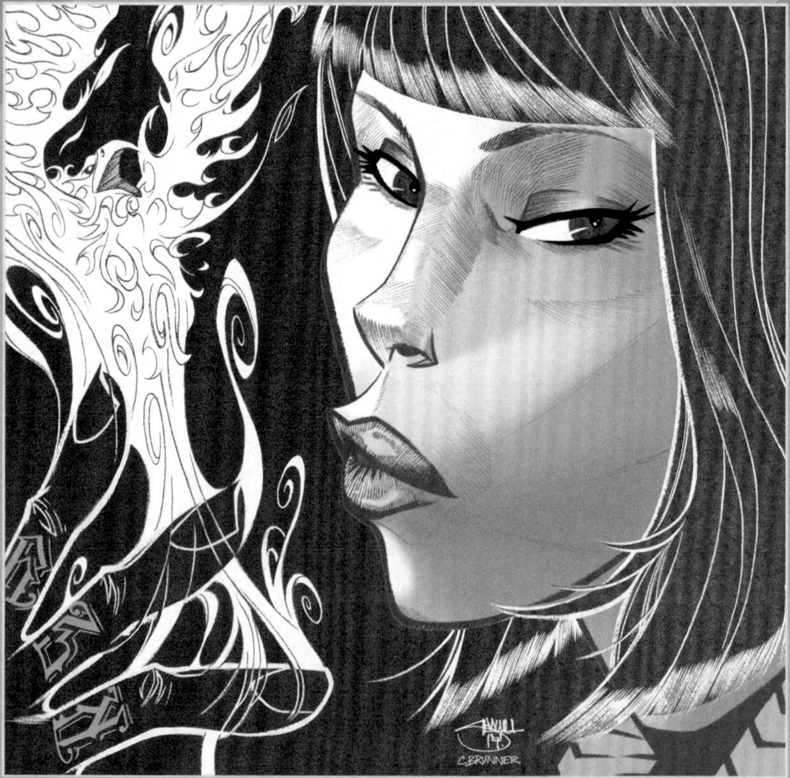

#1 HIP-HOP VARIANT
BY **SHAWN CRYSTAL**
& **CHRIS BRUNNER**

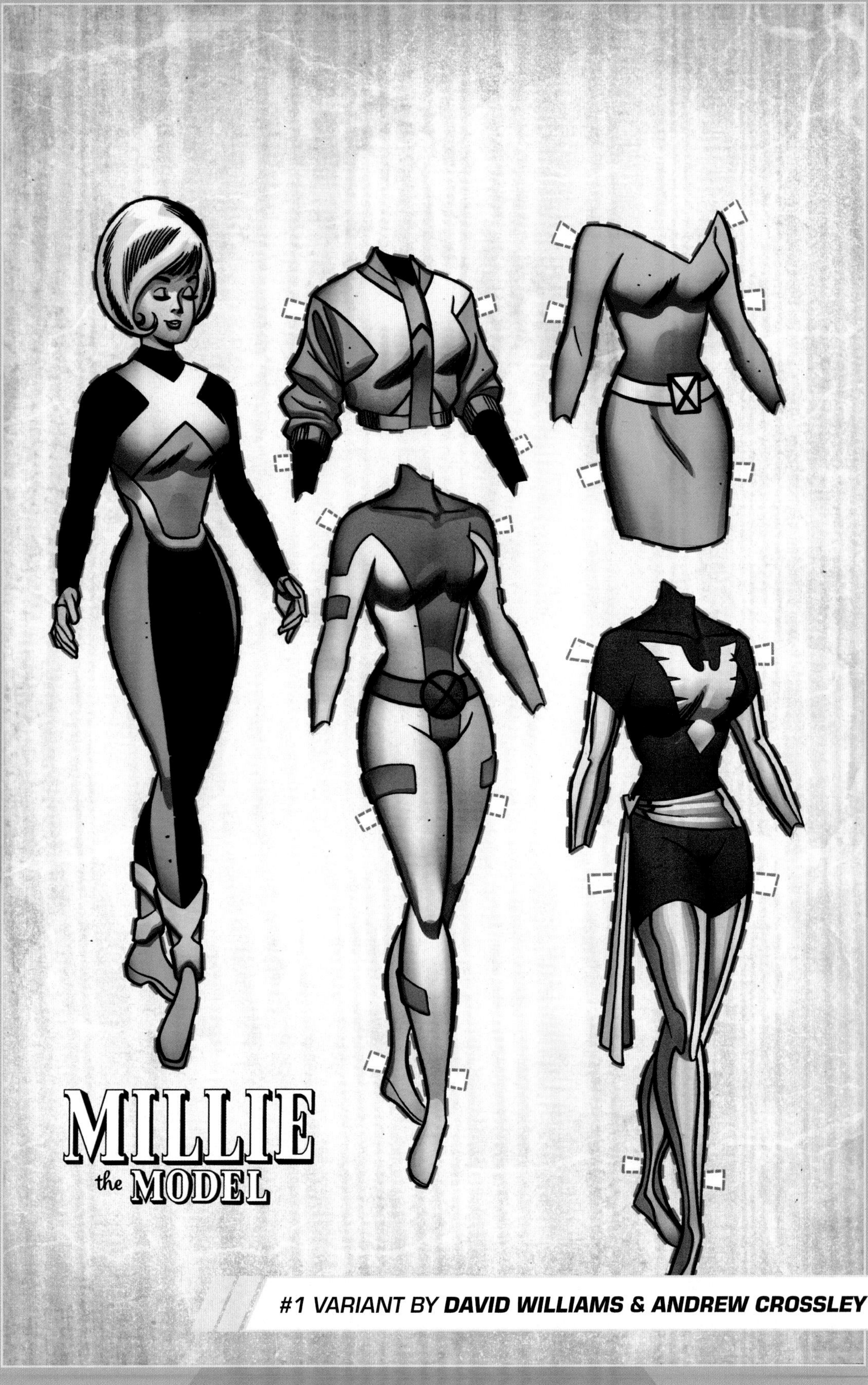

MILLIE
the MODEL

#1 VARIANT BY **DAVID WILLIAMS & ANDREW CROSSLEY**

#2 VARIANT BY **DAVID YARDIN**

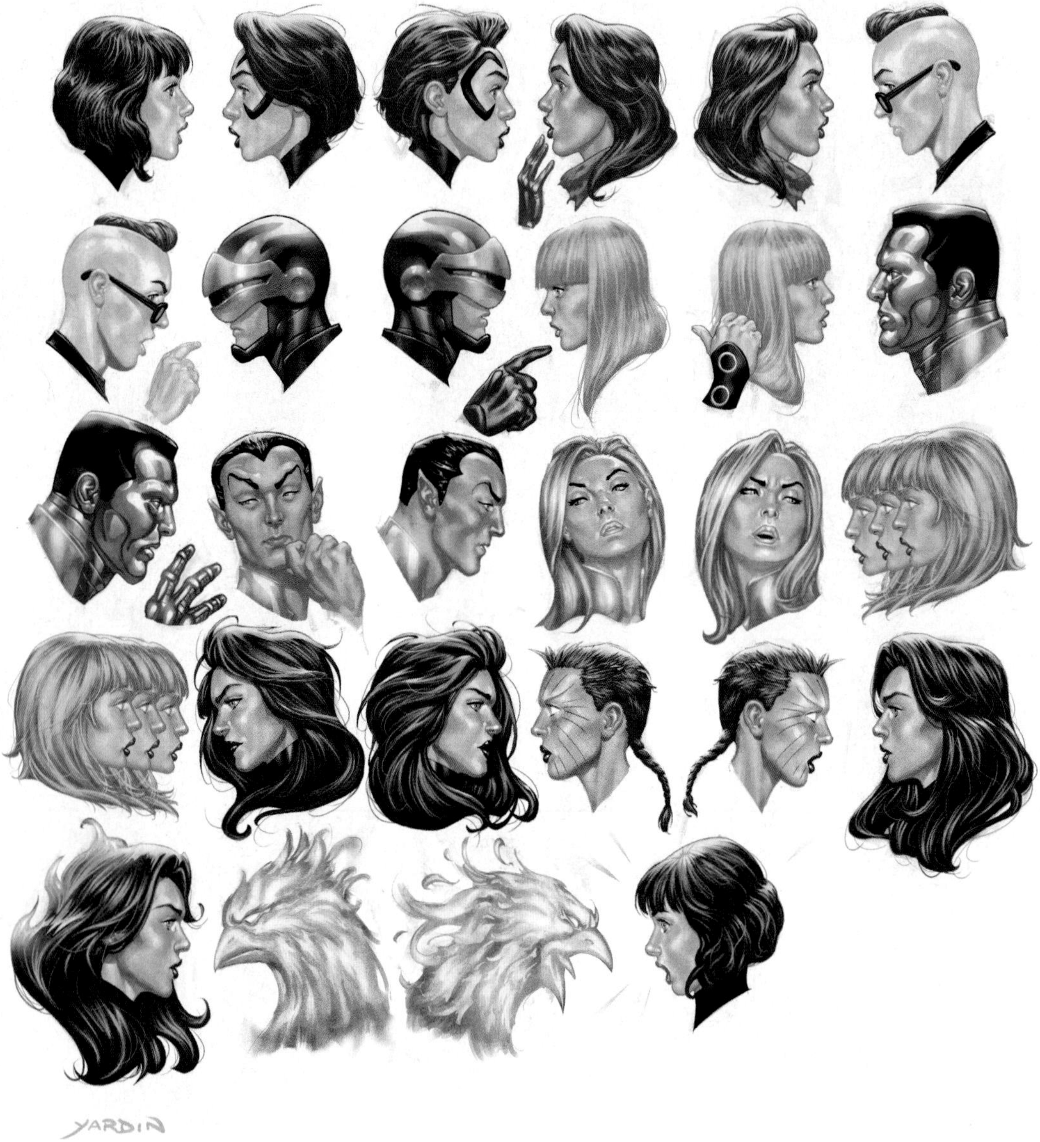
YARDIN

#3 VARIANT BY **RUSSELL DAUTERMAN** & **MATTHEW WILSON**

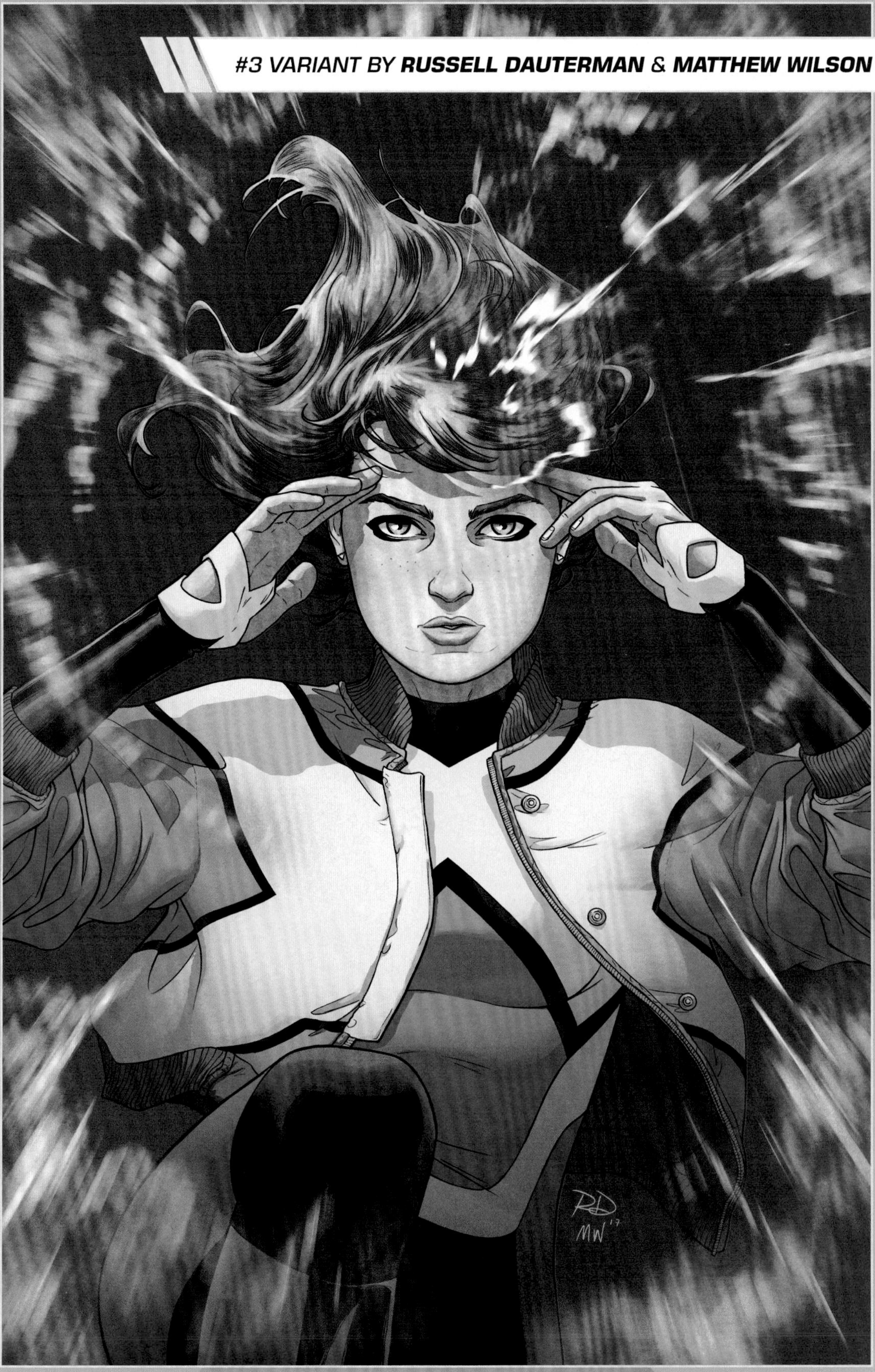

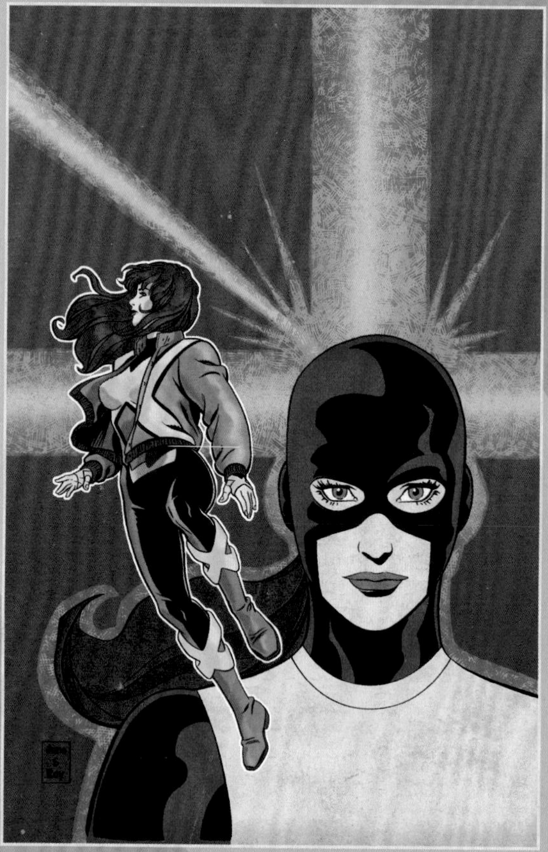

#4 VARIANT
BY **JUNE BRIGMAN**

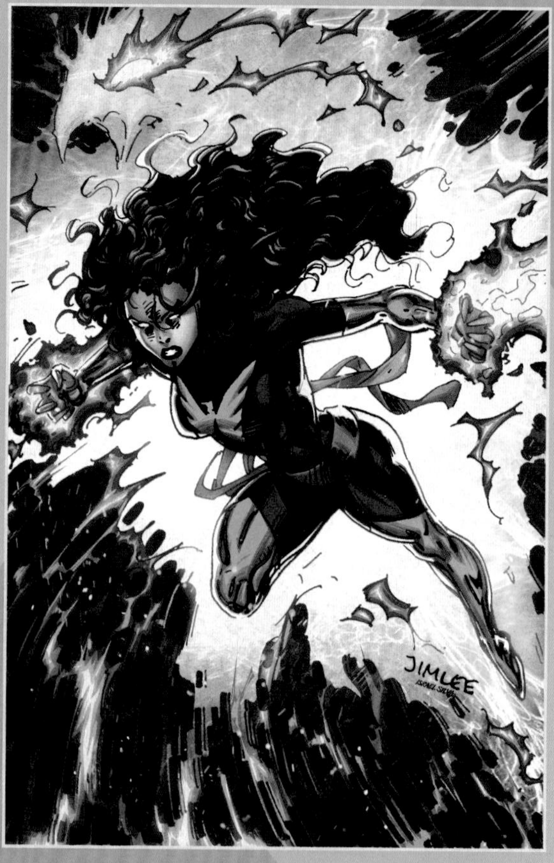
JIMLEE

#4 VARIANT
BY **JIM LEE** & **ISREAL SILVA**
WITH **MICHAEL KELLEHER**